**Publisher**
Jim Scheikofer
*The Family Handyman®*

**Director, Publication Services**
Sue Baalman-Pohlman
*HDA, Inc. (Home Design Alternatives)*

**Publication Manager**
Kimberly King
*HDA, Inc. (Home Design Alternatives)*

**Newsstand Sales**
David Algire
*Reader's Digest Association, Inc.*

**Marketing Manager**
Andrea Vecchio
*The Family Handyman*

**Production Manager**
Judy Rodriguez
*The Family Handyman*

**Home Plans Manager**
Curtis Cadenhead
*HDA, Inc. (Home Design Alternatives)*

Copyright 2005 by
Home Service Publications, Inc.,
publishers of
*The Family Handyman* Magazine,
2915 Commers Drive, Suite 700,
Eagan, MN 55121.
Plan copyrights held by home
designer/architect.

# The Family Handyman Contents

Vol. 19, No. 9

## Featured Homes

Plan #717-027D-0007 is featured on page 182
Photo courtesy of HDA, Inc.; St. Louis, MO

Plan #717-026D-0122 is featured on page 159
Photo courtesy of Design Basics, Inc.; Omaha, NE

## Sections

*The Family Handyman* magazine and HDA, Inc. (Home Design Alternatives) are pleased to join together to bring you this collection of home plans with curb appeal featuring many different styles for many different budgets from some of the nation's leading designers and architects.

Technical Specifications - At the time the construction drawings were prepared, every effort was made to ensure that these plans and specifications meet nationally recognized building codes (BOCA, Southern Building Code Congress and others). Because national building codes change or vary from area to area some drawing modifications and/or the assistance of a professional designer or architect may be necessary to comply with your local codes or to accommodate specific building conditions. We advise you to consult with your local building official for information regarding codes governing your area.

## On The Cover...

Plan #717-065D-0043 is featured on page 56
Photo courtesy of Studer Residential Designs; Photographer - Exposures Unlimited; Ron and Donna Kolb.

**3,216 total square feet of living area**

## Columns And Dormers Grace Stylish Exterior

### Special features

- All bedrooms include private full baths
- Hearth room and combination kitchen/breakfast area create a large informal gathering area
- Oversized family room boasts a fireplace, wet bar and bay window
- Master bedroom has two walk-in closets and a luxurious bath
- 4 bedrooms, 4 1/2 baths, 3-car side entry garage
- Basement foundation

**Price Code F**

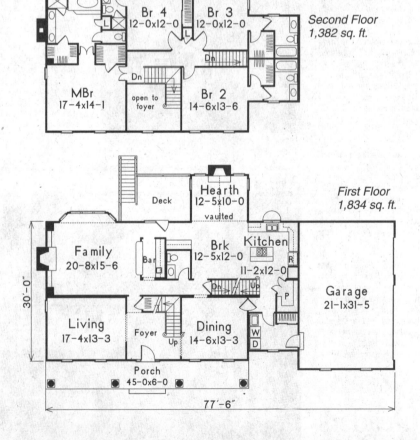

Second Floor
1,382 sq. ft.

Br 4
12-0x12-0

Br 3
12-0x12-0

MBr
17-4x14-1

open to foyer

Br 2
14-6x13-6

First Floor
1,834 sq. ft.

Deck

Hearth
12-5x10-0
vaulted

Family
20-8x15-6

Bar

Brk
12-5x12-0

Kitchen
11-2x12-0

Garage
21-1x31-5

Living
17-4x13-3

Foyer

Dining
14-6x13-3

30'-0"

Porch
45-0x6-0

77'-6"

**TO ORDER BLUEPRINTS USE THE FORM ON PAGE 15 OR CALL TOLL-FREE 1-877-671-6036**
View thousands more home plans online at www.familyhandyman.com/homeplans

2

Chrystine Canova 5/02

© 2003, Garrell Associates, Inc.

**2,135 total square feet of living area**

# Terrific Facade

## Special features

- 10' ceilings throughout the first floor and 9' ceilings on the second floor
- Wonderful angled entry leads through columns into a cozy social room
- Spacious kitchen has a center island with a place for dining as well as food preparation
- Bonus room on the second floor has an additional 247 square feet of living area
- 3 bedrooms, 2 1/2 baths, 2-car rear entry garage
- Slab foundation

### *Price Code H*

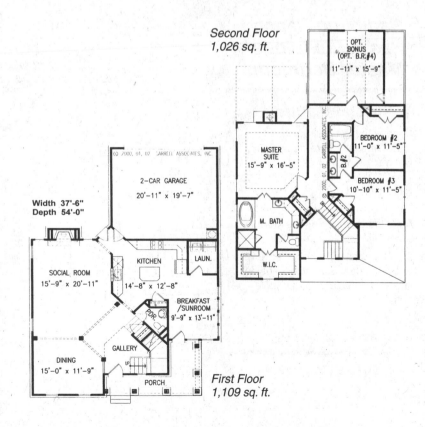

Second Floor
1,026 sq. ft.

OPT. BONUS (OPT. B.R.#4)
11'-11" x 15'-9"

BEDROOM #2
11'-0" x 11'-5"

BEDROOM #3
10'-10" x 11'-5"

MASTER SUITE
15'-9" x 16'-5"

B./2

M. BATH

W.I.C.

© 2000, 01, 02 GARRELL ASSOCIATES, INC.

Width 37'-6"
Depth 54'-0"

© 2000, 01, 02 GARRELL ASSOCIATES, INC.

2-CAR GARAGE
20'-11" x 19'-7"

KITCHEN
14'-8" x 12'-8"

LAUN.

SOCIAL ROOM
15'-9" x 20'-11"

BREAKFAST /SUNROOM
9'-9" x 13'-11"

PDR.

DINING
15'-0" x 11'-9"

GALLERY

UP

PORCH

First Floor
1,109 sq. ft.

**TO ORDER BLUEPRINTS USE THE FORM ON PAGE 15 OR CALL TOLL-FREE 1-877-671-6036**
View thousands more home plans online at www.familyhandyman.com/homeplans

3

**2,523 total square feet of living area**

## Rambling Ranch Has A Luxurious Master Bedroom

### Special features

- Entry with high ceiling leads to massive vaulted great room with wet bar, plant shelves, pillars and fireplace with a harmonious window trio
- Elaborate kitchen with bay and breakfast bar adjoins the morning room with fireplace-in-a-bay
- Vaulted master bedroom features a fireplace, book and plant shelves, large walk-in closet and double baths
- 3 bedrooms, 2 baths, 3-car garage
- Basement foundation

**Price Code D**

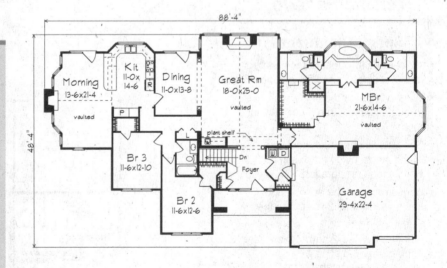

**TO ORDER BLUEPRINTS USE THE FORM ON PAGE 15 OR CALL TOLL-FREE 1-877-671-6036**
View thousands more home plans online at www.familyhandyman.com/homeplans

4

**2,421 total square feet of living area**

## Sprawling Ranch Design

### Special features

- Charming courtyard on the side of the home easily accesses the porch leading into the breakfast area
- French doors throughout home create a sunny atmosphere
- Master bedroom accesses covered porch
- 4 bedrooms, 2 baths, optional 2-car detatched garage
- Crawl space or slab foundation, please specify when ordering

*Price Code D*

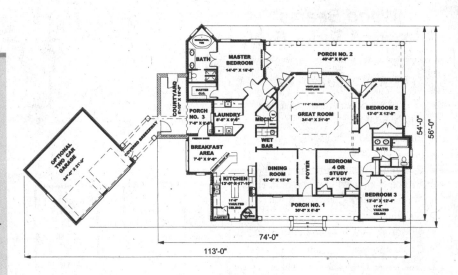

**TO ORDER BLUEPRINTS USE THE FORM ON PAGE 15 OR CALL TOLL-FREE 1-877-671-6036**
View thousands more home plans online at www.familyhandyman.com/homeplans

5

**2,277 total square feet of living area**

## Wood Beams Create A Tudor Feel

### Special features

- Lots of windows in the great room create an inviting feeling
- First floor den/bedroom #4 would make an ideal home office
- Enormous dining area and kitchen combine to create a large gathering area overlooking into the great room
- 4 bedrooms, 3 baths, 2-car garage
- Crawl space foundation

*Price Code E*

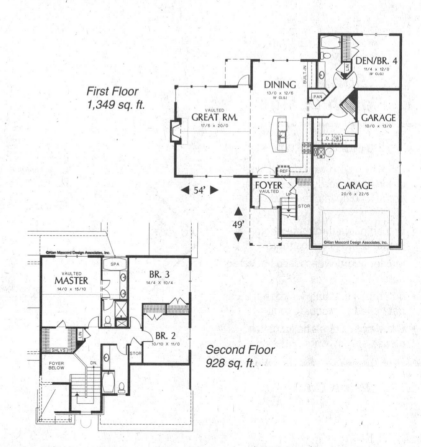

First Floor
1,349 sq. ft.

Second Floor
928 sq. ft.

**TO ORDER BLUEPRINTS USE THE FORM ON PAGE 15 OR CALL TOLL-FREE 1-877-671-6036**
View thousands more home plans online at www.familyhandyman.com/homeplans

**2,920 total square feet of living area**

## Craftsman Style Creates The Feel Of A Great Home

### Special features

- A large, cheerful and private sitting room connects the master bedroom to the master bath
- A cozy den features a unique angled entrance for interest
- The open kitchen flows into the breakfast nook for maximum convenience
- Second floor bonus room is included in the square footage
- 3 bedrooms, 2 1/2 baths, 3-car garage
- Crawl space foundation

***Price Code E***

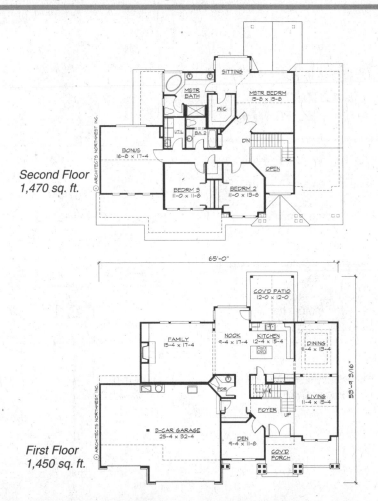

*Second Floor 1,470 sq. ft.*

*First Floor 1,450 sq. ft.*

**TO ORDER BLUEPRINTS USE THE FORM ON PAGE 15 OR CALL TOLL-FREE 1-877-671-6036**
View thousands more home plans online at www.familyhandyman.com/homeplans

7

**1,556 total square feet of living area**

## Country Kitchen Is Center Of Living Activities

### Special features

- A compact home with all the amenities
- Country kitchen combines practicality with access to other areas for eating and entertaining
- Two-way fireplace joins the dining and living areas
- Plant shelf and vaulted ceiling highlight the master bedroom
- 3 bedrooms, 2 1/2 baths, 2-car garage
- Basement foundation

**Price Code B**

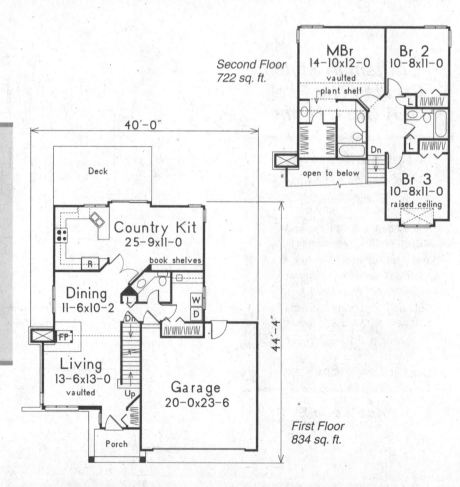

Second Floor
722 sq. ft.

MBr
14-10x12-0
vaulted
plant shelf

Br 2
10-8x11-0

open to below

Dn

Br 3
10-8x11-0
raised ceiling

40'-0"

Deck

Country Kit
25-9x11-0
book shelves

Dining
11-6x10-2

W
D

Living
13-6x13-0
vaulted

FP

Dn

Up

Garage
20-0x23-6

44'-4"

Porch

First Floor
834 sq. ft.

**TO ORDER BLUEPRINTS USE THE FORM ON PAGE 15 OR CALL TOLL-FREE 1-877-671-6036**
View thousands more home plans online at www.familyhandyman.com/homeplans

8

**2,689 total square feet of living area**

## Terrific Home For A Sloping Lot

### Special features

- A private parlor and dining area off the kitchen are perfect for entertaining
- All bedrooms are on the second floor for extra privacy
- A see-through fireplace warms both the family room and the den
- 3 bedrooms, 2 1/2 baths, 3-car drive-under garage
- Crawl space foundation

### *Price Code E*

©Alan Mascord Design Associates, Inc.

BR. 2
10/0 X 12/8

BR. 3
11/0 X 12/8

LINEN

*Second Floor*
*986 sq. ft.*

VAULTED
MASTER
15/2 X 15/8 +/-

OPEN TO FAMILY ROOM BELOW

DECK

STOR

©Alan Mascord Design Associates, Inc.

NOOK
11/0 X 13/6
(9' CLG)

KIT.
13/6 X 13/4

DINING
10/10 X 13/7
(VAULTED)

DEN
13/10 X 11/10
(9' CLG)

2 STORY
FAMILY RM.
15/6 X 20/6 +/-

PARLOR
13/4 X 15/6
(VAULTED)

BUILT-IN

LINEN

*First Floor*
*1,703 sq. ft.*

DECK OVER

WINDOW SEAT

STOR

◄56'-6"►

37'

**TO ORDER BLUEPRINTS USE THE FORM ON PAGE 15 OR CALL TOLL-FREE 1-877-671-6036**
View thousands more home plans online at www.familyhandyman.com/homeplans

9

**1,587 total square feet of living area**

## Large Open Living Areas

### Special features

- The large front porch opens to the spacious great room
- The kitchen is conveniently split around a center island for maximum use of space
- The master bedroom features a large walk-in closet and private bath with double-bowl vanity
- Daily traffic moves easily through the great room, kitchen and dining area
- 3 bedrooms, 2 baths
- Slab or crawl space foundation, please specify when ordering

*Price Code B*

CLO

LAUNDRY

**MASTER BEDROOM**
15'-0" X 14'-0"

**DINING AREA**
13'-6" X 8'-2"

**BEDROOM NO. 2**
11'-0" X14'-0"

**BATH 2**

**BATH 1**

STOVE

**KITCHEN**
13'-6" X 12'-6"

REF

CLO

HVAC

HALL

LINEN

**GREAT ROOM**
19'-0" X 18'-0"

**BEDROOM NO. 3**
12'-0" X 14'-0"

CLO

**PORCH**

**Width: 34'-0"**
**Depth: 52'-8"**

**2,840 total square feet of living area**

## Lower Level
## Expands This Ranch

### Special features

- Secluded den has a half bath making it perfect for a home office
- Corner columns separate the formal dining room while maintaining openness
- Built-in bookshelves flank each side of the fireplace in the great room
- 3 bedrooms, 2 1/2 baths, 2-car garage
- Crawl space foundation

*Price Code F*

*First Floor*
*1,744 sq. ft.*

DECK

NOOK
10/0 x 11/4
(9' CLG.)

10/6 x 13/4

GREAT RM.
16/6 X 15/4
(13' CLG.)

MASTER
15/8 X 13/2
(9' CLG.)

BUILT-INS

BUILT-INS

DESK

W. D. REF.

PANTRY

DN.

DINING
11/0 X 13/2
(13' CLG.)

FOYER
(13' CLG.)

BUILT-INS

GARAGE
21/0 X 21/6

DEN
10/6 X 13/4+
(9' CLG.)

©Alan Mascord Design Associates, Inc.

46'

◄ 57'-6" ►

BR. 3
13/4 X 13/4
(9' CLG.)

WET BAR

REC. RM.
18/6 X 15/4
(9' CLG.)

BR. 2
13/4 X 13/4
(9' CLG.)

UP

*Lower Level*
*1,096 sq. ft.*

**TO ORDER BLUEPRINTS USE THE FORM ON PAGE 15 OR CALL TOLL-FREE 1-877-671-6036**
View thousands more home plans online at www.familyhandyman.com/homeplans

11

# Our Blueprint Packages Offer...

*Quality plans for building your future, with extras that provide unsurpassed value, ensure good construction and long-term enjoyment.*

A quality home - one that looks good, functions well, and provides years of enjoyment - is a product of many things - design, materials, craftsmanship.

But it's also the result of outstanding blueprints - the actual plans and specifications that tell the builder exactly how to build your home.

And with our BLUEPRINT PACKAGES you get the absolute best. A complete set of blueprints is available for every design in this book. These "working drawings" are highly detailed, resulting in two key benefits:

☐ Better understanding by the contractor of how to build your home and...

☐ More accurate construction estimates.

Other helpful building aids are also available to help make your dream home a reality.

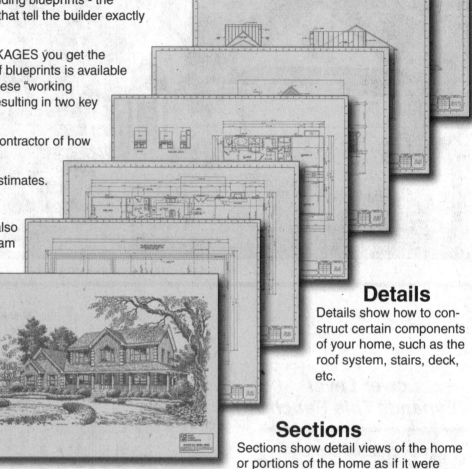

## Cover Sheet
Included with many of the plans, the cover sheet is the artist's rendering of the exterior of the home. It will give you an idea of how your home will look when completed and landscaped.

## Interior Elevations
Interior elevations provide views of special interior elements such as fireplaces, kitchen cabinets, built-in units and other features of the home.

## Foundation Plan
The foundation plan shows the layout of the basement, crawl space, slab or pier foundation. All necessary notations and dimensions are included. See plan page for the foundation types included. If the home plan you choose does not have your desired foundation type, our Customer Service Representatives can advise you on how to customize your foundation to suit your specific needs or site conditions.

## Details
Details show how to construct certain components of your home, such as the roof system, stairs, deck, etc.

## Sections
Sections show detail views of the home or portions of the home as if it were sliced from the roof to the foundation. This sheet shows important areas such as load-bearing walls, stairs, joists, trusses and other structural elements, which are critical for proper construction.

## Floor Plans
The floor plans show the placement of walls, doors, closets, plumbing fixtures, electrical outlets, columns, and beams for each level of the home.

## Exterior Elevations
Exterior elevations illustrate the front, rear and both sides of the house, with all details of exterior materials and the required dimensions.

# What Kind Of Plan Package Do You Need?

*Now that you've found the home you've been looking for, here are some suggestions on how to make your Dream Home a reality. To get started, order the type of plans that fit your particular situation.*

## YOUR CHOICES

☐ **The 1-Set Study Package -** We offer a 1-set plan package so you can study your home in detail. This one set is considered a study set and is marked "not for construction." It is a copyright violation to reproduce blueprints.

☐ **The Minimum 5-Set Package -** If you're ready to start the construction process, this 5-set package is the minimum number of blueprint sets you will need. It will require keeping close track of each set so they can be used by multiple subcontractors and tradespeople.

☐ **The Standard 8-Set Package -** For best results in terms of cost, schedule and quality of construction, we recommend you order eight (or more) sets of blueprints. Besides one set for yourself, additional sets of blueprints will be required by your mortgage lender, local building department, general contractor and all subcontractors working on foundation, electrical, plumbing, heating/air conditioning, carpentry work, etc.

☐ **Reproducible Masters -** If you wish to make some minor design changes, you'll want to order reproducible masters. These drawings contain the same information as the blueprints but are printed on erasable and reproducible paper which clearly indicates your right to copy or reproduce. This will allow your builder or a local design professional to make the necessary drawing changes without the major expense of redrawing the plans. This package also allows you to print copies of the modified plans as needed. The right of building only one structure from these plans is licensed exclusively to the buyer. You may not use this design to build a second or multiple dwelling(s) without purchasing another blueprint. Each violation of the Copyright Law is punishable in a fine.

☐ **Mirror Reverse Sets -** Plans can be printed in mirror reverse. These plans are useful when the house would fit your site better if all the rooms were on the opposite side than shown. They are simply a mirror image of the original drawings causing the lettering and dimensions to read backwards. Therefore, when ordering mirror reverse drawings, you must purchase at least one set of right-reading plans. Some of our plans are offered mirror reverse right-reading. This means the plan, lettering and dimensions are flipped but read correctly. See the Home Plans Index on page 14 for availability.

# Other Helpful Building Aids...

*Your Blueprint Package will contain the necessary construction information to build your home. We also offer the following products and services to save you time and money in the building process.*

## Material Lists
Material lists are available for many of the plans in this book. Each list gives you the quantity, dimensions and description of the building materials necessary to construct your home. You'll get faster and more accurate bids from your contractor while saving money by paying for only the materials you need. See the Home Plans Index on page 14 for availability. **Cost: $125.00**

## Detail Plan Packages
Framing, Plumbing & Electrical Plan Packages: Three separate packages offer homebuilders details for constructing various foundations; numerous floor, wall and roof framing techniques; simple to complex residential wiring; sump and water softener hookups; plumbing connection methods; installation of septic systems and more. Each package includes three-dimensional illustrations and a glossary of terms. Purchase one or all three. **Cost: $20.00 each or all three for $40.00.**
Note: These drawings do not pertain to a specific home plan.

## The Legal Kit™
Our Legal Kit provides contracts and legal forms to help protect you from the potential pitfalls inherent in the building process. The Kit supplies commonly used forms and contracts suitable for homeowners and builders. It can save you a considerable amount of time and help protect you and your assets during and after construction. **Cost: $35.00**

## Express Delivery
Most orders are processed within 24 hours of receipt. Please allow 7-10 business days for delivery. If you need to place a rush order, please call us by 11:00 a.m. Monday-Friday CST and ask for express service (allow 1-2 business days).

## Technical Assistance
If you have questions, call our technical support line at 1-314-770-2228 between 8:00 a.m. and 5:00 p.m. Monday-Friday CST. Whether it involves design modifications or field assistance, our designers are extremely familiar with all of our designs and will be happy to help you. We want your home to be everything you expect it to be.

**HOME DESIGN ALTERNATIVES, INC.**

# Home Plans Index

| Plan Number | Square Feet | Price Code | Page | Mat. List | Right Read. Reverse | Can. Shipping |
|---|---|---|---|---|---|---|
| 717-001D-0007 | 2,874 | E | 100 | • | | |
| 717-001D-0008 | 2,935 | E | 320 | • | | |
| 717-001D-0012 | 3,368 | F | 106 | • | | |
| 717-001D-0013 | 1,882 | D | 288 | • | | |
| 717-001D-0024 | 1,360 | A | 192 | • | | |
| 717-001D-0031 | 1,501 | B | 95 | • | | |
| 717-001D-0034 | 1,642 | B | 18 | • | | |
| 717-001D-0037 | 3,216 | F | 2 | • | | |
| 717-001D-0038 | 3,144 | E | 114 | • | | |
| 717-001D-0059 | 2,050 | C | 210 | • | | |
| 717-001D-0067 | 1,285 | B | 305 | • | | |
| 717-001D-0077 | 1,769 | B | 286 | • | | |
| 717-003D-0001 | 2,058 | C | 190 | • | | |
| 717-003D-0002 | 1,676 | B | 202 | • | | |
| 717-003D-0004 | 3,357 | F | 99 | • | | |
| 717-003D-0005 | 1,708 | B | 93 | • | | |
| 717-004D-0001 | 2,505 | D | 195 | • | | |
| 717-004D-0002 | 1,823 | C | 20 | • | | |
| 717-005D-0001 | 1,400 | B | 290 | • | | |
| 717-006D-0002 | 3,222 | F | 103 | • | | |
| 717-006D-0003 | 1,674 | B | 113 | • | | |
| 717-006D-0004 | 1,996 | C | 209 | • | | |
| 717-007D-0001 | 2,597 | E | 75 | • | | |
| 717-007D-0002 | 3,814 | G | 300 | • | | |
| 717-007D-0003 | 2,806 | E | 306 | • | | |
| 717-007D-0004 | 2,531 | D | 287 | • | | |
| 717-007D-0006 | 2,624 | E | 193 | • | | |
| 717-007D-0007 | 2,523 | D | 4 | • | | |
| 717-007D-0008 | 2,452 | D | 47 | • | | |
| 717-007D-0010 | 1,721 | C | 191 | • | | |
| 717-007D-0011 | 2,182 | D | 96 | • | | |
| 717-007D-0015 | 2,828 | F | 17 | • | | |
| 717-007D-0016 | 3,850 | F | 115 | • | | |
| 717-007D-0017 | 1,882 | C | 212 | • | | |
| 717-007D-0028 | 1,711 | B | 319 | • | | |
| 717-007D-0030 | 1,140 | AA | 284 | • | | |
| 717-007D-0031 | 1,092 | AA | 189 | • | | |
| 717-007D-0032 | 1,294 | A | 94 | • | | |
| 717-007D-0038 | 1,524 | B | 22 | • | | |
| 717-007D-0040 | 632 | AAA | 118 | • | | |
| 717-007D-0046 | 1,712 | B | 194 | • | | |
| 717-007D-0048 | 2,758 | E | 215 | • | | |
| 717-007D-0049 | 1,791 | C | 281 | • | | |
| 717-007D-0050 | 2,723 | E | 186 | • | | |
| 717-007D-0051 | 2,614 | E | 92 | • | | |
| 717-007D-0052 | 2,521 | D | 19 | • | | |
| 717-007D-0054 | 1,575 | B | 121 | • | | |
| 717-007D-0055 | 2,029 | D | 217 | • | | |
| 717-007D-0056 | 3,199 | E | 279 | • | | |
| 717-007D-0057 | 2,808 | F | 183 | • | | |
| 717-007D-0058 | 4,826 | G | 90 | • | | |
| 717-007D-0059 | 3,169 | F | 293 | • | | |
| 717-007D-0060 | 1,268 | B | 24 | • | | |
| 717-007D-0062 | 2,483 | D | 124 | • | | |
| 717-007D-0063 | 3,138 | E | 220 | • | | |
| 717-007D-0064 | 2,967 | E | 309 | • | | |
| 717-007D-0065 | 2,218 | D | 276 | • | | |
| 717-007D-0066 | 2,408 | D | 181 | • | | |
| 717-007D-0067 | 1,761 | B | 88 | • | | |
| 717-007D-0068 | 1,384 | B | 26 | • | | |
| 717-007D-0071 | 3,657 | F | 126 | • | | |
| 717-007D-0072 | 2,900 | E | 223 | • | | |
| 717-007D-0075 | 1,684 | B | 273 | • | | |
| 717-007D-0077 | 1,977 | C | 179 | • | | |
| 717-007D-0078 | 2,514 | D | 86 | • | | |
| 717-007D-0079 | 2,727 | E | 28 | • | | |
| 717-007D-0080 | 2,900 | E | 129 | • | | |
| 717-007D-0084 | 3,420 | F | 226 | • | | |
| 717-007D-0085 | 1,787 | B | 270 | • | | |
| 717-007D-0088 | 1,299 | A | 176 | • | | |
| 717-007D-0089 | 2,125 | C | 84 | • | | |
| 717-007D-0098 | 2,397 | D | 142 | • | | |
| 717-007D-0100 | 2,409 | D | 30 | • | | |
| 717-007D-0102 | 1,452 | A | 132 | • | | |
| 717-007D-0103 | 1,231 | A | 229 | • | | |
| 717-007D-0105 | 1,084 | AA | 108 | • | | |
| 717-007D-0107 | 1,161 | AA | 268 | • | | |
| 717-007D-0113 | 2,547 | D | 174 | • | | |
| 717-007D-0117 | 2,695 | E | 82 | • | | |
| 717-007D-0118 | 1,991 | C | 33 | • | | |
| 717-007D-0124 | 1,944 | C | 135 | | | |
| 717-007D-0132 | 4,370 | G | 239 | | | |
| 717-007D-0140 | 1,591 | B | 232 | • | | |
| 717-007D-0146 | 1,929 | C | 265 | | | |
| 717-007D-0149 | 5,321 | H | 172 | | | |
| 717-010D-0006 | 1,170 | AA | 291 | • | • | |
| 717-011D-0009 | 2,840 | F | 11 | | • | |
| 717-011D-0029 | 2,689 | E | 9 | | • | |
| 717-011D-0042 | 2,561 | F | 21 | | • | |
| 717-011D-0045 | 2,850 | F | 117 | | • | |
| 717-011D-0046 | 2,277 | E | 6 | | • | |
| 717-013D-0015 | 1,787 | B | 211 | | | |
| 717-013D-0019 | 1,992 | C | 308 | • | | |
| 717-013D-0022 | 1,992 | C | 285 | • | • | |
| 717-013D-0025 | 2,097 | C | 188 | • | | |
| 717-013D-0027 | 2,184 | C | 80 | | | |
| 717-013D-0037 | 2,564 | D | 32 | • | | |
| 717-016D-0009 | 1,416 | A | 119 | • | | |
| 717-016D-0021 | 1,892 | D | 206 | • | | |
| 717-016D-0048 | 2,567 | F | 213 | • | | |
| 717-016D-0049 | 1,793 | B | 97 | • | | |
| 717-016D-0051 | 1,945 | D | 282 | • | | |
| 717-016D-0055 | 1,040 | B | 107 | • | | |
| 717-016D-0058 | 2,874 | G | 187 | • | | |
| 717-017D-0005 | 1,367 | B | 91 | • | | |
| 717-017D-0006 | 3,006 | E | 313 | • | | |
| 717-017D-0007 | 1,567 | C | 23 | • | | |
| 717-017D-0010 | 1,660 | C | 123 | • | | |
| 717-018D-0001 | 3,494 | F | 214 | • | | |
| 717-019D-0010 | 1,890 | C | 260 | | | |
| 717-019D-0012 | 1,993 | C | 160 | | | |
| 717-019D-0014 | 2,586 | D | 283 | | | |
| 717-019D-0016 | 2,678 | E | 73 | | | |
| 717-019D-0021 | 2,838 | E | 185 | | | |
| 717-020D-0003 | 1,420 | A | 78 | | | |
| 717-020D-0009 | 2,123 | E | 49 | | | |
| 717-020D-0015 | 1,191 | AA | 34 | | | |
| 717-021D-0004 | 1,800 | C | 144 | • | | |
| 717-021D-0006 | 1,600 | C | 116 | • | | |
| 717-021D-0012 | 1,672 | C | 219 | • | | |
| 717-021D-0016 | 1,600 | B | 310 | • | | |
| 717-021D-0019 | 2,605 | E | 277 | • | | |
| 717-021D-0021 | 3,153 | E | 241 | • | | |
| 717-022D-0001 | 1,039 | AA | 184 | • | | |
| 717-022D-0002 | 1,246 | A | 76 | • | | |
| 717-022D-0009 | 1,851 | D | 25 | • | | |
| 717-022D-0011 | 1,630 | B | 315 | • | | |
| 717-022D-0014 | 1,556 | B | 8 | • | | |
| 717-022D-0019 | 1,283 | A | 101 | • | | |
| 717-022D-0020 | 988 | AA | 125 | • | | |
| 717-023D-0001 | 3,149 | E | 216 | • | | |
| 717-023D-0006 | 2,357 | D | 275 | • | | |
| 717-023D-0009 | 2,333 | D | 104 | • | | |
| 717-023D-0010 | 2,558 | D | 175 | • | | |
| 717-023D-0016 | 1,609 | B | 74 | • | | |
| 717-024D-0031 | 3,266 | H | 27 | | | |
| 717-024D-0032 | 3,444 | G | 196 | | | |
| 717-024D-0034 | 3,493 | H | 120 | | | |
| 717-024D-0036 | 4,187 | H | 105 | | | |
| 717-024D-0037 | 4,380 | H | 301 | | | |
| 717-025D-0010 | 1,677 | B | 218 | | | |
| 717-025D-0018 | 1,979 | C | 110 | | | |
| 717-025D-0028 | 2,350 | D | 280 | | | |
| 717-025D-0033 | 2,416 | D | 295 | | | |
| 717-025D-0051 | 3,369 | F | 177 | | | |
| 717-026D-0096 | 1,341 | A | 258 | • | | |
| 717-026D-0112 | 1,911 | C | 72 | • | • | |
| 717-026D-0121 | 2,270 | D | 36 | • | | |
| 717-026D-0122 | 1,850 | C | 159 | • | • | |
| 717-026D-0142 | 2,188 | C | 71 | • | | |
| 717-026D-0154 | 1,392 | A | 127 | • | | |
| 717-027D-0005 | 2,135 | D | 221 | • | | |
| 717-027D-0006 | 2,076 | C | 271 | • | | |
| 717-027D-0007 | 2,444 | D | 182 | • | | |
| 717-028D-0004 | 1,785 | B | 302 | | • | |
| 717-028D-0008 | 2,156 | C | 50 | | • | |
| 717-028D-0011 | 2,123 | C | 89 | | • | |
| 717-028D-0015 | 2,421 | D | 5 | | | |
| 717-028D-0025 | 1,587 | B | 10 | | • | |
| 717-029D-0002 | 1,619 | B | 29 | • | | |
| 717-030D-0001 | 1,374 | A | 146 | | | |
| 717-030D-0002 | 1,429 | A | 242 | | | |
| 717-030D-0004 | 1,791 | B | 317 | | | |
| 717-032D-0033 | 1,484 | A | 98 | • | • | • |
| 717-032D-0040 | 1,480 | A | 122 | • | • | • |
| 717-032D-0050 | 840 | AAA | 111 | • | • | • |
| 717-033D-0001 | 2,733 | F | 254 | • | | |
| 717-033D-0002 | 1,859 | D | 200 | • | | |
| 717-033D-0012 | 1,546 | C | 158 | • | | |
| 717-035D-0011 | 1,945 | C | 69 | • | | |
| 717-035D-0021 | 1,978 | C | 51 | • | | |
| 717-035D-0028 | 1,779 | B | 147 | • | | |
| 717-035D-0029 | 2,349 | D | 243 | • | | |
| 717-035D-0032 | 1,856 | C | 256 | • | | |
| 717-035D-0035 | 2,322 | D | 157 | • | | |
| 717-035D-0036 | 2,193 | C | 67 | • | | |
| 717-035D-0040 | 2,126 | C | 53 | • | | |
| 717-035D-0042 | 2,311 | D | 149 | • | | |
| 717-035D-0045 | 1,749 | B | 225 | • | | |
| 717-035D-0047 | 1,818 | C | 312 | • | | |
| 717-035D-0048 | 1,915 | C | 245 | • | | |
| 717-035D-0050 | 1,342 | A | 252 | • | | |
| 717-035D-0051 | 1,491 | A | 155 | • | | |
| 717-035D-0056 | 2,246 | D | 278 | • | | |
| 717-036D-0020 | 2,787 | E | 65 | | | |
| 717-036D-0037 | 3,870 | F | 180 | | | |
| 717-036D-0048 | 1,830 | C | 70 | | | |
| 717-036D-0058 | 2,529 | D | 38 | | | |
| 717-036D-0059 | 2,674 | E | 131 | | | |
| 717-036D-0060 | 1,760 | B | 227 | | | |
| 717-037D-0004 | 2,449 | E | 197 | • | | |
| 717-037D-0006 | 1,772 | C | 274 | • | | |
| 717-037D-0009 | 2,059 | C | 173 | • | | |
| 717-037D-0013 | 2,213 | E | 52 | • | | |
| 717-037D-0014 | 2,932 | F | 148 | • | | |
| 717-037D-0021 | 2,260 | D | 87 | • | | |
| 717-037D-0031 | 1,923 | C | 244 | • | | |
| 717-038D-0008 | 1,738 | B | 31 | • | • | |
| 717-038D-0037 | 1,434 | A | 128 | | | |
| 717-038D-0039 | 1,771 | B | 203 | • | | |
| 717-038D-0040 | 1,642 | B | 294 | • | | |
| 717-038D-0044 | 1,982 | C | 231 | • | | |
| 717-038D-0045 | 2,044 | C | 272 | • | | |
| 717-039D-0001 | 1,253 | A | 178 | • | | |
| 717-039D-0002 | 1,333 | A | 85 | • | | |
| 717-039D-0004 | 1,406 | A | 35 | • | | |
| 717-040D-0001 | 1,814 | D | 204 | • | | |
| 717-040D-0003 | 1,475 | B | 130 | • | | |
| 717-040D-0005 | 2,665 | E | 289 | • | | |
| 717-040D-0006 | 1,759 | B | 222 | • | | |
| 717-040D-0007 | 2,073 | D | 251 | • | | |
| 717-040D-0019 | 1,854 | D | 156 | • | | |
| 717-040D-0024 | 1,874 | C | 314 | • | | |
| 717-040D-0026 | 1,393 | B | 266 | • | | |
| 717-040D-0027 | 1,597 | C | 170 | • | | |
| 717-043D-0007 | 2,788 | E | 63 | | | |
| 717-043D-0008 | 1,496 | A | 68 | | | |
| 717-043D-0018 | 3,502 | F | 40 | | | |
| 717-043D-0020 | 2,880 | E | 133 | | | |
| 717-047D-0019 | 1,783 | B | 59 | • | | |
| 717-047D-0051 | 2,962 | E | 150 | • | | |
| 717-047D-0052 | 3,098 | F | 109 | | | |
| 717-047D-0054 | 3,144 | F | 207 | | | |
| 717-047D-0058 | 3,106 | E | 246 | • | | |
| 717-047D-0059 | 3,556 | F | 250 | • | | |
| 717-047D-0060 | 3,570 | F | 224 | | | |
| 717-048D-0001 | 1,865 | D | 269 | • | | |
| 717-048D-0004 | 2,397 | E | 168 | • | | |
| 717-048D-0008 | 2,089 | C | 154 | • | | |
| 717-048D-0011 | 1,550 | B | 83 | • | | |
| 717-049D-0005 | 1,389 | A | 42 | • | | |
| 717-049D-0006 | 1,771 | B | 137 | • | | |
| 717-049D-0007 | 1,118 | AA | 233 | • | | |
| 717-049D-0008 | 1,937 | C | 267 | • | | |
| 717-049D-0009 | 1,673 | B | 171 | • | | |
| 717-049D-0010 | 1,669 | B | 81 | | | |
| 717-051D-0039 | 1,976 | C | 44 | | | |
| 717-051D-0046 | 2,991 | E | 134 | | | |
| 717-051D-0060 | 1,591 | B | 228 | | | |
| 717-051D-0066 | 3,321 | F | 307 | | | |
| 717-051D-0166 | 2,477 | E | 263 | | | |
| 717-051D-0180 | 3,470 | G | 169 | | | |
| 717-052D-0011 | 1,325 | A | 66 | • | | |
| 717-052D-0046 | 1,869 | C | 46 | • | | |
| 717-052D-0048 | 1,870 | C | 292 | • | | |
| 717-053D-0002 | 1,668 | C | 61 | • | | |
| 717-053D-0003 | 1,992 | C | 55 | • | | |
| 717-053D-0017 | 2,529 | E | 304 | • | | |
| 717-053D-0029 | 1,220 | A | 139 | • | | |
| 717-053D-0030 | 1,657 | B | 198 | • | | |
| 717-053D-0032 | 1,404 | A | 151 | • | | |
| 717-053D-0050 | 2,718 | E | 235 | • | | |
| 717-053D-0052 | 2,513 | D | 247 | • | | |
| 717-053D-0058 | 1,818 | C | 261 | • | | |
| 717-055D-0017 | 1,525 | B | 166 | • | • | |
| 717-055D-0023 | 4,237 | G | 79 | • | • | |
| 717-055D-0026 | 1,538 | B | 37 | • | • | |
| 717-055D-0030 | 2,107 | C | 296 | • | • | |
| 717-055D-0032 | 2,439 | D | 136 | • | • | |
| 717-055D-0053 | 1,957 | C | 230 | • | • | |
| 717-055D-0097 | 2,975 | E | 259 | • | • | |
| 717-055D-0103 | 2,716 | E | 299 | • | • | |
| 717-055D-0109 | 2,217 | C | 163 | • | • | |
| 717-055D-0118 | 2,789 | E | 201 | • | • | |
| 717-056D-0002 | 2,135 | B | 3 | | | |
| 717-056D-0005 | 2,111 | H | 249 | | | |
| 717-056D-0007 | 1,985 | G | 153 | | | |
| 717-056D-0019 | 2,737 | E | 64 | | | |
| 717-058D-0016 | 1,558 | B | 39 | | | |
| 717-058D-0020 | 1,428 | A | 138 | • | | |
| 717-058D-0021 | 1,477 | A | 234 | • | | |
| 717-058D-0023 | 1,883 | C | 257 | • | | |
| 717-058D-0026 | 1,819 | C | 167 | • | | |
| 717-058D-0027 | 2,516 | D | 62 | • | | |
| 717-058D-0033 | 1,440 | A | 41 | • | | |
| 717-058D-0048 | 3,556 | F | 141 | • | | |
| 717-060D-0007 | 2,079 | C | 236 | | | |
| 717-060D-0008 | 2,281 | D | 316 | | | |
| 717-060D-0010 | 2,600 | E | 264 | | | |
| 717-060D-0030 | 1,455 | A | 164 | | | |
| 717-062D-0041 | 1,541 | B | 60 | • | • | • |
| 717-062D-0043 | 2,750 | E | 43 | • | | • |
| 717-062D-0046 | 2,632 | E | 57 | • | | • |
| 717-062D-0048 | 1,543 | B | 143 | • | | • |
| 717-062D-0050 | 1,408 | A | 102 | • | • | • |
| 717-062D-0052 | 1,795 | B | 237 | • | • | • |
| 717-065D-0009 | 2,403 | D | 112 | • | | |
| 717-065D-0024 | 4,652 | G | 205 | | | |
| 717-065D-0026 | 2,269 | D | 311 | | | |
| 717-065D-0036 | 2,587 | D | 152 | • | | |
| 717-065D-0041 | 3,171 | E | 297 | • | | |
| 717-065D-0042 | 2,362 | D | 248 | • | | |
| 717-065D-0043 | 3,816 | F | 56 | | | |
| 717-067D-0003 | 1,841 | C | 54 | | | |
| 717-068D-0002 | 2,266 | D | 255 | • | | |
| 717-068D-0003 | 1,784 | B | 165 | • | | |
| 717-068D-0004 | 1,969 | C | 58 | • | | |
| 717-068D-0006 | 1,399 | A | 45 | • | | |
| 717-068D-0010 | 1,849 | C | 145 | • | | |
| 717-069D-0012 | 1,594 | B | 240 | • | | |
| 717-069D-0017 | 1,926 | C | 262 | • | | |
| 717-069D-0018 | 2,069 | C | 162 | • | | |
| 717-071D-0001 | 2,920 | E | 7 | | • | |
| 717-071D-0002 | 2,770 | E | 77 | | • | |
| 717-071D-0003 | 2,890 | E | 303 | | • | |
| 717-071D-0006 | 3,746 | G | 199 | | • | |
| 717-071D-0008 | 4,100 | G | 48 | | • | |
| 717-071D-0010 | 5,250 | H | 208 | | • | |
| 717-071D-0011 | 5,800 | H | 140 | | • | |
| 717-077D-0002 | 1,855 | D | 238 | • | | |
| 717-077D-0003 | 1,896 | D | 298 | | | |
| 717-077D-0004 | 2,024 | D | 318 | • | | |
| 717-077D-0006 | 2,307 | D | 253 | | | |
| 717-077D-0007 | 2,805 | E | 161 | • | | |

## Important Information To Know Before You Order

■ **Exchange Policies -** Since blueprints are printed in response to your order, we cannot honor requests for refunds. However, if for some reason you find that the plan you have purchased does not meet your requirements, you may exchange that plan for another plan in our collection within 90 days of purchase. At the time of the exchange, you will be charged a processing fee of 25% of your original plan package price, plus the difference in price between the plan packages (if applicable) and the cost to ship the new plans to you.

*Please note: Reproducible drawings can only be exchanged if the package is unopened.*

■ **Building Codes & Requirements -** At the time the construction drawings were prepared, every effort was made to ensure that these plans and specifications meet nationally recognized codes. Our plans conform to most national building codes. Because building codes vary from area to area, some drawing modifications and/or the assistance of a professional designer or architect may be necessary to comply with your local codes or to accommodate specific building site conditions. We advise you to consult with your local building official for information regarding codes governing your area.

### Questions?  Call Our Customer Service Number
### 1-877-671-6036

### Blueprint Price Schedule — BEST VALUE

| Price Code | 1-Set* | SAVE $110 5-Sets | SAVE $200 8-Sets | Reproducible Masters |
|---|---|---|---|---|
| AAA | $225 | $295 | $340 | $440 |
| AA | $325 | $395 | $440 | $540 |
| A | $385 | $455 | $500 | $600 |
| B | $445 | $515 | $560 | $660 |
| C | $500 | $570 | $615 | $715 |
| D | $560 | $630 | $675 | $775 |
| E | $620 | $690 | $735 | $835 |
| F | $675 | $745 | $790 | $890 |
| G | $765 | $835 | $880 | $980 |
| H | $890 | $960 | $1005 | $1105 |

**Plan prices guaranteed through June 30, 2006.**
**Please note that plans are not refundable.**

■ **Additional Sets* -** Additional sets of the plan ordered are available for $45.00 each. Five-set, eight-set, and reproducible packages offer considerable savings.

■ **Mirror Reverse Plans* -** Available for an additional $15.00 per set, these plans are simply a mirror image of the original drawings causing the dimensions and lettering to read backwards. Therefore, when ordering mirror reverse plans, you must purchase at least one set of right-reading plans. Some of our plans are offered mirror reverse right-reading. This means the plan, lettering and dimensions are flipped but read correctly. To purchase a mirror reverse right-reading set, the cost is an additional $150.00. See the Home Plans Index on page 14 for availability.

■ **One-Set Study Package* -** We offer a one-set plan package so you can study your home in detail. This one set is considered a study set and is marked "not for construction." It is a copyright violation to reproduce blueprints.

*Available only within 90 days after purchase of plan package or reproducible masters of same plan.

## Shipping & Handling Charges

| U.S. SHIPPING - HI and AK express only | 1-4 Sets | 5-7 Sets | 8 Sets or Reproducibles |
|---|---|---|---|
| Regular (allow 7-10 business days) | $15.00 | $17.50 | $25.00 |
| Priority (allow 3-5 business days) | $25.00 | $30.00 | $35.00 |
| Express* (allow 1-2 business days) | $35.00 | $40.00 | $45.00 |

| CANADA SHIPPING (to/from) - Plans with suffix 032D or 62D | 1-4 Sets | 5-7 Sets | 8 Sets or Reproducibles |
|---|---|---|---|
| Standard (allow 8-12 business days) | $25.00 | $30.00 | $35.00 |
| Express* (allow 3-5 business days) | $40.00 | $40.00 | $45.00 |

Overseas Shipping/International - Call, fax, or e-mail (plans@hdainc.com) for shipping costs.

* For express delivery please call us by 11:00 a.m. Monday-Friday CST

---

# How To Order

### For fastest service, Call Toll-Free
## 1-877-671-6036
### 24 HOURS A DAY

**Three Easy Ways To Order**

1. CALL toll-free 1-877-671-6036 for credit card orders. MasterCard, Visa, Discover and American Express are accepted.

2. FAX your order to 1-314-770-2226.

3. MAIL the Order Form to:

    HDA, Inc.
    944 Anglum Road
    St. Louis, MO  63042

## Order Form

*Please send me -*

**PLAN NUMBER  717BT -** _____

PRICE CODE _____ (see page 14)

Specify Foundation Type (see plan page for availability)
- ☐ Slab        ☐ Crawl space        ☐ Pier
- ☐ Basement   ☐ Walk-out basement

- ☐ Reproducible Masters ........................ $ _____
- ☐ Eight-Set Plan Package ...................... $ _____
- ☐ Five-Set Plan Package ....................... $ _____
- ☐ One-Set Study Package (no mirror reverse) $ _____
- ☐ Additional Plan Sets*
    _____ (Qty.) at $45.00 each ............... $ _____

Mirror Reverse*
- ☐ Right-reading $150 one-time charge
    (see index on page 14 for availability) ...... $ _____
- ☐ Print in Mirror Reverse (where right-reading is not available)
    _____ (Qty.) at $15.00 each ............... $ _____
- ☐ Material List* $125 (see page 14 for avail.) $ _____
- ☐ Legal Kit (see page 13) ....................... $ _____

Detail Plan Packages: (see page 13)
- ☐ Framing   ☐ Electrical   ☐ Plumbing  $ _____

  **SUBTOTAL** $ _____

Sales Tax - MO residents add 6% ............... $ _____
- ☐ Shipping / Handling (see chart at left) ..... $ _____

  **TOTAL ENCLOSED** (US funds only) ........ $ _____

I hereby authorize HDA, Inc. to charge this purchase to my credit card account (check one):

☐ MasterCard    ☐ VISA    ☐ DISCOVER    ☐ American Express

Credit Card number _____

Expiration date _____

Signature _____

Name _____
(Please print or type)

Street Address _____
(Please **do not** use PO Box)

City _____

State _____  Zip _____

Daytime phone number ( ___ ) - _____

I'm a ☐ Builder/Contractor    I ☐ have
      ☐ Homeowner            ☐ have not
      ☐ Renter               selected my
                             general contractor

***Thank you for your order!***

15

# Quick & Easy Customizing
## Make Changes To Your Home Plan In 4 Steps

**Here's an affordable and efficient way to make changes to your plan.**

**1.** Select the house plan that most closely meets your needs. Purchase of a reproducible master is necessary in order to make changes to a plan.

**2.** Call 1-877-671-6036 to place your order. Tell the sales representative you're interested in customizing a plan. A $50 nonrefundable consultation fee will be charged. You will then be instructed to complete a customization checklist indicating all the changes you wish to make to your plan. You may attach sketches if necessary. If you proceed with the custom changes the $50 will be credited to the total amount charged.

**3.** FAX the completed customization checklist to our design consultant at 1-866-477-5173 or e-mail customize@hdainc.com. Within 24-48* business hours you will be provided with a written cost estimate to modify your plan. Our design consultant will contact you by phone if you wish to discuss any of your changes in greater detail.

**4.** Once you approve the estimate, a 75% retainer fee is collected and customization work gets underway. Preliminary drawings can usually be completed within 5-10* business days. Following approval of the preliminary drawings your design changes are completed within 5-10* business days. Your remaining 25% balance due is collected prior to shipment of your completed drawings. You will be shipped five sets of revised blueprints or a reproducible master, plus a customized materials list if required.

## Sample Modification Pricing Guide

The average prices specified below are provided as examples only. They refer to the most commonly requested changes, and are subject to change without notice. Prices for changes will vary or differ, from the prices below, depending on the number of modifications requested, the plan size, style, quality of original plan, format provided to us (originally drawn by hand or computer), and method of design used by the original designer. To obtain a detailed cost estimate or to get more information, please contact us.

| Categories | Average Cost* |
| --- | --- |
| Adding or removing living space | Quote required |
| Adding or removing a garage | Starting at $400 |
| Garage: Front entry to side load or vice versa | Starting at $300 |
| Adding a screened porch | Starting at $280 |
| Adding a bonus room in the attic | Starting at $450 |
| Changing full basement to crawl space or vice versa | Starting at $495 |
| Changing full basement to slab or vice versa | Starting at $495 |
| Changing exterior building material | Starting at $200 |
| Changing roof lines | Starting at $360 |
| Adjusting ceiling height | Starting at $280 |
| Adding, moving or removing an exterior opening | $65 per opening |
| Adding or removing a fireplace | Starting at $90 |
| Modifying a non-bearing wall or room | $65 per room |
| Changing exterior walls from 2"x4" to 2"x6" | Starting at $200 |
| Redesigning a bathroom or a kitchen | Starting at $120 |
| Reverse plan right reading | Quote required |
| Adapting plans for local building code requirements | Quote required |
| Engineering and Architectural stamping and services | Quote required |
| Adjust plan for handicapped accessibility | Quote required |
| Interactive Illustrations (choices of exterior materials) | Quote required |
| Metric conversion of home plan | Starting at $400 |

*Prices and Terms are subject to change without notice.

**2,828 total square feet of living area**

## Five Bedroom Home Embraces Large Family

### Special features

- Popular wrap-around porch gives home country charm
- Secluded, oversized family room with vaulted ceiling and wet bar features many windows
- Any chef would be delighted to cook in this smartly designed kitchen with island and corner windows
- Spectacular master bedroom and bath
- 5 bedrooms, 3 1/2 baths, 2-car side entry garage
- Basement foundation, drawings also include crawl space and slab foundations

**Price Code F**

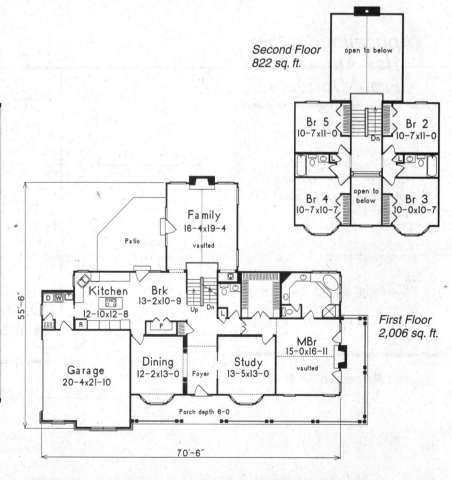

Second Floor
822 sq. ft.

open to below

Br 5
10-7x11-0

Br 2
10-7x11-0

Dn

Br 4
10-7x10-7

open to below

Br 3
10-0x10-7

Family
16-4x19-4
vaulted

Patio

Kitchen
12-10x12-8

Brk
13-2x10-9

Up
Dn

D W

R

First Floor
2,006 sq. ft.

MBr
15-0x16-11
vaulted

Garage
20-4x21-10

Dining
12-2x13-0

P

Foyer

Study
13-5x13-0

55'-6"

Porch depth 6-0

70'-6"

**TO ORDER BLUEPRINTS USE THE FORM ON PAGE 15 OR CALL TOLL-FREE 1-877-671-6036**
View thousands more home plans online at www.familyhandyman.com/homeplans

17

**1,642 total square feet of living area**

## Appealing Ranch Has Attractive Front Dormers

### Special features

- Walk-through kitchen boasts a vaulted ceiling and corner sink overlooking the family room
- Vaulted family room features a cozy fireplace and access to the rear patio
- Master bedroom includes a sloped ceiling, walk-in closet and private bath
- 3 bedrooms, 2 baths, 2-car garage
- Basement foundation, drawings also include slab and crawl space foundations

*Price Code B*

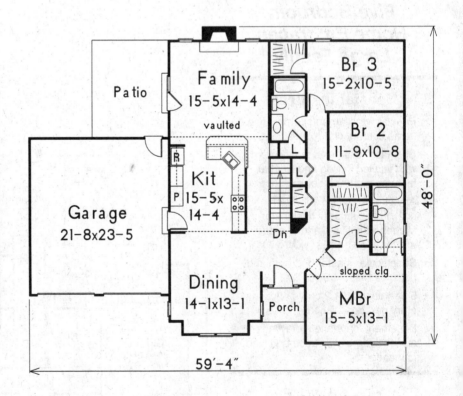

18

**TO ORDER BLUEPRINTS USE THE FORM ON PAGE 15 OR CALL TOLL-FREE 1-877-671-6036**
View thousands more home plans online at www.familyhandyman.com/homeplans

**2,521 total square feet of living area**

## Great Looks Accentuated By Elliptical Brick Arches

### Special features

- Large living and dining rooms are a plus for formal entertaining or large family gatherings
- Informal kitchen, breakfast and family rooms feature a 37' vista and double bay windows
- Generously sized master bedroom and three secondary bedrooms grace the second floor
- 4 bedrooms, 2 1/2 baths, 2-car garage
- Basement foundation

*Price Code D*

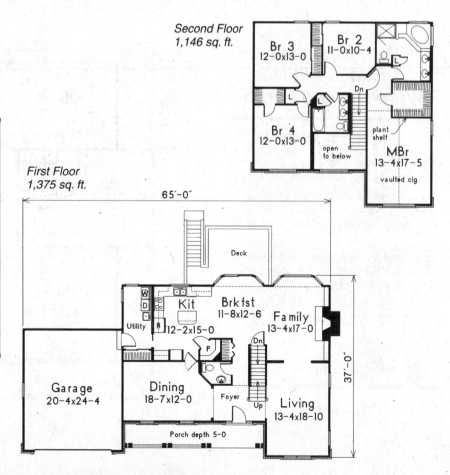

Second Floor
1,146 sq. ft.

Br 3
12-0x13-0

Br 2
11-0x10-4

Br 4
12-0x13-0

Dn

plant shelf

open to below

MBr
13-4x17-5

vaulted clg

First Floor
1,375 sq. ft.

65'-0"

Deck

Kit
12-2x15-0

Brkfst
11-8x12-6

Family
13-4x17-0

Utility

W
D

P

Dn

37'-0"

Garage
20-4x24-4

Dining
18-7x12-0

Foyer

Up

Living
13-4x18-10

Porch depth 5-0

**TO ORDER BLUEPRINTS USE THE FORM ON PAGE 15 OR CALL TOLL-FREE 1-877-671-6036**
View thousands more home plans online at www.familyhandyman.com/homeplans

19

**1,823 total square feet of living area**

## Well-Designed Ranch With Wrap-Around Porch

### Special features

- Vaulted living room is spacious and easily accesses the dining area
- The master bedroom boasts a tray ceiling, large walk-in closet and a private bath with a corner whirlpool tub
- Cheerful dining area is convenient to the U-shaped kitchen and also enjoys patio access
- Centrally located laundry room connects the garage to the living areas
- 3 bedrooms, 2 baths, 2-car garage
- Basement foundation

*Price Code C*

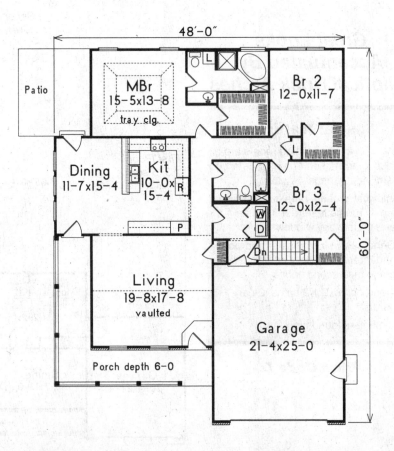

**TO ORDER BLUEPRINTS USE THE FORM ON PAGE 15 OR CALL TOLL-FREE 1-877-671-6036**
View thousands more home plans online at www.familyhandyman.com/homeplans

20

**Plan #717-011D-0042**

**2,561 total square feet of living area**

## Sophisticated Southern Style

### Special features

- Sunny vaulted breakfast nook
- Dormers are a charming touch in the second floor bedrooms
- Columns throughout the first floor help separate rooms while creating a feeling of openness
- Bonus room on the second floor has an additional 232 square feet of living area
- 4 bedrooms, 2 1/2 baths, 2-car side entry garage
- Crawl space foundation

*Price Code F*

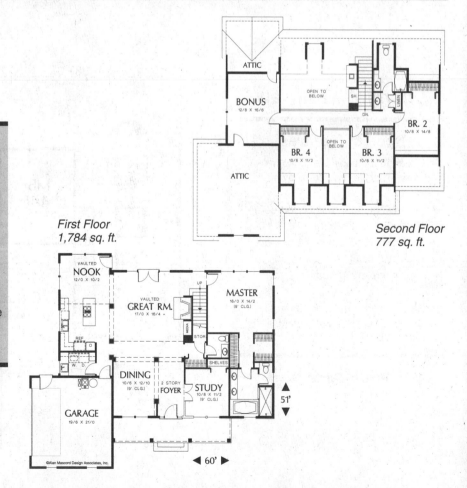

First Floor
1,784 sq. ft.

Second Floor
777 sq. ft.

**TO ORDER BLUEPRINTS USE THE FORM ON PAGE 15 OR CALL TOLL-FREE 1-877-671-6036**
View thousands more home plans online at www.familyhandyman.com/homeplans

21

**1,524 total square feet of living area**

## Dining With A View

### Special features

- Delightful balcony overlooks two-story entry illuminated by oval window
- Roomy first floor master bedroom offers quiet privacy
- All bedrooms feature one or more walk-in closets
- 3 bedrooms, 2 1/2 baths, 2-car garage
- Basement foundation, drawings also include crawl space and slab foundations

*Price Code B*

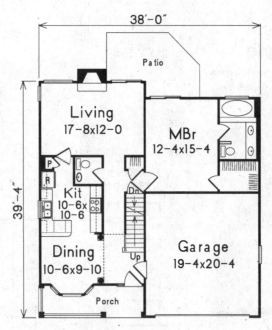

First Floor
951 sq. ft.

Second Floor
573 sq. ft.

**1,567 total square feet of living area**

## Pillared Front Porch Generates Charm And Warmth

### Special features

- Living room flows into the dining room shaped by an angled pass-through into the kitchen
- Cheerful, windowed dining area
- Future area available on the second floor has an additional 338 square feet of living area
- Master bedroom is separated from other bedrooms for privacy
- 3 bedrooms, 2 baths, 2-car side entry garage
- Partial basement/crawl space foundation, drawings also include slab foundation

### *Price Code C*

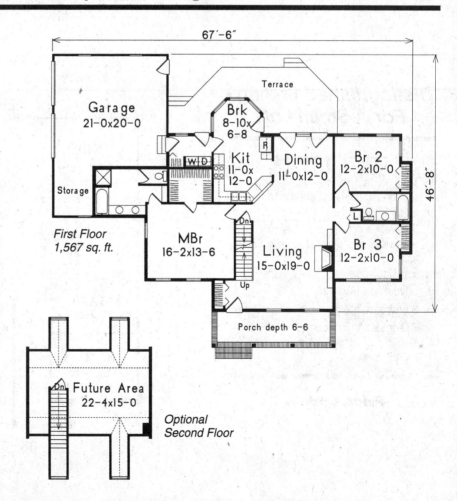

67'-6"

46'-8"

Terrace

Garage
21-0x20-0

Storage

W D

Brk
8-10x
6-8

Kit
11-0x
12-0

R

Dining
11-0x12-0

Br 2
12-2x10-0

First Floor
1,567 sq. ft.

MBr
16-2x13-6

Dn

Up

Living
15-0x19-0

Br 3
12-2x10-0

Porch depth 6-6

Dn

Future Area
22-4x15-0

*Optional
Second Floor*

**TO ORDER BLUEPRINTS USE THE FORM ON PAGE 15 OR CALL TOLL-FREE 1-877-671-6036**
View thousands more home plans online at www.familyhandyman.com/homeplans

23

**1,268 total square feet of living area**

## Distinguished Styling For A Small Lot

### Special features

- Multiple gables, large porch and arched windows create a classy exterior
- Innovative design provides openness in the great room, kitchen and breakfast room
- Secondary bedrooms have a private hall with bath
- 3 bedrooms, 2 baths, 2-car garage
- Basement foundation, drawings also include crawl space and slab foundations

### *Price Code B*

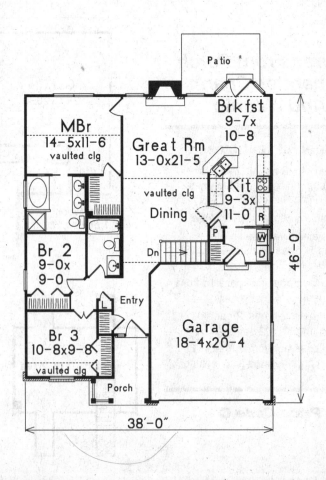

**1,851 total square feet of living area**

## Vaulted Great Room With Open Entrance

### Special features

- High-impact entrance to great room also leads directly to the second floor
- First floor master bedroom suite features a corner window and walk-in closet
- Kitchen/breakfast room has center work island and pass-through to the dining room
- Second floor bedrooms share a bath
- 4 bedrooms, 2 1/2 baths, 2-car garage
- Basement foundation

**Price Code D**

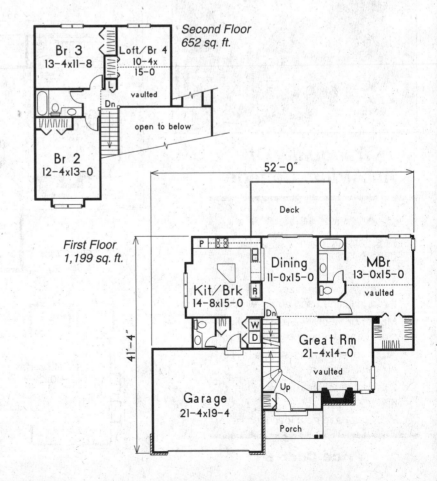

Second Floor 652 sq. ft.

Br 3 13-4x11-8

Loft/Br 4 10-4x 15-0

vaulted

Br 2 12-4x13-0

Dn

open to below

First Floor 1,199 sq. ft.

52'-0"

41'-4"

Deck

Dining 11-0x15-0

MBr 13-0x15-0 vaulted

Kit/Brk 14-8x15-0

Great Rm 21-4x14-0 vaulted

Dn

W D

Up

Garage 21-4x19-4

Porch

**1,384 total square feet of living area**

*Rear View*

# Tranquility Of An Atrium Cottage

## Special features

- Wrap-around country porch for peaceful evenings
- Great room has a large bay window, stone fireplace, pass-through kitchen and atrium window
- Master bedroom features a walk-in closet and a fabulous bath
- Atrium opens to 611 square feet of optional living area below
- 2 bedrooms, 2 baths, 1-car side entry garage
- Walk-out basement foundation

*Price Code B*

55'-8"

Atrium below

Dn

Dining Area

Kit
10-2x
11-9

Garage
22-0x11-9

Great Rm
18-0x21-8
vaulted

Laundry

46'-0"

Cover porch depth 6-0

MBr
12-8x15-0

Br 2
11-4x12-6

**First Floor**
1,384 sq. ft.

Up

Patio

Family Rm
25-0x21-4

Unexcavated

*Optional Lower Level*

Unfinished Basement

**3,266 total square feet of living area**

## Beautiful Entrance Is Graced With Southern Charm

### Special features

- Screen porch has double-door entrances from the living room
- Sunny breakfast room has lots of windows for a cheerful atmosphere
- All bedrooms on the second floor have spacious walk-in closets
- Multimedia room makes a great casual family room
- 5 bedrooms, 3 1/2 baths, 2-car drive under garage
- Two-story pier foundation

**Price Code H**

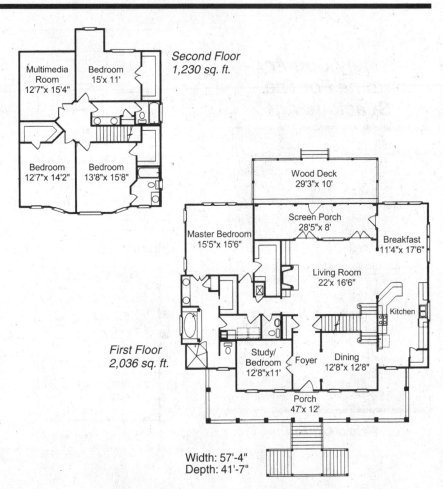

Second Floor
1,230 sq. ft.

Multimedia Room 12'7"x 15'4"

Bedroom 15'x 11'

Bedroom 12'7"x 14'2"

Bedroom 13'8"x 15'8"

First Floor
2,036 sq. ft.

Wood Deck 29'3"x 10'

Screen Porch 28'5"x 8'

Master Bedroom 15'5"x 15'6"

Breakfast 11'4"x 17'6"

Living Room 22'x 16'6"

Kitchen

Study/Bedroom 12'8"x11'

Foyer

Dining 12'8"x 12'8"

Porch 47'x 12'

Width: 57'-4"
Depth: 41'-7"

**TO ORDER BLUEPRINTS USE THE FORM ON PAGE 15 OR CALL TOLL-FREE 1-877-671-6036**
View thousands more home plans online at www.familyhandyman.com/homeplans

27

## 2,727 total square feet of living area

## Stately Country Home For The "Spacious Age"

### Special features

- Wrap-around porch and large foyer create an impressive entrance
- A state-of-the-art vaulted kitchen has a walk-in pantry and is open to the breakfast room and adjoining screen porch
- A walk-in wet bar, fireplace, bay window and deck access are features of the family room
- Vaulted master bedroom enjoys a luxurious bath with skylight and an enormous 13' deep walk-in closet
- 4 bedrooms, 2 1/2 baths, 2-car side entry garage
- Walk-out basement foundation

### Price Code E

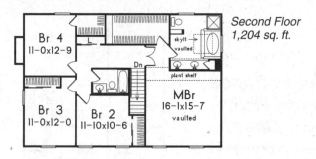

*Second Floor*
*1,204 sq. ft.*

Br 4
11-0x12-9

Br 3
11-0x12-0

Br 2
11-10x10-6

MBr
16-1x15-7
vaulted

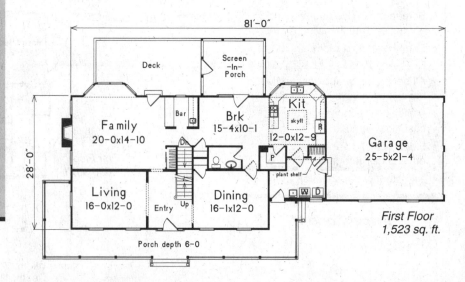

81'-0"

Deck

Screen-In-Porch

Family
20-0x14-10

Bar

Brk
15-4x10-1

Kit
12-0x12-9

Garage
25-5x21-4

28'-0"

Living
16-0x12-0

Entry

Dining
16-1x12-0

Porch depth 6-0

*First Floor*
*1,523 sq. ft.*

**1,619 total square feet of living area**

## Country-Style Porch Adds Charm

### Special features

- Private second floor bedroom and bath
- Kitchen features a snack bar and adjacent dining area
- Master bedroom has a private bath
- Centrally located washer and dryer
- 3 bedrooms, 3 baths
- Basement foundation, drawings also include crawl space and slab foundations

### *Price Code B*

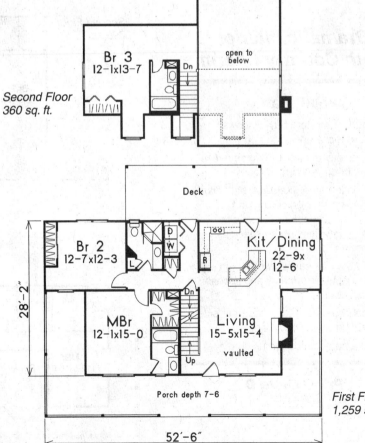

Second Floor
360 sq. ft.

Br 3
12-1x13-7

open to below

Dn

Deck

Br 2
12-7x12-3

Kit/Dining
22-9x
12-6

28'-2"

MBr
12-1x15-0

Dn

Living
15-5x15-4

vaulted

Up

Porch depth 7-6

First Floor
1,259 sq. ft.

52'-6"

**TO ORDER BLUEPRINTS USE THE FORM ON PAGE 15 OR CALL TOLL-FREE 1-877-671-6036**
View thousands more home plans online at www.familyhandyman.com/homeplans

29

**2,409 total square feet of living area**

## Dramatic Interior With Country Charm

### Special features

- Double two-story bay windows adorn the wrap-around porch
- A grand-scale foyer features a 40' view through morning room
- An eating area, fireplace, palladian windows, vaulted ceiling and balcony overlook are among the many amenities of the spacious morning room
- Bedroom #2 enjoys two walk-in closets, a bay window and access to hall bath
- 4 bedrooms, 2 1/2 baths, 2-car side entry garage with storage
- Basement foundation

### Price Code D

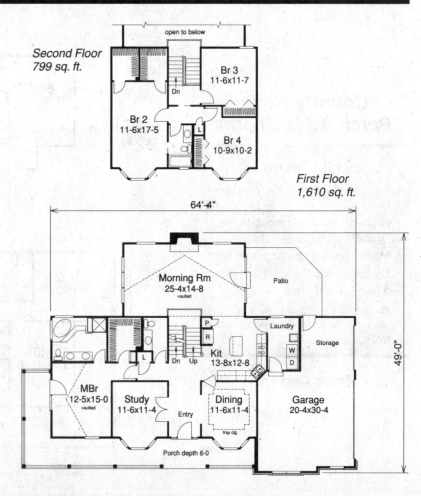

Second Floor 799 sq. ft.

open to below

Br 3 11-6x11-7

Br 2 11-6x17-5

Br 4 10-9x10-2

Dn

First Floor 1,610 sq. ft.

64'-4"

49'-0"

Morning Rm 25-4x14-8 vaulted

Patio

Laundry

Storage

Kit 13-8x12-8

W D

MBr 12-5x15-0 vaulted

Study 11-6x11-4

Dining 11-6x11-4 tray clg.

Garage 20-4x30-4

Entry

Dn Up

Porch depth 6-0

**TO ORDER BLUEPRINTS USE THE FORM ON PAGE 15 OR CALL TOLL-FREE 1-877-671-6036**
View thousands more home plans online at www.familyhandyman.com/homeplans

**1,738 total square feet of living area**

*Rear View*

## Ideal Compact Ranch

### Special features

- A den in the front of the home can easily be converted to a third bedroom
- Kitchen includes an eating nook for family gatherings
- Master bedroom has an unforgettable bath with a super skylight
- Large sunken great room is centralized with a cozy fireplace
- 2 bedrooms, 2 baths, 3-car garage
- Basement, crawl space or slab foundation, please specify when ordering

### *Price Code B*

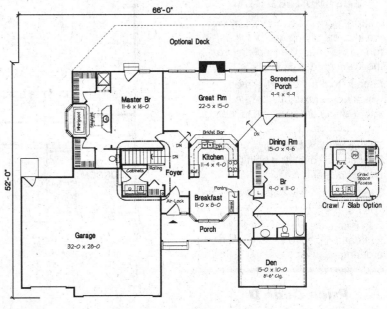

**TO ORDER BLUEPRINTS USE THE FORM ON PAGE 15 OR CALL TOLL-FREE 1-877-671-6036**
View thousands more home plans online at www.familyhandyman.com/homeplans

31

2,564 total square feet of living area

## Grand Arched Entry

### Special features

- Hearth room is surrounded by the kitchen, dining and breakfast rooms making it the focal point of the living areas

- Escape to the master bedroom which has a luxurious private bath and a sitting area leading to the deck outdoors

- The secondary bedrooms share a Jack and Jill bath and both have a walk-in closet

- 3 bedrooms, 2 1/2 baths, 2-car side entry garage

- Basement, crawl space or slab foundation, please specify when ordering

*Price Code D*

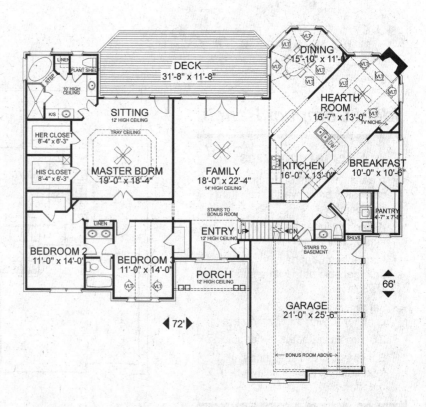

32

**TO ORDER BLUEPRINTS USE THE FORM ON PAGE 15 OR CALL TOLL-FREE 1-877-671-6036**
View thousands more home plans online at www.familyhandyman.com/homeplans

**1,991 total square feet of living area**

## Impressive Home For Country Living

### Special features

- A large porch with roof dormers and flanking stonework creates a distinctive country appeal
- The highly functional U-shaped kitchen is open to the dining and living rooms defined by a colonnade
- Large bay windows are enjoyed by both the living room and master bedroom
- Every bedroom features spacious walk-in closets and its own private bath
- 3 bedrooms, 3 1/2 baths, 2-car side entry garage
- Basement foundation

**Price Code C**

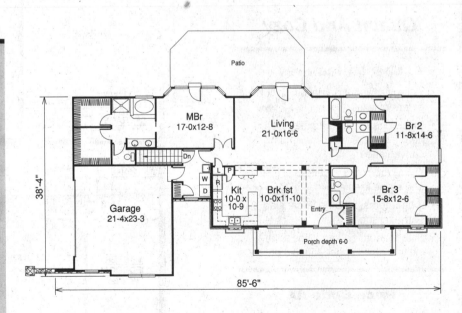

Patio

MBr
17-0x12-8

Living
21-0x16-6

Br 2
11-8x14-6

Dn

Garage
21-4x23-3

Kit
10-0 x
10-9

Brk fst
10-0x11-10

Br 3
15-8x12-6

Entry

Porch depth 6-0

38'-4"

85'-6"

**TO ORDER BLUEPRINTS USE THE FORM ON PAGE 15 OR CALL TOLL-FREE 1-877-671-6036**
View thousands more home plans online at www.familyhandyman.com/homeplans

33

**1,191 total square feet of living area**

## Quaint And Cozy

### Special features

• Energy efficient home with 2" x 6" exterior walls

• Master bedroom is located near living areas for maximum convenience

• Living room has a cathedral ceiling and stone fireplace

• 3 bedrooms, 2 baths, 2-car side entry garage

• Slab foundation, drawings also include crawl space foundation

### Price Code AA

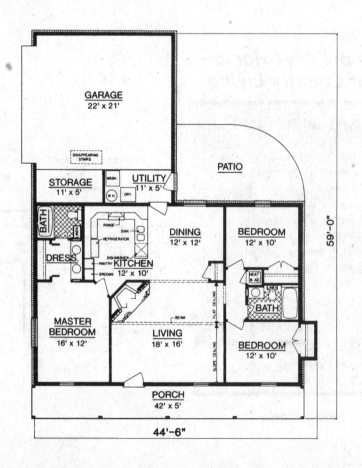

**1,406 total square feet of living area**

## Covered Breezeway To Garage

### Special features

- Master bedroom has a sloped ceiling
- Kitchen and dining area merge becoming a gathering place
- Enter the family room from the charming covered front porch to find a fireplace and lots of windows
- 3 bedrooms, 2 baths, 2-car detached garage
- Slab or crawl space foundation, please specify when ordering

*Price Code A*

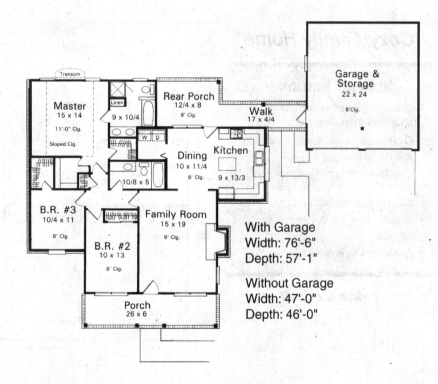

Transom

Master
15 x 14
11'-0" Clg.
Sloped Clg.

Linen

9 x 10/4

Rear Porch
12/4 x 8
8' Clg.

Walk
17 x 4/4

Garage & Storage
22 x 24
8' Clg.

w   d

10/8 x 5

Dining
10 x 11/4
8' Clg.

Kitchen
9 x 13/3

B.R. #3
10/4 x 11
8' Clg.

Family Room
15 x 19
9' Clg.

B.R. #2
10 x 13
8' Clg.

Porch
26 x 6

With Garage
Width: 76'-6"
Depth: 57'-1"

Without Garage
Width: 47'-0"
Depth: 46'-0"

**2,270 total square feet of living area**

## Cozy Family Home

### Special features

- Great room and hearth room share a see-through fireplace
- Oversized rooms throughout
- First floor has a terrific floor plan for entertaining featuring a large kitchen, breakfast area and adjacent great room
- 4 bedrooms, 2 1/2 baths, 2-car garage
- Basement foundation

### Price Code D

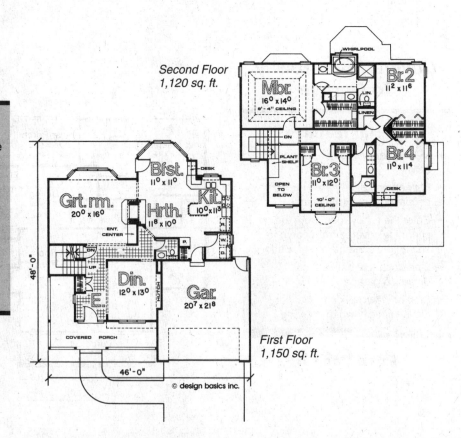

Second Floor
1,120 sq. ft.

First Floor
1,150 sq. ft.

© design basics inc.

**1,538 total square feet of living area**

## *Bayed Dining Room*

### Special features

- Dining and great rooms are highlighted in this design
- Master suite has many amenities
- Kitchen and laundry room are accessible from any room in the house
- 3 bedrooms, 2 baths, 2-car garage
- Walk-out basement, basement, crawl space or slab foundation, please specify when ordering

*Price Code B*

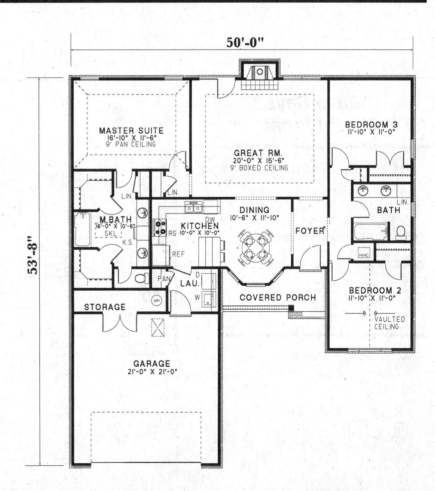

**TO ORDER BLUEPRINTS USE THE FORM ON PAGE 15 OR CALL TOLL-FREE 1-877-671-6036**
View thousands more home plans online at www.familyhandyman.com/homeplans

37

**2,529 total square feet of living area**

## Double Bays Accent Front

### Special features

- Kitchen and breakfast area are located between the family and living rooms for easy access
- Master bedroom includes a sitting area, private bath and access to the covered patio
- 4 bedrooms, 3 baths, 3-car side entry garage
- Slab foundation

*Price Code D*

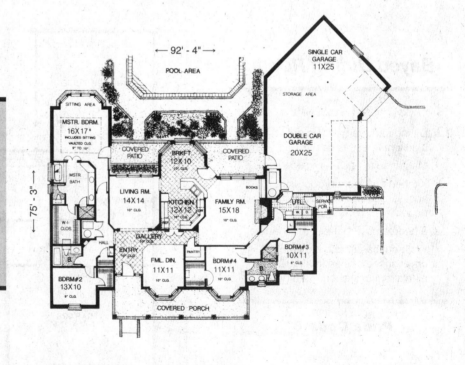

**1,558 total square feet of living area**

## Lovely, Spacious Floor Plan

### Special features

- The spacious utility room is located conveniently between the garage and kitchen/dining area
- Bedrooms are separated from the living area by a hallway
- Enormous living area with fireplace and vaulted ceiling opens to the kitchen and dining area
- Master bedroom is enhanced with a large bay window, walk-in closet and private bath
- 3 bedrooms, 2 baths, 2-car garage
- Basement foundation

*Price Code B*

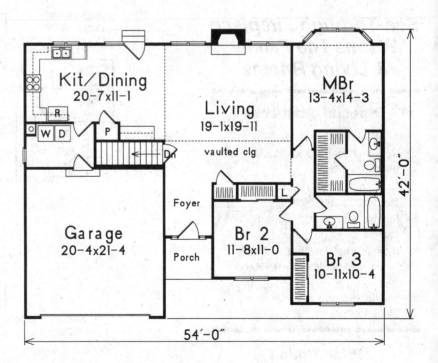

Kit/Dining
20-7x11-1

R
W D

P

Living
19-1x19-11

vaulted clg

MBr
13-4x14-3

Garage
20-4x21-4

Foyer

Porch

Br 2
11-8x11-0

Br 3
10-11x10-4

Dn
L

42'-0"

54'-0"

**TO ORDER BLUEPRINTS USE THE FORM ON PAGE 15 OR CALL TOLL-FREE 1-877-671-6036**
View thousands more home plans online at www.familyhandyman.com/homeplans

39

# Plan #717-043D-0018

**3,502 total square feet of living area**

## See-Through Fireplace Warms The Family & Living Rooms

### Special features

- 12' ceiling in the dining room
- Column accents and display niches grace the interior
- Living and family rooms share a see-through fireplace
- Master bath has double walk-in closets
- 4 bedrooms, 2 full baths, 2 half baths, 3-car side entry garage
- Basement foundation, drawings also include crawl space foundation

**Price Code F**

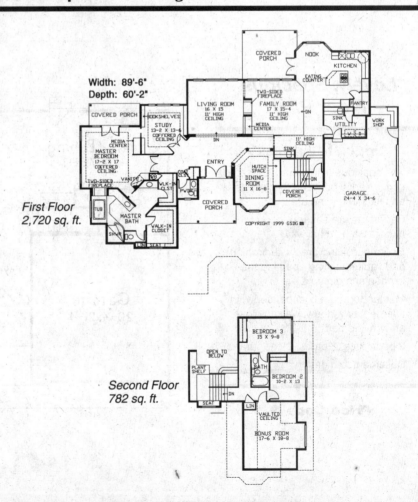

Width: 89'-6"
Depth: 60'-2"

First Floor
2,720 sq. ft.

Second Floor
782 sq. ft.

**1,440 total square feet of living area**

### Flexible Design Is Popular

#### Special features

- Open floor plan with access to covered porches in front and back
- Lots of linen, pantry and closet space throughout
- Laundry/mud room between kitchen and garage is a convenient feature
- 2 bedrooms, 2 baths, 2-car side entry garage
- Basement foundation

*Price Code A*

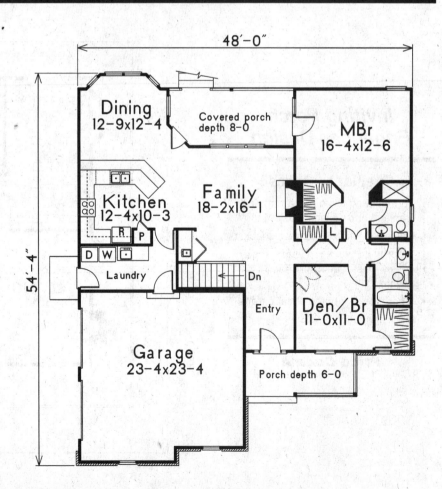

48'-0"

54'-4"

Dining
12-9x12-4

Covered porch
depth 8-0

MBr
16-4x12-6

Kitchen
12-4x10-3

Family
18-2x16-1

D W

Laundry

R
P

Dn

Entry

Den/Br
11-0x11-0

Garage
23-4x23-4

Porch depth 6-0

**TO ORDER BLUEPRINTS USE THE FORM ON PAGE 15 OR CALL TOLL-FREE 1-877-671-6036**
View thousands more home plans online at www.familyhandyman.com/homeplans

41

**1,389 total square feet of living area**

## Inviting Porch Enhances Design

### Special features

- Formal living room has a warming fireplace and delightful bay window
- U-shaped kitchen shares a snack bar with the bayed family room
- Lovely master bedroom has its own private bath
- 3 bedrooms, 2 baths, 2-car garage
- Slab foundation

***Price Code A***

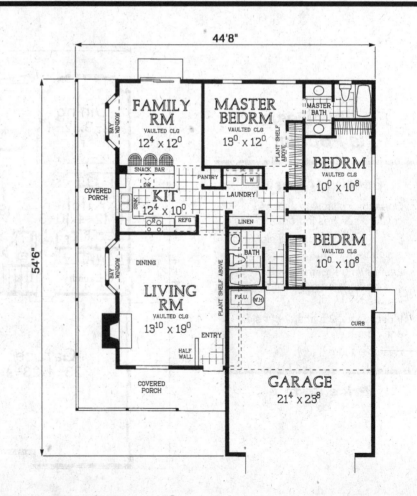

**42**

**TO ORDER BLUEPRINTS USE THE FORM ON PAGE 15 OR CALL TOLL-FREE 1-877-671-6036**
View thousands more home plans online at www.familyhandyman.com/homeplans

# Plan #717-062D-0043

**2,750 total square feet of living area**

## Victorian Accents Create A Custom Feel

### Special features

- Spacious dining room is connected to the kitchen for ease and also has access onto the wrap-around porch
- A double-door entry leads into the master bedroom enhanced with a spacious walk-in closet and a private bath with whirlpool tub
- Secluded den is an ideal place for a home office
- 4 bedrooms, 2 1/2 baths, 2-car side entry garage
- Basement or crawl space foundation, please specify when ordering

**Price Code E**

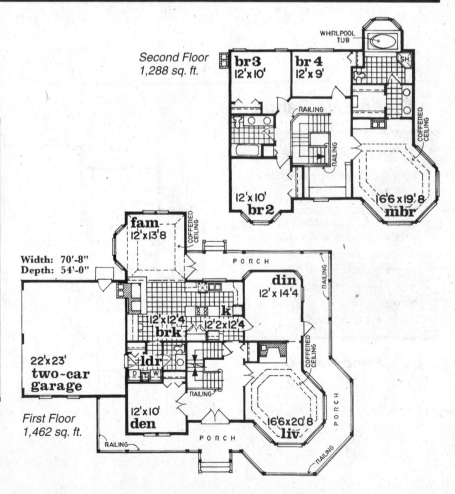

Second Floor 1,288 sq. ft.

Width: 70'-8"
Depth: 54'-0"

First Floor 1,462 sq. ft.

**TO ORDER BLUEPRINTS USE THE FORM ON PAGE 15 OR CALL TOLL-FREE 1-877-671-6036**
View thousands more home plans online at www.familyhandyman.com/homeplans

43

**1,976 total square feet of living area**

## Distinctive Ranch

### Special features

- Formal dining room has a butler's pantry for entertaining
- Open living room offers a fireplace, built-in cabinetry and an exceptional view to the outdoors
- Kitchen has work island and planning desk
- 3 bedrooms, 2 1/2 baths, 3-car garage
- Basement foundation

*Price Code C*

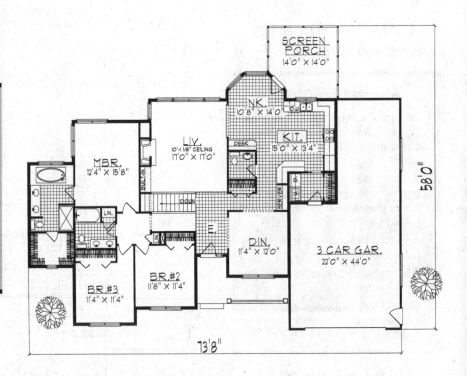

**1,399 total square feet of living area**

## Covered Porch Surrounds Home

### Special features

- Living room overlooks dining area through arched columns
- Laundry room contains a handy half bath
- Spacious master bedroom includes a sitting area, walk-in closet and plenty of sunlight
- 3 bedrooms, 1 1/2 baths, 1-car garage
- Basement foundation, drawings also include crawl space and slab foundations

**Price Code A**

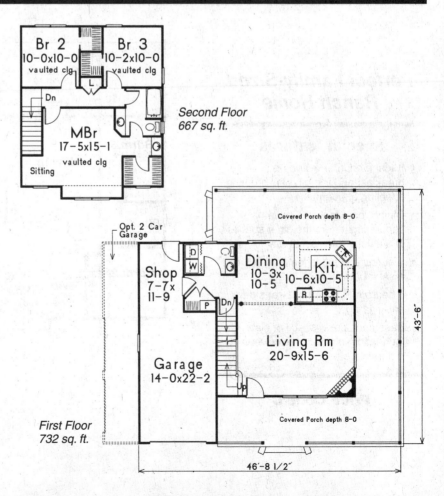

Br 2
10-0x10-0
vaulted clg

Br 3
10-2x10-0
vaulted clg

Dn

MBr
17-5x15-1
vaulted clg

Sitting

*Second Floor 667 sq. ft.*

Opt. 2 Car Garage

Covered Porch depth 8-0

Shop
7-7x
11-9

Dining
10-3x
10-5

Kit
10-6x10-5

Dn

Garage
14-0x22-2

Living Rm
20-9x15-6

43'-6"

Covered Porch depth 8-0

*First Floor 732 sq. ft.*

46'-8 1/2"

**TO ORDER BLUEPRINTS USE THE FORM ON PAGE 15 OR CALL TOLL-FREE 1-877-671-6036**
View thousands more home plans online at www.familyhandyman.com/homeplans

45

**1,869 total square feet of living area**

## Perfect Family-Sized Ranch Home

### Special features

- Kitchen counter overlooks breakfast and living rooms creating a feeling of openness
- Dining room features columns separating it from the other spaces in a unique and formal way
- A sunny spa tub is featured in the master bath
- 3 bedrooms, 2 baths, 2-car side entry garage
- Basement, crawl space or slab foundation, please specify when ordering

*Price Code C*

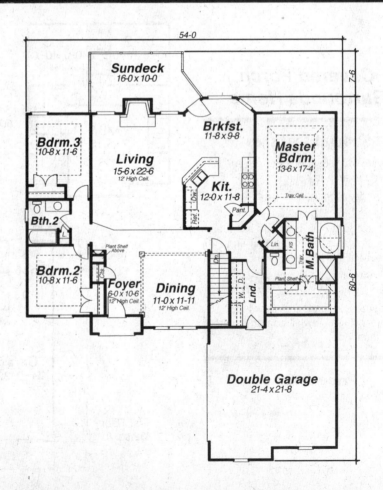

**2,452 total square feet of living area**

## Charming Design Features Home Office

### Special features

- Spacious home office with private entrance and bath, two closets, vaulted ceiling and transomed window is perfect shown as is or used as a fourth bedroom
- Delightful great room features a vaulted ceiling, fireplace, storage closets and patio doors to deck
- Extra-large kitchen boasts a walk-in pantry, cooktop island and charming bay window
- Vaulted master bedroom includes transomed windows, walk-in closet and luxurious bath
- 3 bedrooms, 2 1/2 baths, 3-car garage
- Basement foundation

*Price Code D*

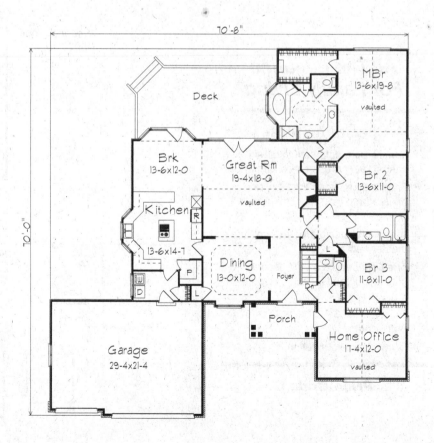

**TO ORDER BLUEPRINTS USE THE FORM ON PAGE 15 OR CALL TOLL-FREE 1-877-671-6036**
View thousands more home plans online at www.familyhandyman.com/homeplans

47

**4,100 total square feet of living area**

## All The Luxuries For Family Living

### Special features

- Family room connects to other casual living areas for convenience
- French doors keep the cozy den private from the rest of the first floor
- A beautiful sitting area extends the master bedroom
- The bonus room on the second floor is included in the square footage
- 4 bedrooms, 3 1/2 baths, 3-car side entry garage
- Crawl space foundation

**Price Code G**

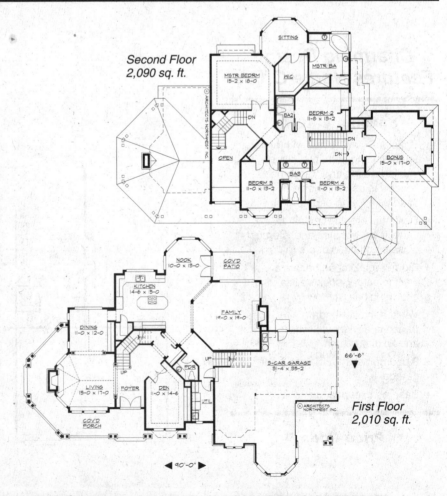

Second Floor 2,090 sq. ft.

First Floor 2,010 sq. ft.

**2,123 total square feet of living area**

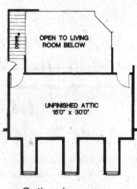

*Optional
Second Floor*

## Expansive
## Counterspace

### Special features

- Energy efficient home with 2" x 6" exterior walls
- Living room has a wood burning fireplace, built-in bookshelves and a wet bar
- Skylights make the sunporch bright and comfortable
- Unfinished attic has an additional 450 square feet of living area
- 3 bedrooms, 2 1/2 baths, 2-car side entry garage
- Crawl space foundation, drawings also include slab and basement foundations

### *Price Code E*

*First Floor
2,123 sq. ft.*

**TO ORDER BLUEPRINTS USE THE FORM ON PAGE 15 OR CALL TOLL-FREE 1-877-671-6036**
View thousands more home plans online at www.familyhandyman.com/homeplans

49

**2,156 total square feet of living area**

## Award-Winning Style With This Design

### Special features

- Secluded master bedroom has a spa-style bath with a corner whirlpool tub, large shower, double sinks and a walk-in closet
- Kitchen overlooks the rear patio
- Plenty of windows add an open, airy feel to the great room
- 4 bedrooms, 3 baths, 2-car side entry garage
- Basement, crawl space or slab foundation, please specify when ordering

**Price Code C**

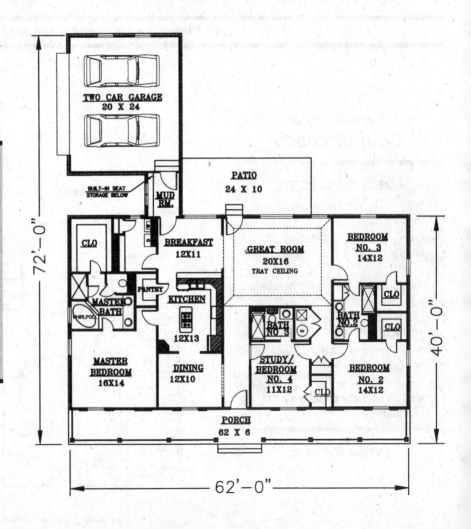

**1,978 total square feet of living area**

## Secluded Living Room

### Special features

- Elegant arched openings throughout interior
- Vaulted living room off foyer
- Master suite features a cheerful sitting room and a private bath
- 3 bedrooms, 2 1/2 baths, 2-car garage
- Walk-out basement, slab or crawl space foundation, please specify when ordering

### Price Code C

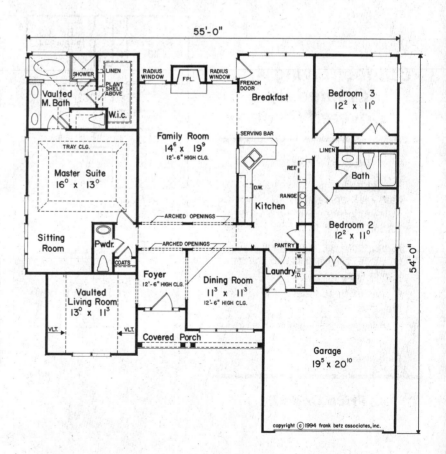

**TO ORDER BLUEPRINTS USE THE FORM ON PAGE 15 OR CALL TOLL-FREE 1-877-671-6036**
View thousands more home plans online at www.familyhandyman.com/homeplans

51

**2,213 total square feet of living area**

## Outdoor Living Area Created By Covered Porch

### Special features

- Master bedroom features a full bath with separate vanities, large walk-in closet and access to the veranda
- Living room is enhanced by a fireplace, bay window and columns framing the gallery
- 9' ceilings throughout home add to the open feeling
- 4 bedrooms, 2 1/2 baths, 2-car side entry garage
- Slab foundation

### Price Code E

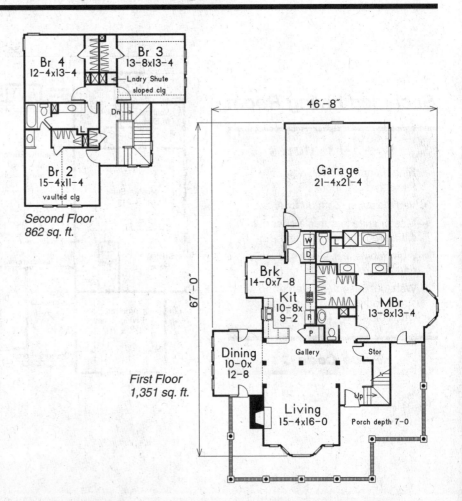

Br 4
12-4x13-4

Br 3
13-8x13-4

Lndry Shute
sloped clg

Br 2
15-4x11-4
vaulted clg

*Second Floor*
*862 sq. ft.*

Dn

46'-8"

Garage
21-4x21-4

W
D

Brk
14-0x7-8

Kit
10-8x
9-2

MBr
13-8x13-4

67'-0"

Dining
10-0x
12-8

Gallery

Stor

*First Floor*
*1,351 sq. ft.*

Living
15-4x16-0

Up

Porch depth 7-0

**TO ORDER BLUEPRINTS USE THE FORM ON PAGE 15 OR CALL TOLL-FREE 1-877-671-6036**
View thousands more home plans online at www.familyhandyman.com/homeplans

**2,126 total square feet of living area**

## Second Floor Overlook

### Price Code C

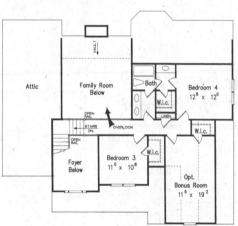

*Second Floor 543 sq. ft.*

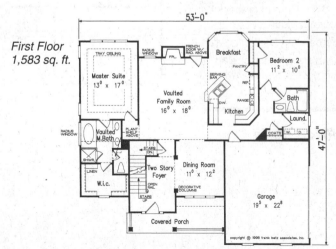

*First Floor 1,583 sq. ft.*

**TO ORDER BLUEPRINTS USE THE FORM ON PAGE 15 OR CALL TOLL-FREE 1-877-671-6036**
View thousands more home plans online at www.familyhandyman.com/homeplans

53

**1,841 total square feet of living area**

## Ranch Has A Contemporary Feel

### Special features

- Corner fireplace warms the vaulted living room
- Sliding glass doors in the dining room lead to a covered patio
- Extended counter has a snack bar with seating for four
- 3 bedrooms, 2 baths, 2-car garage
- Basement, crawl space or slab foundation, please specify when ordering

*Price Code C*

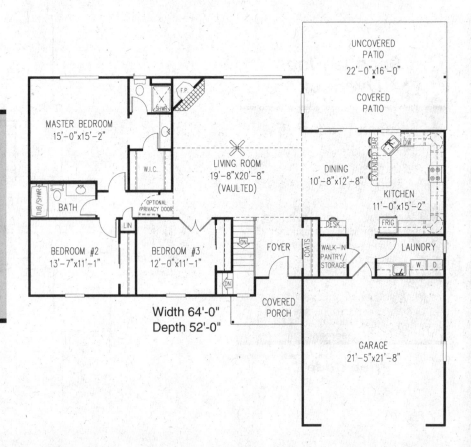

Width 64'-0"
Depth 52'-0"

**1,992 total square feet of living area**

## Double Bay Window Enhances Front Entry

### Special features

- Distinct living, dining and breakfast areas
- Master bedroom boasts a full-end bay window and a cathedral ceiling
- Storage and laundry area are located adjacent to the garage
- Bonus room over the garage for future office or playroom is included in the square footage
- 3 bedrooms, 2 1/2 baths, 2-car garage
- Crawl space foundation, drawings also include basement foundation

*Price Code C*

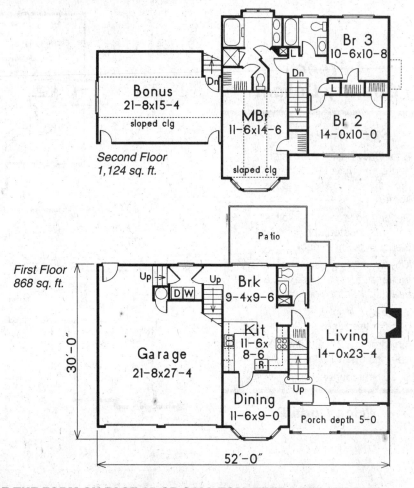

Br 3
10-6x10-8

Bonus
21-8x15-4
sloped clg

MBr
11-6x14-6

Br 2
14-0x10-0

*Second Floor*
*1,124 sq. ft.*

sloped clg

*First Floor*
*868 sq. ft.*

Patio

Up

Brk
9-4x9-6

Kit
11-6x
8-6

Living
14-0x23-4

Garage
21-8x27-4

Dining
11-6x9-0

Porch depth 5-0

30'-0"

52'-0"

**TO ORDER BLUEPRINTS USE THE FORM ON PAGE 15 OR CALL TOLL-FREE 1-877-671-6036**
View thousands more home plans online at www.familyhandyman.com/homeplans

55

**3,816 total square feet of living area**

## A French Country Delight

### Special features

- Beautifully designed master bedroom enjoys a lavish dressing area as well as access to the library
- Second floor computer loft is centrally located and includes plenty of counterspace
- The two-story great room has an impressive arched opening and a beautiful beamed ceiling
- The outdoor covered deck has a popular fireplace
- 4 bedrooms, 3 1/2 baths, 3-car side entry garage
- Basement foundation

*Price Code F*

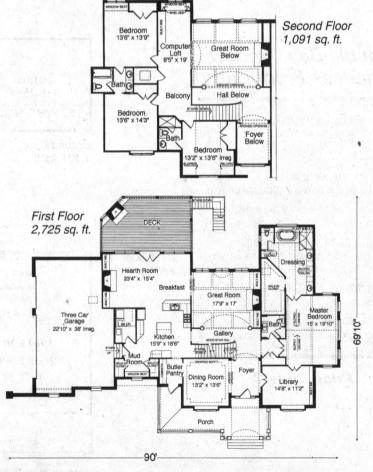

Second Floor
1,091 sq. ft.

First Floor
2,725 sq. ft.

56

**TO ORDER BLUEPRINTS USE THE FORM ON PAGE 15 OR CALL TOLL-FREE 1-877-671-6036**
View thousands more home plans online at www.familyhandyman.com/homeplans

**2,632 total square feet of living area**

## Rich With Victorian Details

### Special features

- Energy efficient home with 2" x 6" exterior walls
- Master bedroom has a cheerful octagon-shaped sitting area
- Arched entrances create a distinctive living room with a lovely tray ceiling and help define the dining room
- 4 bedrooms, 2 1/2 baths, 2-car garage
- Basement or crawl space foundation, please specify when ordering

### *Price Code E*

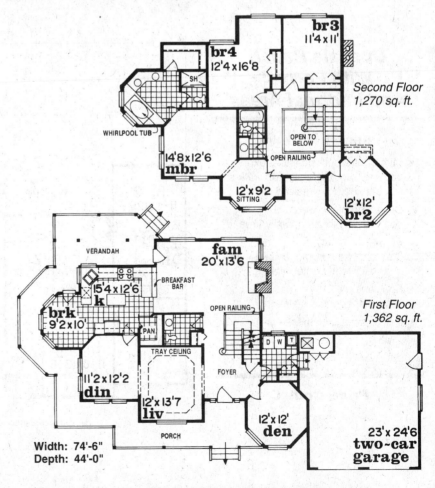

br3
11'4 x 11'

br4
12'4 x 16'8

SH

WHIRLPOOL TUB

Second Floor
1,270 sq. ft.

OPEN TO BELOW

OPEN RAILING

14'8 x 12'6
**mbr**

12' x 9'2
SITTING

12' x 12'
**br2**

VERANDAH

**fam**
20' x 13'6

BREAKFAST BAR

15'4 x 12'6
**k**

**brk**
9'2 x 10'

PAN.

OPEN RAILING

First Floor
1,362 sq. ft.

D W T

FOYER

TRAY CEILING

11'2 x 12'2
**din**

12' x 13'7
**liv**

PORCH

12' x 12'
**den**

23' x 24'6
**two-car garage**

Width: 74'-6"
Depth: 44'-0"

**TO ORDER BLUEPRINTS USE THE FORM ON PAGE 15 OR CALL TOLL-FREE 1-877-671-6036**
View thousands more home plans online at www.familyhandyman.com/homeplans

57

**1,969 total square feet of living area**

## Upscale Ranch With Formal And Informal Areas

### Special features

- Master bedroom boasts a luxurious bath with double sinks, two walk-in closets and an oversized tub
- Corner fireplace warms a conveniently located family area
- Formal living and dining areas in the front of the home lend a touch of privacy when entertaining
- Spacious utility room has counterspace and a sink
- 3 bedrooms, 2 baths, 2-car garage
- Crawl space foundation, drawings also include slab foundation

*Price Code C*

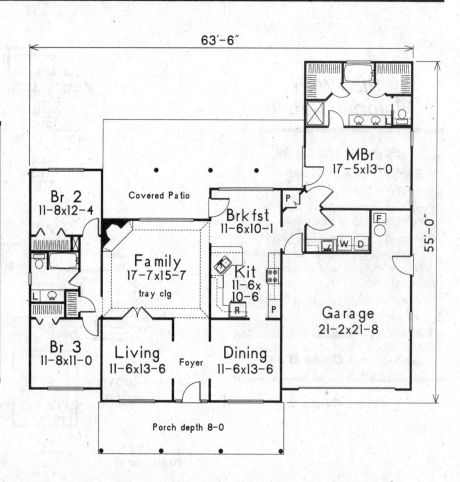

63'-6"

55'-0"

Covered Patio

Br 2
11-8x12-4

MBr
17-5x13-0

Brkfst
11-6x10-1

Family
17-7x15-7
tray clg

Kit
11-6x
10-6

Garage
21-2x21-8

Br 3
11-8x11-0

Living
11-6x13-6

Foyer

Dining
11-6x13-6

Porch depth 8-0

**TO ORDER BLUEPRINTS USE THE FORM ON PAGE 15 OR CALL TOLL-FREE 1-877-671-6036**
View thousands more home plans online at www.familyhandyman.com/homeplans

**1,783 total square feet of living area**

## Private Master Bedroom

### Special features

- Grand foyer leads to the family room
- Walk-in pantry in the kitchen
- Master bath has a step-down doorless shower, huge vanity and a large walk-in closet
- 3 bedrooms, 2 baths, 2-car garage
- Slab foundation

### Price Code B

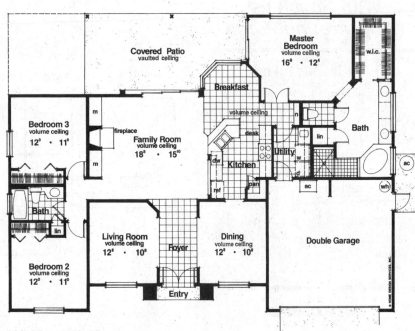

Width: 60'-0"
Depth: 45'-0"

**TO ORDER BLUEPRINTS USE THE FORM ON PAGE 15 OR CALL TOLL-FREE 1-877-671-6036**
View thousands more home plans online at www.familyhandyman.com/homeplans

59

**1,541 total square feet of living area**

# Country Ranch With Spacious Wrap-Around Porch

## Special features

- Dining area offers access to a screened porch for outdoor dining and entertaining
- Country kitchen features a center island and a breakfast bay for casual meals
- Great room is warmed by a woodstove
- 3 bedrooms, 2 baths, 2-car garage
- Basement or crawl space foundation, please specify when ordering

### Price Code B

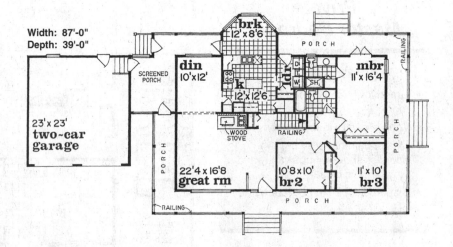

Width: 87'-0"
Depth: 39'-0"

SCREENED PORCH

23' x 23'
**two-car garage**

brk 12' x 8'6"

din 10'x12'

k 12' x 12'6"

ldr

mbr 11' x 16'4"

PORCH

RAILING

WOOD STOVE

RAILING

PORCH

22'4 x 16'8 **great rm**

10'8 x 10' **br2**

11' x 10' **br3**

PORCH

RAILING

PORCH

**1,668 total square feet of living area**

## Bay Window Graces Luxury Master Bedroom

### Special features

- Large bay windows grace the breakfast area, master bedroom and dining room
- Extensive walk-in closets and storage spaces are throughout the home
- Handy covered entry porch
- Large living room has a fireplace, built-in bookshelves and sloped ceiling
- 3 bedrooms, 2 baths, 2-car drive under garage
- Basement foundation

*Price Code C*

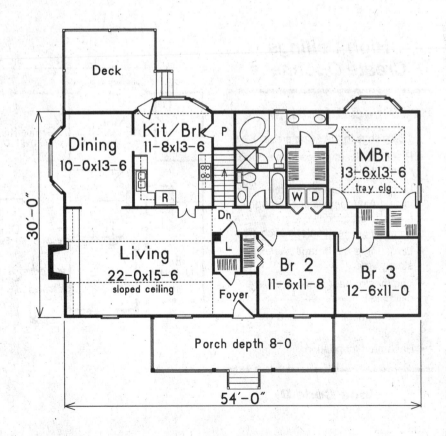

Deck

Kit/Brk
11-8x13-6

Dining
10-0x13-6

P

MBr
13-6x13-6
tray clg

R

W D

Dn

Living
22-0x15-6
sloped ceiling

L

Br 2
11-6x11-8

Br 3
12-6x11-0

Foyer

30'-0"

Porch depth 8-0

54'-0"

**TO ORDER BLUEPRINTS USE THE FORM ON PAGE 15 OR CALL TOLL-FREE 1-877-671-6036**
View thousands more home plans online at www.familyhandyman.com/homeplans

61

**2,516 total square feet of living area**

## High Ceilings
## Create Openness

### Special features

- 12' ceilings in the living areas
- Plenty of closet space in this open ranch plan
- Large kitchen/breakfast area joins great room via see-through fireplace creating two large entering spaces flanking each side
- Large three-car garage has extra storage area
- The master bedroom has an eye-catching bay window
- 3 bedrooms, 2 1/2 baths, 3-car garage
- Basement foundation

**Price Code D**

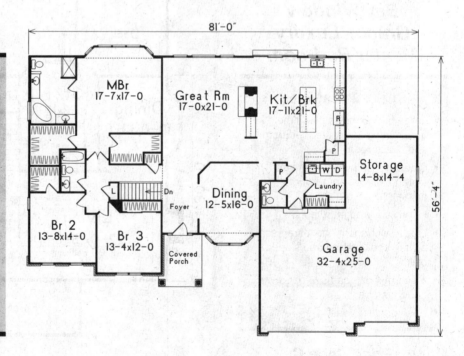

**2,788 total square feet of living area**

## Many Decorative Touches Throughout

### Special features

- Breakfast nook is flooded with sunlight from skylights
- Fireplace in great room is framed by media center and shelving
- Large game room is secluded for active children
- 3 bedrooms, 2 1/2 baths, 3-car side entry garage
- Crawl space foundation

*Price Code E*

**Width: 76'-6"**
**Depth: 72'-0"**

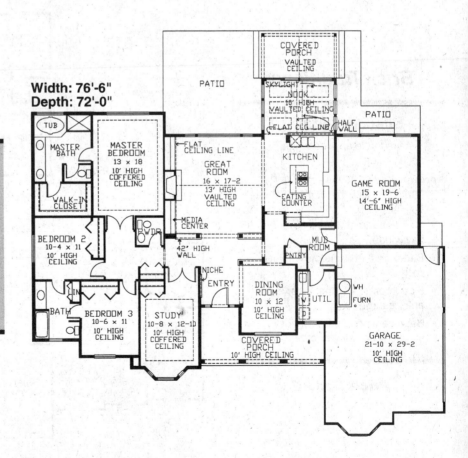

**TO ORDER BLUEPRINTS USE THE FORM ON PAGE 15 OR CALL TOLL-FREE 1-877-671-6036**
View thousands more home plans online at www.familyhandyman.com/homeplans

63

**2,737 total square feet of living area**

## Brick Traditional

### Special features

- T-stairs make any room easily accessible
- Two-story ceilings in foyer and grand room create a spacious feeling
- Master bedroom has a gorgeous bay window and sitting area
- Bedroom #4 has its own private bath
- 5 bedrooms, 4 baths, 2-car side entry garage
- Basement or slab foundation, please specify when ordering

**Price Code E**

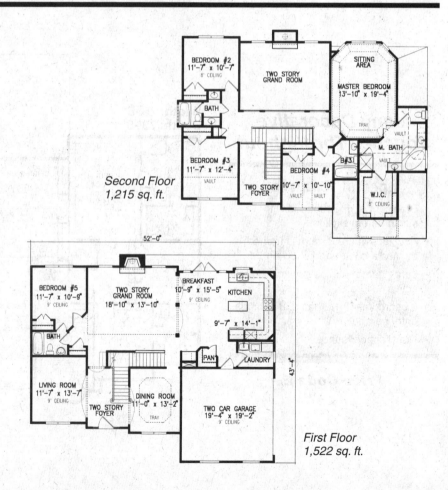

*Second Floor*
1,215 sq. ft.

*First Floor*
1,522 sq. ft.

**2,787 total square feet of living area**

## Extraordinary Charm

### Special features

- 9' ceilings on the first and second floors
- Enormous shop area in the garage is ideal for hobbies, workshop or extra storage
- Interesting gallery is the focal point of the entry
- Optional second floor has an additional 636 square feet of living area
- 4 bedrooms, 2 1/2 baths, 3-car side entry garage
- Crawl space, basement or slab foundation, please specify when ordering

*Price Code E*

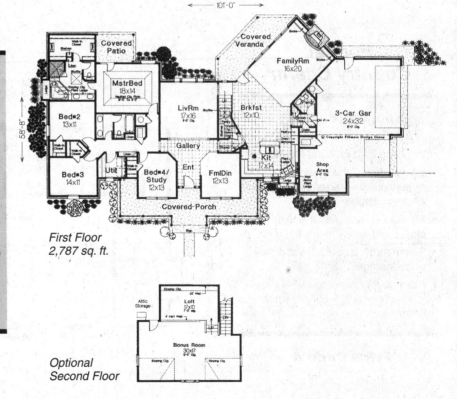

*First Floor*
*2,787 sq. ft.*

*Optional*
*Second Floor*

**TO ORDER BLUEPRINTS USE THE FORM ON PAGE 15 OR CALL TOLL-FREE 1-877-671-6036**
View thousands more home plans online at www.familyhandyman.com/homeplans

65

**1,325 total square feet of living area**

## Formal Country Charm

### Special features

- Sloped ceiling and a fireplace in the living area create a cozy feeling
- Formal dining and breakfast areas have an efficiently designed kitchen between them
- Master bedroom has a walk-in closet and luxurious private bath
- 3 bedrooms, 2 baths, 2-car drive under garage
- Basement or crawl space foundation, please specify when ordering

**Price Code A**

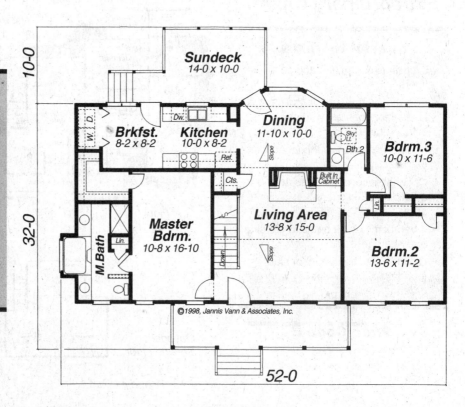

Sundeck 14-0 x 10-0

Brkfst. 8-2 x 8-2

Kitchen 10-0 x 8-2

Dining 11-10 x 10-0

Bdrm.3 10-0 x 11-6

Master Bdrm. 10-8 x 16-10

M.Bath

Living Area 13-8 x 15-0

Bdrm.2 13-6 x 11-2

©1998, Jannis Vann & Associates, Inc.

10-0

32-0

52-0

# Plan #717-035D-0036

**2,193 total square feet of living area**

## Kitchen Is A Chef's Dream

### Special features

- Master suite includes a sitting room
- Dining room has decorative columns and overlooks the family room
- Kitchen has lots of storage
- Optional bonus room with bath on the second floor has an additional 400 square feet of living area
- 3 bedrooms, 3 baths, 2-car side entry garage
- Walk-out basement, crawl space or slab foundation, please specify when ordering

**Price Code C**

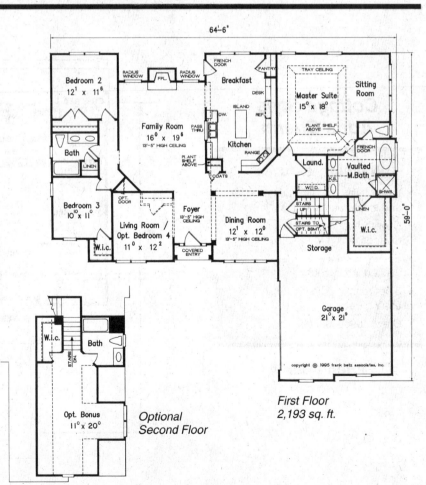

Optional Second Floor

First Floor
2,193 sq. ft.

**TO ORDER BLUEPRINTS USE THE FORM ON PAGE 15 OR CALL TOLL-FREE 1-877-671-6036**
View thousands more home plans online at www.familyhandyman.com/homeplans

67

**1,496 total square feet of living area**

## Cottage Style Adds Charm

### Special features

- Large utility room includes a sink and extra counterspace
- Covered patio off breakfast nook extends dining to the outdoors
- Eating counter in kitchen overlooks vaulted family room
- 3 bedrooms, 2 baths, 2-car side entry garage
- Crawl space foundation

### Price Code A

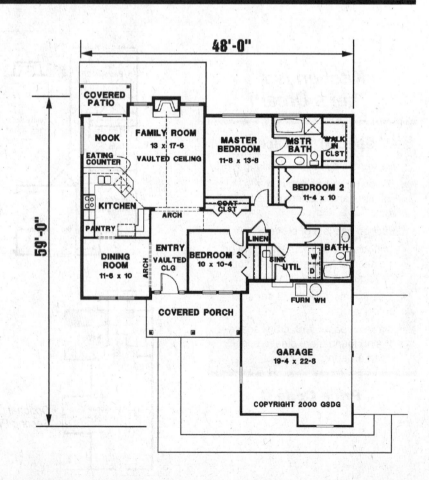

**68**

**TO ORDER BLUEPRINTS USE THE FORM ON PAGE 15 OR CALL TOLL-FREE 1-877-671-6036**
View thousands more home plans online at www.familyhandyman.com/homeplans

**1,945 total square feet of living area**

## Plenty Of Detail

### Special features

- Master suite is separate from other bedrooms for privacy
- Vaulted breakfast room is directly off great room
- Kitchen includes a built-in desk area
- Elegant dining room has an arched window
- 4 bedrooms, 2 baths, 2-car side entry garage
- Walk-out basement, crawl space or slab foundation, please specify when ordering

*Price Code C*

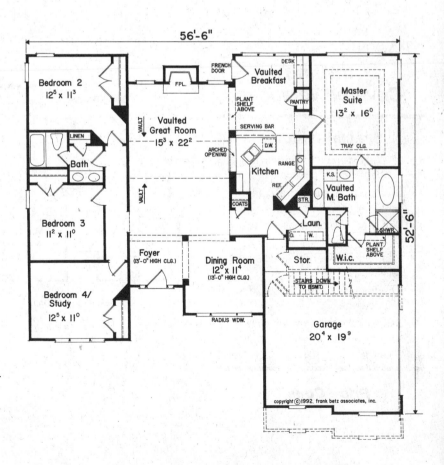

**TO ORDER BLUEPRINTS USE THE FORM ON PAGE 15 OR CALL TOLL-FREE 1-877-671-6036**
View thousands more home plans online at www.familyhandyman.com/homeplans

69

**1,830 total square feet of living area**

## Inviting Covered Verandas

### Special features

- Inviting covered verandas in the front and rear of the home
- Great room has a fireplace and cathedral ceiling
- Handy service porch allows easy access
- Master bedroom has a vaulted ceiling and private bath
- 3 bedrooms, 2 baths, 3-car side entry garage
- Basement, crawl space or slab foundation, please specify when ordering

**Price Code C**

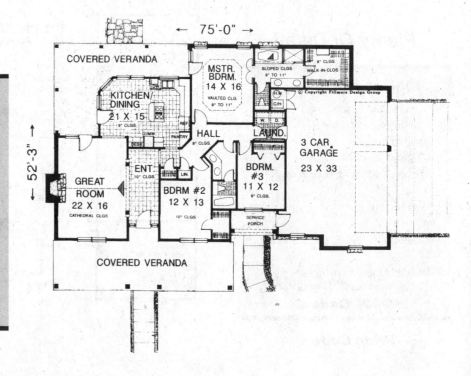

**TO ORDER BLUEPRINTS USE THE FORM ON PAGE 15 OR CALL TOLL-FREE 1-877-671-6036**
View thousands more home plans online at www.familyhandyman.com/homeplans

**2,188 total square feet of living area**

## Master Bedroom With Sitting Area

### Special features

- Master bedroom includes a private covered porch, sitting area and two large walk-in closets
- Spacious kitchen has center island, snack bar and laundry access
- Great room has a 10' ceiling and a dramatic corner fireplace
- 3 bedrooms, 2 baths, 3-car side entry garage
- Basement foundation

*Price Code C*

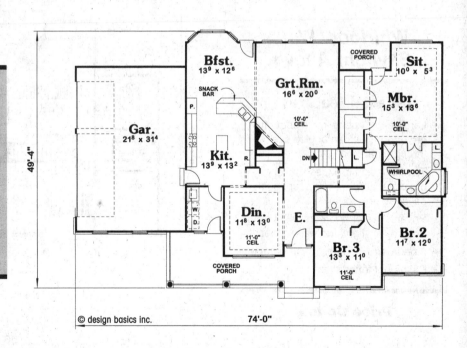

**1,911 total square feet of living area**

## Whirlpool With Skylight Above

### Special features

- Large entry opens into a beautiful great room with an angled see-through fireplace
- Terrific design includes kitchen and breakfast area with adjacent sunny bayed hearth room
- Private master bedroom with bath features skylight and walk-in closet
- 3 bedrooms, 2 baths, 2-car garage
- Basement foundation

*Price Code C*

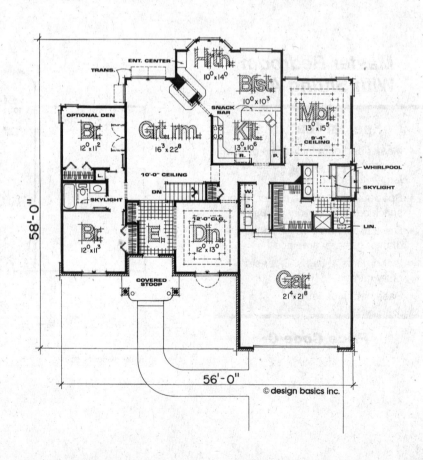

© design basics inc.

**72**

**TO ORDER BLUEPRINTS USE THE FORM ON PAGE 15 OR CALL TOLL-FREE 1-877-671-6036**
View thousands more home plans online at www.familyhandyman.com/homeplans

**2,678 total square feet of living area**

## Step Up Into The Master Bath Tub

### Special features

- An elegant arched opening graces the entrance
- Kitchen has double ovens, walk-in pantry and an eating bar
- Master bedroom has a beautiful bath spotlighting a step-up tub
- 4 bedrooms, 2 1/2 baths, 2-car side entry garage
- Crawl space foundation, drawings also include slab foundation

*Price Code E*

**TO ORDER BLUEPRINTS USE THE FORM ON PAGE 15 OR CALL TOLL-FREE 1-877-671-6036**
View thousands more home plans online at www.familyhandyman.com/homeplans

73

**1,609 total square feet of living area**

## Charming Home Arranged For Open Living

### Special features

- Kitchen captures full use of space with pantry, ample cabinets and workspace
- Master bedroom is well-secluded with a walk-in closet and private bath
- Large utility room includes a sink and extra storage
- Attractive bay window in the dining area provides light
- 3 bedrooms, 2 1/2 baths, 2-car garage
- Slab foundation

### Price Code B

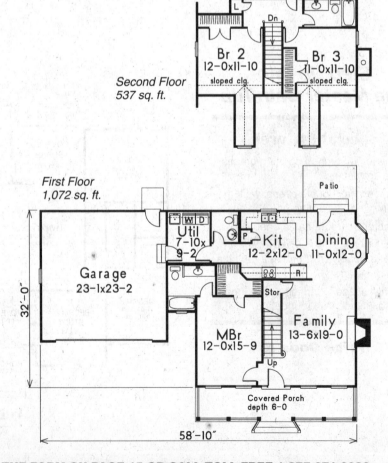

Second Floor 537 sq. ft.

attic

**Br 2** 12-0x11-10 sloped clg.

**Br 3** 11-0x11-10 sloped clg.

Dn

First Floor 1,072 sq. ft.

Patio

**Util** 7-10x 9-2

W D

**Kit** 12-2x12-0

P

**Dining** 11-0x12-0

**Garage** 23-1x23-2

Stor

R

**MBr** 12-0x15-9

**Family** 13-6x19-0

Up

32'-0"

Covered Porch depth 6-0

58'-10"

**2,597 total square feet of living area**

## Outstanding Floor Plan For Year-Round Entertaining

### Special features

- Large U-shaped kitchen features an island cooktop and breakfast bar
- Entry and great room are enhanced by sweeping balcony
- Bedrooms #2 and #3 share a bath, while the fourth bedroom has a private bath
- Vaulted great room includes transomed arch windows
- 4 bedrooms, 3 1/2 baths, 2-car side entry garage
- Walk-out basement foundation, drawings also include crawl space and slab foundations

*Price Code E*

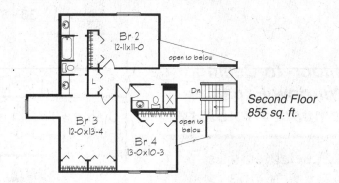

Br. 2
12-11x11-0

open to below

Br. 3
12-0x13-4

Dn

open to below

Br. 4
13-0x10-3

*Second Floor*
*855 sq. ft.*

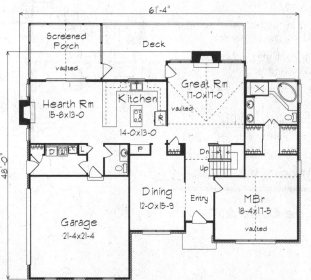

61'-4"

Screened Porch
vaulted

Deck

Great Rm
17-0x17-0
vaulted

Hearth Rm
15-8x13-0

Kitchen
14-0x13-0

48'-0"

Dn

Up

Dining
12-0x15-9

Entry

MBr
18-4x17-5
vaulted

Garage
21-4x21-4

*First Floor*
*1,742 sq. ft.*

**TO ORDER BLUEPRINTS USE THE FORM ON PAGE 15 OR CALL TOLL-FREE 1-877-671-6036**
View thousands more home plans online at www.familyhandyman.com/homeplans

75

**1,246 total square feet of living area**

## Floor-To-Ceiling Window Expands Compact Two-Story

### Special features

- Corner living room window adds openness and light
- Out-of-the-way kitchen with dining area accesses the outdoors
- Private first floor master bedroom has a corner window
- Large walk-in closet is located in bedroom #3
- Easily built perimeter allows economical construction
- 3 bedrooms, 2 baths, 2-car garage
- Basement foundation

### Price Code A

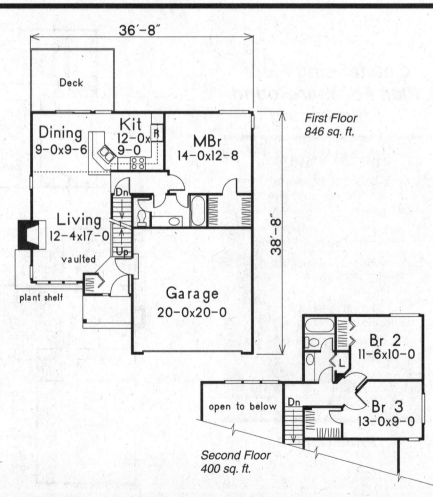

36'-8"

Deck

Dining 9-0x9-6

Kit 12-0x 9-0

MBr 14-0x12-8

Dn

Living 12-4x17-0 vaulted

Up

plant shelf

Garage 20-0x20-0

38'-8"

First Floor 846 sq. ft.

Br 2 11-6x10-0

open to below

Dn

Br 3 13-0x9-0

Second Floor 400 sq. ft.

**76**

**TO ORDER BLUEPRINTS USE THE FORM ON PAGE 15 OR CALL TOLL-FREE 1-877-671-6036**
View thousands more home plans online at www.familyhandyman.com/homeplans

**2,770 total square feet of living area**

## Outdoor Living Areas Surround Home

### Special features

- Formal living and dining areas combine for optimal entertaining possibilities including access outdoors and a fireplace

- The cheerful family and breakfast rooms connect for added spaciousness

- A double-door entry into the master bedroom leads to a private covered deck, sitting area and luxurious bath

- 4 bedrooms, 2 1/2 baths, 3-car side entry garage

- Crawl space foundation

**Price Code E**

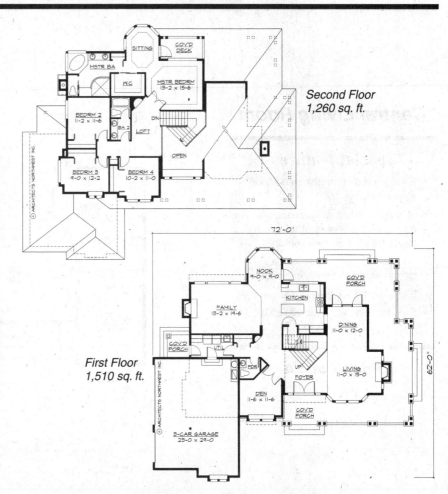

Second Floor
1,260 sq. ft.

First Floor
1,510 sq. ft.

**TO ORDER BLUEPRINTS USE THE FORM ON PAGE 15 OR CALL TOLL-FREE 1-877-671-6036**
View thousands more home plans online at www.familyhandyman.com/homeplans

77

**1,420 total square feet of living area**

## *Central Living Room*

### Special features

- Energy efficient home with 2" x 6" exterior walls
- Living room has a 12' ceiling, corner fireplace and atrium doors leading to the covered porch
- Secluded master suite has a garden bath and walk-in closet
- 3 bedrooms, 2 baths, 2-car garage
- Slab foundation, drawings also include crawl space foundation

### *Price Code A*

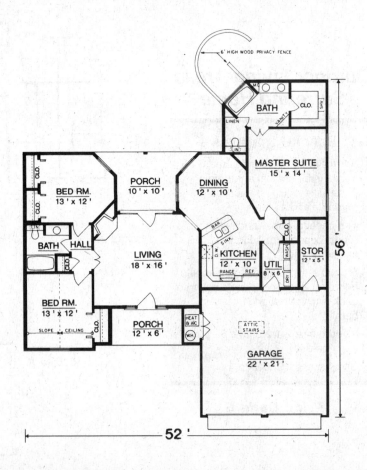

**4,237 total square feet of living area**

## Grand-Scale Design

### Special features

- Grand entrance has a vaulted two-story foyer
- Fireplaces warm the formal living room and master bedroom
- Second floor bedrooms have their own window seats
- Bonus room above the garage has an additional 497 square feet of living area
- 4 bedrooms, 3 1/2 baths, 3-car side entry garage
- Basement, crawl space or slab foundation, please specify when ordering

*Price Code G*

*First Floor*
*2,651 sq. ft.*

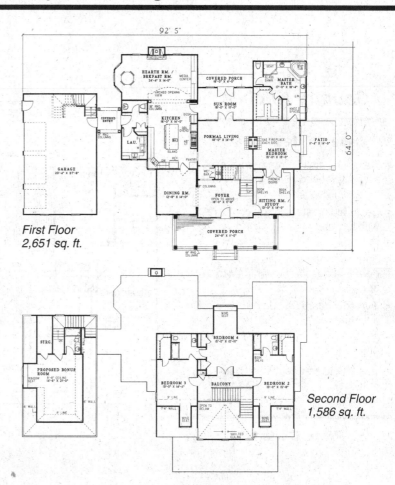

*Second Floor*
*1,586 sq. ft.*

**TO ORDER BLUEPRINTS USE THE FORM ON PAGE 15 OR CALL TOLL-FREE 1-877-671-6036**
View thousands more home plans online at www.familyhandyman.com/homeplans

79

**2,184 total square feet of living area**

## Spacious Country Kitchen

### Special features

- Delightful family room has access to the screened porch for enjoyable outdoor living
- Secluded master suite is complete with a sitting area and luxurious bath
- Formal living room has a double-door entry easily converting it to a study or home office
- Two secondary bedrooms share a full bath
- 3 bedrooms, 3 baths, 2-car side entry garage
- Basement, crawl space or slab foundation, please specify when ordering

*Price Code C*

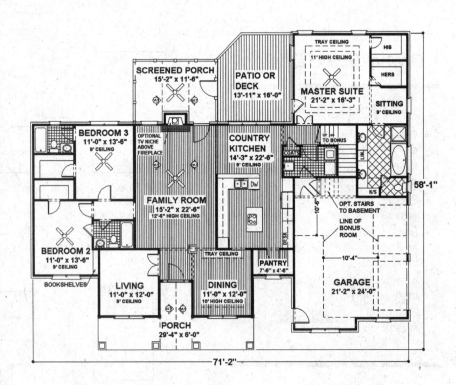

**80**

**TO ORDER BLUEPRINTS USE THE FORM ON PAGE 15 OR CALL TOLL-FREE 1-877-671-6036**
View thousands more home plans online at www.familyhandyman.com/homeplans

**1,669 total square feet of living area**

## A Great Country Farmhouse

### Special features

- Windows add exciting visual elements to the exterior as well as plenty of natural light to the interior
- Two-story great room has a raised hearth
- Second floor loft/study would easily make a terrific home office
- 3 bedrooms, 2 baths
- Crawl space foundation

**Price Code B**

*Second Floor*
*576 sq. ft.*

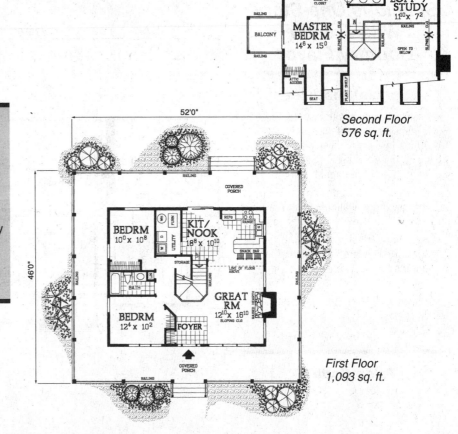

*First Floor*
*1,093 sq. ft.*

**TO ORDER BLUEPRINTS USE THE FORM ON PAGE 15 OR CALL TOLL-FREE 1-877-671-6036**
View thousands more home plans online at www.familyhandyman.com/homeplans

81

**2,695 total square feet of living area**

## Spacious One-Story With French Country Flavor

### Special features

- A grand-scale great room features a fireplace with flanking shelves, handsome entry foyer with staircase and opens to a large kitchen and breakfast room
- Roomy master bedroom has a bay window, huge walk-in closet and bath with a shower built for two
- Bedrooms #2 and #3 are generously oversized with walk-in closets and a Jack and Jill style bath
- 3 bedrooms, 2 1/2 baths, 2-car side entry garage
- Basement foundation

**Price Code E**

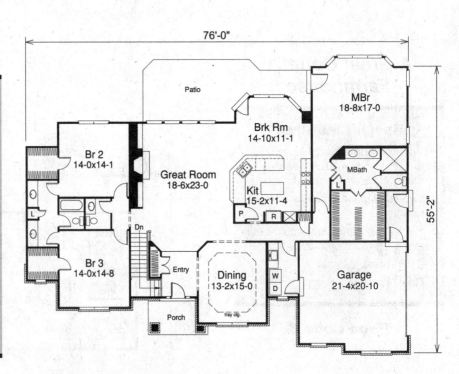

**TO ORDER BLUEPRINTS USE THE FORM ON PAGE 15 OR CALL TOLL-FREE 1-877-671-6036**
View thousands more home plans online at www.familyhandyman.com/homeplans

**1,550 total square feet of living area**

## Vaulted Ceilings
## Add Dimension

### Special features

- Alcove in the family room can be used as a cozy corner fireplace or as a media center.
- Master bedroom features a large walk-in closet, skylight and separate tub and shower
- Convenient laundry closet
- Kitchen with pantry and breakfast bar connects to the family room
- Family room and master bedroom access the covered patio
- 3 bedrooms, 2 baths, 2-car garage
- Slab foundation

*Price Code B*

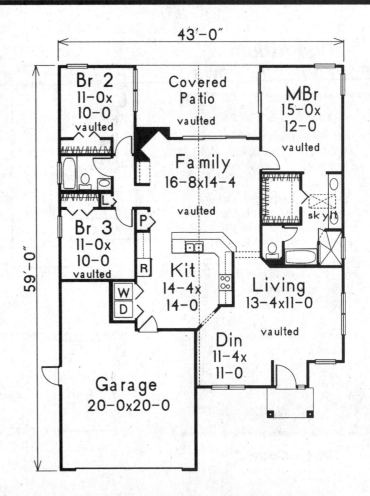

43'-0"

59'-0"

Br 2
11-0x
10-0
vaulted

Covered
Patio
vaulted

MBr
15-0x
12-0
vaulted

Family
16-8x14-4
vaulted

sky lt

Br 3
11-0x
10-0
vaulted

P

R

Kit
14-4x
14-0

Living
13-4x11-0

vaulted

W
D

Din
11-4x
11-0

Garage
20-0x20-0

**TO ORDER BLUEPRINTS USE THE FORM ON PAGE 15 OR CALL TOLL-FREE 1-877-671-6036**
View thousands more home plans online at www.familyhandyman.com/homeplans

83

**2,125 total square feet of living area**

## Duo Atrium
## For Fantastic Views

### Special features

- A cozy porch leads to the vaulted great room with fireplace through the entry which has a walk-in closet and bath

- Large and well-arranged kitchen offers spectacular views from its cantilevered sink cabinetry through a two-story atrium window wall

- Master bedroom boasts a sitting room, large walk-in closet and bath with garden tub overhanging a brightly lit atrium

- 1,047 square feet of optional living area on the lower level featuring a study and family room with walk-in bar and full bath below the kitchen

- 3 bedrooms, 2 1/2 baths, 2-car side entry garage

- Walk-out basement foundation

*Price Code C*

First Floor
2,125 sq. ft.

*Optional
Lower Level*

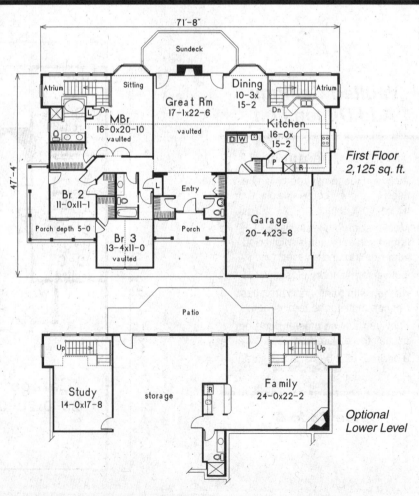

**TO ORDER BLUEPRINTS USE THE FORM ON PAGE 15 OR CALL TOLL-FREE 1-877-671-6036**
View thousands more home plans online at www.familyhandyman.com/homeplans

**1,333 total square feet of living area**

## Carport With Storage

### Special features

- Country charm with a covered front porch
- Dining area looks into the family room with fireplace
- Master suite has a walk-in closet and private bath
- 3 bedrooms, 2 baths, 2-car attached carport
- Slab or crawl space foundation, please specify when ordering

*Price Code A*

Width: 55'-6"
Depth: 64'-3"

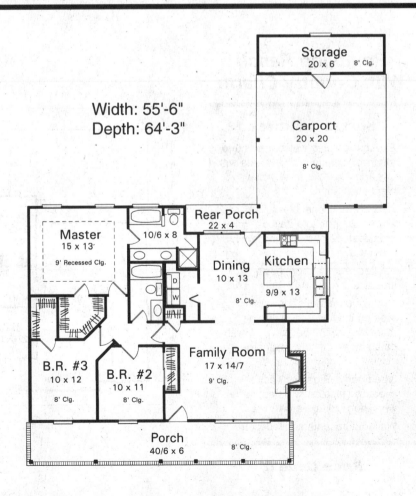

**TO ORDER BLUEPRINTS USE THE FORM ON PAGE 15 OR CALL TOLL-FREE 1-877-671-6036**
View thousands more home plans online at www.familyhandyman.com/homeplans

85

**2,514 total square feet of living area**

## Rambling Ranch With Country Charm

### Special features

- Expansive porch welcomes you to the foyer, spacious dining area with bay and a gallery-sized hall with plant shelf above

- A highly functional U-shaped kitchen is open to a bayed breakfast room, study and family room with a 46' vista

- Vaulted rear sunroom has a fireplace

- 1,509 square feet of optional living area on the lower level with a recreation room, bedroom #4 with bath and an office with storage closet

- 3 bedrooms, 2 baths, 3-car oversized side entry garage with workshop/storage area

- Walk-out basement foundation

*Price Code D*

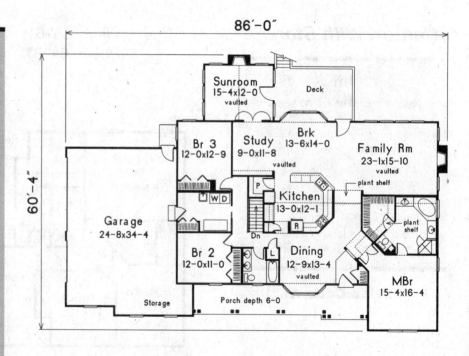

**2,260 total square feet of living area**

# Dramatic Roof Line Accents This Ranch

## Special features

- Luxurious master bedroom includes a raised ceiling, bath with oversized tub, separate shower and large walk-in closet
- Convenient kitchen and breakfast area enjoys ample pantry storage
- Formal foyer leads into the large living room with warming fireplace
- Convenient secondary entrance for everyday traffic
- 3 bedrooms, 2 baths, 2-car garage
- Slab foundation

*Price Code D*

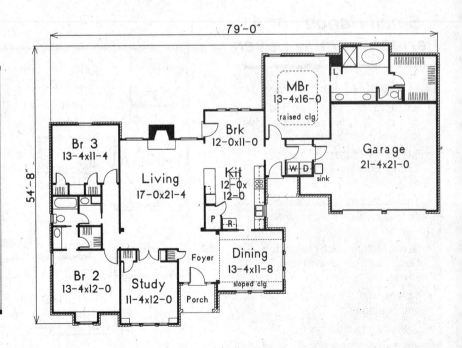

79'-0"

54'-8"

Br 3 13-4x11-4

MBr 13-4x16-0 raised clg.

Brk 12-0x11-0

Garage 21-4x21-0

Living 17-0x21-4

Kit 12-0x 12-0

W D sink

Br 2 13-4x12-0

Study 11-4x12-0

Foyer

Porch

Dining 13-4x11-8 sloped clg.

**TO ORDER BLUEPRINTS USE THE FORM ON PAGE 15 OR CALL TOLL-FREE 1-877-671-6036**
View thousands more home plans online at www.familyhandyman.com/homeplans

87

**1,761 total square feet of living area**

## Small Ranch For A Perfect Country Haven

### Special features

- Exterior window dressing, roof dormers and planter boxes provide visual warmth and charm
- Great room boasts a vaulted ceiling, fireplace and opens to a pass-through kitchen
- The vaulted master bedroom includes a luxury bath and walk-in closet
- Home features eight separate closets with an abundance of storage
- 4 bedrooms, 2 baths, 2-car side entry garage
- Basement foundation

*Price Code B*

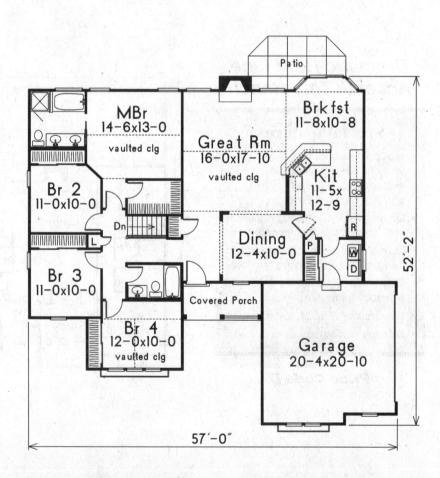

**88**

**TO ORDER BLUEPRINTS USE THE FORM ON PAGE 15 OR CALL TOLL-FREE 1-877-671-6036**
View thousands more home plans online at www.familyhandyman.com/homeplans

**2,123 total square feet of living area**

## Spacious Country Home

### Special features

- L-shaped porch extends the entire length of this home creating lots of extra space for outdoor living
- Master bedroom is secluded for privacy and has two closets, double vanity in bath and a double-door entry onto covered porch
- Efficiently designed kitchen
- 3 bedrooms, 2 1/2 baths
- Crawl space or slab foundation, please specify when ordering

*Price Code C*

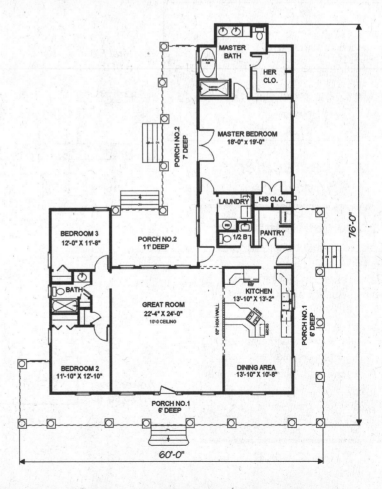

MASTER BATH

HER CLO.

PORCH NO.2
7' DEEP

MASTER BEDROOM
18'-0" x 19'-0"

LAUNDRY | HIS CLO.

1/2 B | PANTRY

BEDROOM 3
12'-0" X 11'-8"

PORCH NO.2
11' DEEP

REF KITCHEN
13'-10" X 13'-2"

BATH

GREAT ROOM
22'-4" X 24'-0"
10'-0 CEILING

STOVE
MICRO

PORCH NO.1
6' DEEP

BEDROOM 2
11'-10" X 12'-10"

DINING AREA
13'-10" X 10'-8"

PORCH NO.1
6' DEEP

76'-0"

60'-0"

**TO ORDER BLUEPRINTS USE THE FORM ON PAGE 15 OR CALL TOLL-FREE 1-877-671-6036**
View thousands more home plans online at www.familyhandyman.com/homeplans

89

**4,826 total square feet of living area**

*Great Room/Atrium
Interior View*

## A Spectacular Showplace

### Special features

- Great room with balcony and bay-shaped atrium
- Master bedroom has sitting area, walk-in closets, atrium overlook and luxury bath
- Lower level has family room/atrium, home theater area with wet bar, game room and guest bedroom
- 4 bedrooms, 3 1/2 baths, 3-car side entry garage
- Walk-out basement foundation with lawn and garden workroom

**Price Code G**

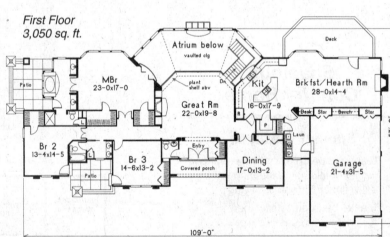

First Floor
3,050 sq. ft.

Atrium below
vaulted clg

Deck

MBr
23-0x17-0

plant
shelf abv

Kit
16-0x17-9

Brkfst/Hearth Rm
28-0x14-4

Great Rm
22-0x19-8

Desk  Stor  Bench  Stor

Patio

Br 2
13-4x14-5

Entry

Laun

Br 3
14-6x13-2

Dining
17-0x13-2

Garage
21-4x31-5

Covered porch

Patio

109'-0"

57'-6"

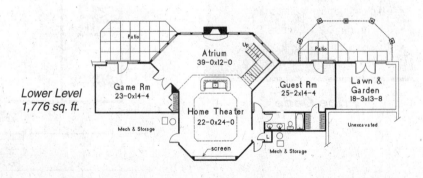

Lower Level
1,776 sq. ft.

Patio

Patio

Atrium
39-0x12-0

Up

Game Rm
23-0x14-4

Guest Rm
25-2x14-4

Lawn &
Garden
18-3x13-8

Home Theater
22-0x24-0

Mech & Storage

Mech & Storage

Unexcavated

screen

**TO ORDER BLUEPRINTS USE THE FORM ON PAGE 15 OR CALL TOLL-FREE 1-877-671-6036**
View thousands more home plans online at www.familyhandyman.com/homeplans

**1,367 total square feet of living area**

## Comfortable Country Home

### Special features

- Neat front porch shelters the entrance
- Dining room has a full wall of windows and convenient storage area
- Breakfast area leads to the rear terrace through sliding doors
- Large living room with high ceiling, skylight and fireplace
- 3 bedrooms, 2 baths, 2-car garage
- Basement foundation, drawings also include slab foundation

**Price Code B**

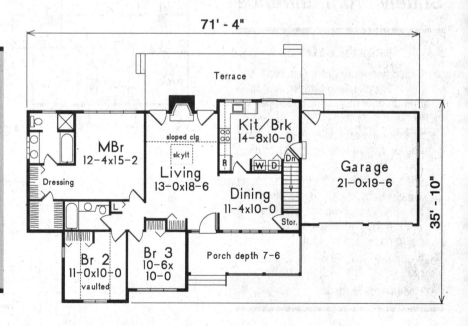

**TO ORDER BLUEPRINTS USE THE FORM ON PAGE 15 OR CALL TOLL-FREE 1-877-671-6036**
View thousands more home plans online at www.familyhandyman.com/homeplans

91

**2,614 total square feet of living area**

## Stately Front Entrance

### Special features

- Grand two-story entry features majestic palladian window, double French doors to parlor and access to powder room
- State-of-the-art kitchen has corner sink with two large archtop windows, island snack bar, menu desk and walk-in pantry
- Master bath is vaulted and offers a luxurious step-up tub, palladian window, built-in shelves and columns with plant shelf
- 4 bedrooms, 2 1/2 baths, 2-car garage
- Basement foundation

**Price Code E**

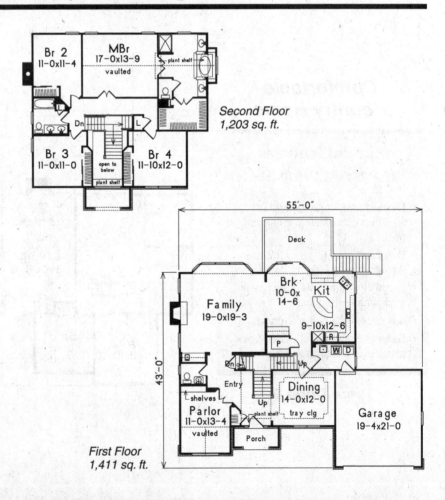

*Second Floor*
*1,203 sq. ft.*

*First Floor*
*1,411 sq. ft.*

**1,708 total square feet of living area**

## Private Breakfast Room Provides Casual Dining

### Special features

- Massive family room is enhanced with several windows, a fireplace and access to the porch
- Deluxe master bath is accented by a step-up corner tub flanked by double vanities
- Closets throughout maintain organized living
- Bedrooms are isolated from living areas
- 3 bedrooms, 2 baths, 2-car garage
- Basement foundation, drawings also include crawl space foundation

*Price Code B*

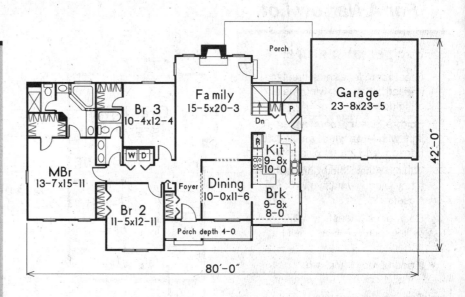

**TO ORDER BLUEPRINTS USE THE FORM ON PAGE 15 OR CALL TOLL-FREE 1-877-671-6036**
View thousands more home plans online at www.familyhandyman.com/homeplans

93

**1,294 total square feet of living area**

## Trendsetting Appeal For A Narrow Lot

### Special features

- Great room features a fireplace and large bay with windows and patio doors
- Enjoy a laundry room immersed in light with large windows, arched transom and attractive planter box
- Vaulted master bedroom features a bay window and two walk-in closets
- Bedroom #2 boasts a vaulted ceiling, plant shelf and half bath, perfect for a studio
- 2 bedrooms, 1 full bath, 2 half baths, 1-car rear entry garage
- Basement foundation

**Price Code A**

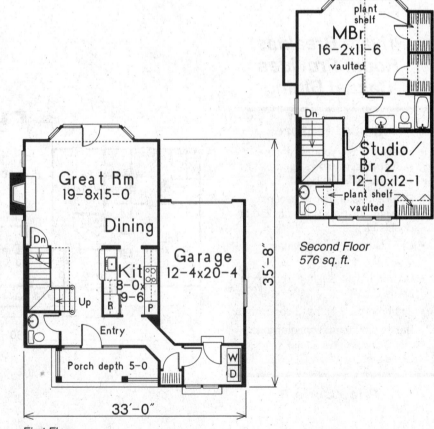

Great Rm
19-8x15-0

Dining

Kit
8-0x
9-6

Garage
12-4x20-4

Dn

Up

Entry

Porch depth 5-0

W
D

35'-8"

33'-0"

*First Floor*
*718 sq. ft.*

plant shelf

MBr
16-2x11-6
vaulted

Dn

Studio/
Br 2
12-10x12-1
plant shelf
vaulted

*Second Floor*
*576 sq. ft.*

**1,501 total square feet of living area**

## Country-Style Home With Large Front Porch

### Special features

- Spacious kitchen with dining area is open to the outdoors
- Convenient utility room is adjacent to garage
- Master bedroom features a private bath, dressing area and access to the large covered porch
- Large family room creates openness
- 3 bedrooms, 2 baths, 2-car side entry garage
- Basement foundation, drawings also include crawl space and slab foundations

### *Price Code B*

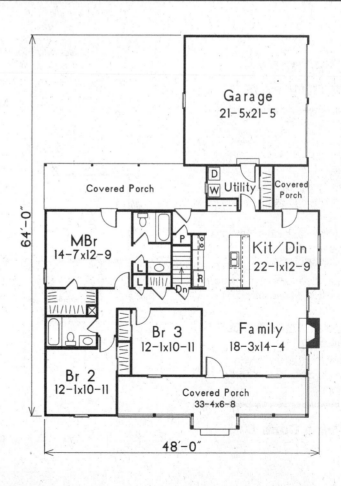

Garage
21-5x21-5

Covered Porch

Utility

Covered Porch

MBr
14-7x12-9

Kit/Din
22-1x12-9

Br 3
12-1x10-11

Family
18-3x14-4

Br 2
12-1x10-11

Covered Porch
33-4x6-8

64'-0"

48'-0"

**TO ORDER BLUEPRINTS USE THE FORM ON PAGE 15 OR CALL TOLL-FREE 1-877-671-6036**
View thousands more home plans online at www.familyhandyman.com/homeplans

95

**2,182 total square feet of living area**

## Distinctive Country Porch

### Special features

- Meandering porch creates an inviting look
- Generous great room has four double-hung windows and gliding doors to exterior
- Highly functional kitchen features island/breakfast bar, menu desk and convenient pantry
- Each secondary bedroom includes generous closet space and a private bath
- 3 bedrooms, 3 1/2 baths, 2-car side entry garage
- Basement foundation, drawings also include crawl space and slab foundations

### Price Code D

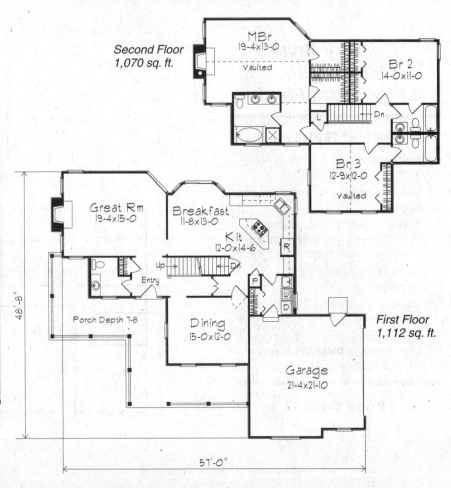

Second Floor 1,070 sq. ft.

MBr 19-4x13-0 Vaulted

Br 2 14-0x11-0

Br 3 12-9x12-0 Vaulted

Great Rm 19-4x15-0

Breakfast 11-8x13-0

Kit 12-0x14-6

Entry

Porch Depth 7-8

Dining 15-0x12-0

Garage 21-4x21-10

First Floor 1,112 sq. ft.

48'-8"

51'-0"

**TO ORDER BLUEPRINTS USE THE FORM ON PAGE 15 OR CALL TOLL-FREE 1-877-671-6036**
View thousands more home plans online at www.familyhandyman.com/homeplans

**1,793 total square feet of living area**

## Porch Adds To Farmhouse Style

### Special features

- Beautiful foyer leads into the great room that has a fireplace flanked by two sets of beautifully transomed doors both leading to a large covered porch
- Dramatic eat-in kitchen includes an abundance of cabinets and workspace in an exciting angled shape
- Delightful master bedroom has many amenities
- Optional bonus room above the garage has an additional 779 square feet of living area
- 3 bedrooms, 2 baths, 2-car side entry garage
- Basement, crawl space or slab foundation, please specify when ordering

*Price Code B*

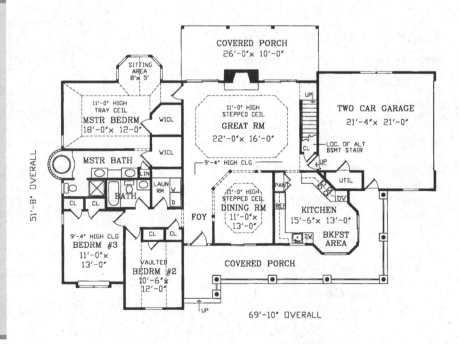

**TO ORDER BLUEPRINTS USE THE FORM ON PAGE 15 OR CALL TOLL-FREE 1-877-671-6036**
View thousands more home plans online at www.familyhandyman.com/homeplans

97

**1,484 total square feet of living area**

## Four Seasons Cottage

### Special features

- Energy efficient home with 2" x 6" exterior walls
- Useful screened porch is ideal for dining and relaxing
- Corner fireplace warms the living room
- Snack bar adds extra counterspace in the kitchen
- 3 bedrooms, 2 baths
- Basement foundation

**Price Code A**

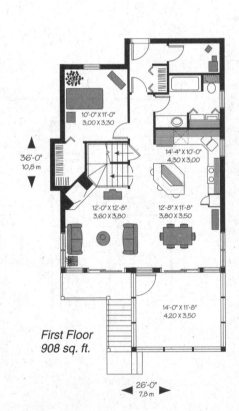

36'-0"
10,8 m

10'-0" X 11'-0"
3,00 X 3,30

14'-4" X 10'-0"
4,30 X 3,00

12'-0" X 12'-8"
3,60 X 3,80

12'-8" X 11'-8"
3,80 X 3,50

14'-0" X 11'-8"
4,20 X 3,50

*First Floor*
*908 sq. ft.*

26'-0"
7,8 m

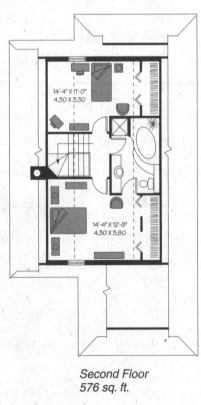

14'-4" X 11'-0"
4,30 X 3,30

14'-4" X 12'-8"
4,30 X 3,80

*Second Floor*
*576 sq. ft.*

**3,357 total square feet of living area**

## Elegant Entrance

### Special features

- Attractive balcony overlooks entry foyer and living area
- Balcony area could easily convert to a fifth bedroom
- Spacious kitchen also opens into a sunken family room with a fireplace
- First floor master bedroom boasts a large walk-in closet and dressing area
- Convenient 2nd floor laundry chute leads to the central laundry room
- 4 bedrooms, 2 full baths, 2 half baths, 2-car side entry garage
- Basement foundation, drawings also include crawl space and slab foundations

*Price Code F*

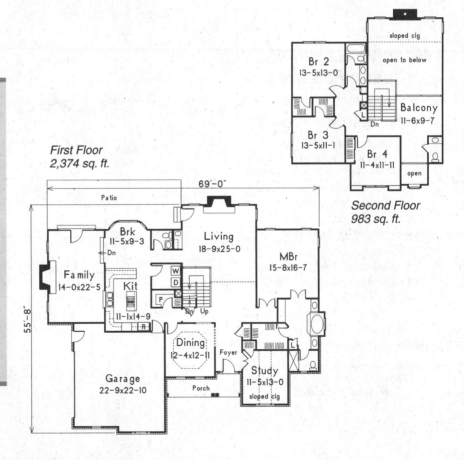

*First Floor 2,374 sq. ft.*

*Second Floor 983 sq. ft.*

**TO ORDER BLUEPRINTS USE THE FORM ON PAGE 15 OR CALL TOLL-FREE 1-877-671-6036**
View thousands more home plans online at www.familyhandyman.com/homeplans

99

**2,874 total square feet of living area**

## Massive Ranch With Classy Features

### Special features

- Large family room with sloped ceiling and wood beams adjoins the kitchen and breakfast area with windows on two walls
- Large foyer opens to family room with massive stone fireplace and open stairs to the basement
- Private master bedroom includes a raised tub under the bay window, dramatic dressing area and a huge walk-in closet
- 4 bedrooms, 2 1/2 baths, 2-car side entry garage
- Basement foundation

*Price Code E*

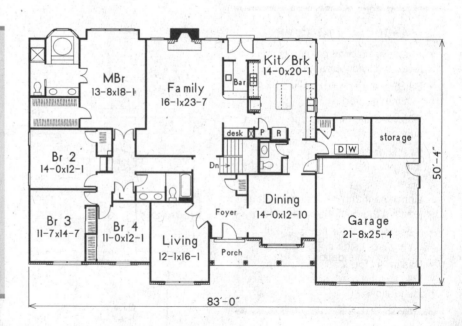

MBr
13-8x18-1

Family
16-1x23-7

Kit/Brk
14-0x20-1

Bar

Br 2
14-0x12-1

desk   P   R

Dn

storage

D W

Br 3
11-7x14-7

Br 4
11-0x12-1

Living
12-1x16-1

Foyer

Dining
14-0x12-10

Porch

Garage
21-8x25-4

50'-4"

83'-0"

**100**

**TO ORDER BLUEPRINTS USE THE FORM ON PAGE 15 OR CALL TOLL-FREE 1-877-671-6036**
View thousands more home plans online at www.familyhandyman.com/homeplans

**1,283 total square feet of living area**

## Large Corner Deck Lends Way To Outdoor Living Area

### Special features

- Vaulted breakfast room has sliding doors that open onto the deck
- Kitchen features a convenient corner sink and pass-through to dining room
- Open living atmosphere in dining area and great room
- Vaulted great room features a fireplace
- 3 bedrooms, 2 baths, 2-car garage
- Basement foundation

### Price Code A

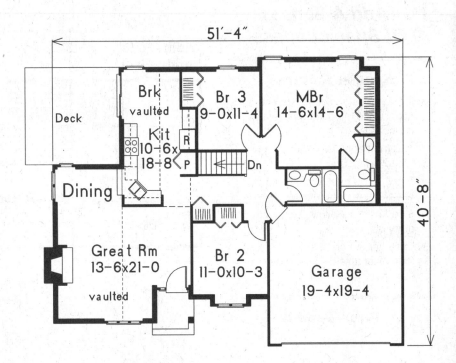

51'-4"

40'-8"

Deck

Brk
vaulted

Br 3
9-0x11-4

MBr
14-6x14-6

Kit
10-6x
18-8

R

P

Dn

Dining

Great Rm
13-6x21-0
vaulted

Br 2
11-0x10-3

Garage
19-4x19-4

**1,408 total square feet of living area**

## Vaulted Ceilings Add A Sense Of Spaciousness

### Special features

- A bright country kitchen boasts an abundance of counterspace and cupboards
- The front entry is sheltered by a broad verandah
- A spa tub is brightened by a box-bay window in the master bath
- 3 bedrooms, 2 baths, 2-car side entry garage
- Basement or crawl space foundation, please specify when ordering

*Price Code A*

Width: 70'-0"
Depth: 28'-0"

DECK

SOAKER TUB    BOX WINDOW

WORKSHOP

D
T  LDR
W

country k
18'11 x 13'4
vaulted

WORK ISLAND

RAILING

P

DN

mbr
12' x 14'4

SKYLIGHT

ART NICHE

LAUNDRY CHUTE

two-car garage
21'6 x 19'6

POT LEDGE OVER CLOSETS

grt rm
20' x 13'4
vaulted

L
CLS

br3
12' x 10'

br2
12' x 10'

VERANDA

RAILING

**3,222 total square feet of living area**

## Arched Elegance

### Special features

- Two-story foyer features central staircase and views to the second floor and the dining and living rooms

- Built-in breakfast booth is surrounded by windows

- Gourmet kitchen includes a view to the great room

- Two-story great room features large fireplace and arched openings to the second floor

- Elegant master bedroom has a separate reading room with bookshelves and a fireplace

- 4 bedrooms, 3 1/2 baths, 2-car side entry garage

- Basement foundation, drawings also include crawl space and slab foundations

**Price Code F**

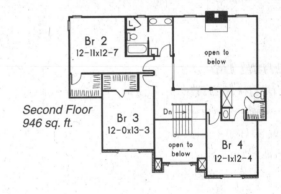

*Second Floor*
*946 sq. ft.*

Br 2
12-11x12-7

Br 3
12-0x13-3

Br 4
12-1x12-4

open to below

open to below

Dn

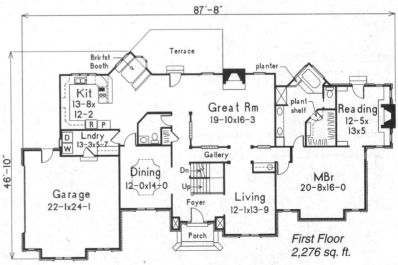

87'-8"

46'-10"

Brkfst Booth

Terrace

Kit
13-8x
12-2

Lndry
13-3x5-7

Dining
12-0x14-0

Garage
22-1x24-1

Foyer

Porch

Living
12-1x13-9

Dn
Up

Gallery

Great Rm
19-10x16-3

planter

plant shelf

Reading
12-5x
13x5

MBr
20-8x16-0

*First Floor*
*2,276 sq. ft.*

**TO ORDER BLUEPRINTS USE THE FORM ON PAGE 15 OR CALL TOLL-FREE 1-877-671-6036**
View thousands more home plans online at www.familyhandyman.com/homeplans

103

**2,333 total square feet of living area**

## Double French Doors Grace Living Room

### Special features

- 9' ceilings on the first floor
- Master bedroom features a large walk-in closet and an inviting double-door entry into a spacious bath
- Convenient laundry room is located near the kitchen
- 4 bedrooms, 3 baths, 2-car side entry garage
- Slab foundation, drawings also include crawl space and partial crawl space/basement foundations

### Price Code D

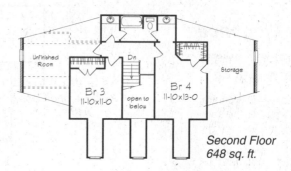

*Second Floor
648 sq. ft.*

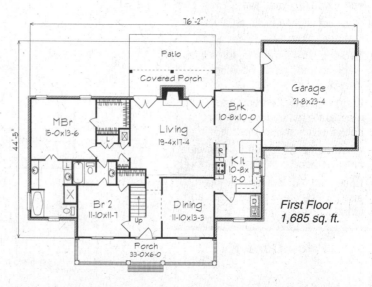

*First Floor
1,685 sq. ft.*

**4,187 total square feet of living area**

## Colossal Southern Colonial

### Special features

- 10' ceilings on the first floor and 9' ceilings on the second floor
- Secluded bedroom on the first floor has its own private bath and could easily be converted to a mother-in-law suite
- Second floor sitting area accesses outdoor balcony through lovely French doors
- Octagon-shaped breakfast room is a nice focal point
- Future gameroom over garage has an additional 551 square feet of living area
- 4 bedrooms, 4 1/2 baths, 3-car side entry garage
- Slab foundation

**Price Code H**

*First Floor 3,129 sq. ft.*

Ext. Storage

Garage 21'4"x45'8"

Patio

Utility

Bedroom 12'9"x12'2"

Screened Porch

Width: 68'-0"
Depth: 117'-10"

Master Bedroom 15'2"x25'5"

WIC

Family 19'11"x25'7"

Kitchen 15'3"x19'8"

Master Bath

Breakfast 13'7"x14'2"

Dining 11'3"x14'

Study 11'5"x 12'1"

WIC

Foyer

Porch

*Second Floor 1,058 sq. ft.*

Gameroom 20'x29'8"

WIC

Media Room 12'8"x11'1"

WIC

WIC

Bedroom 11'5"x 16'11"

Sitting

Bedroom 11'5"x 16'11"

**TO ORDER BLUEPRINTS USE THE FORM ON PAGE 15 OR CALL TOLL-FREE 1-877-671-6036**
View thousands more home plans online at www.familyhandyman.com/homeplans

105

**3,368 total square feet of living area**

## A Great Manor House, Spacious Inside And Out

### Special features

- Sunken great room with cathedral ceiling, wooden beams, skylights and a masonry fireplace
- Octagon-shaped breakfast room has domed ceiling with beams, large windows and door to patio
- Private master bedroom has a deluxe bath and dressing area
- Oversized walk-in closets and storage areas in each bedroom
- 4 bedrooms, 3 full baths, 2 half baths, 2-car side entry garage
- Basement foundation

**Price Code F**

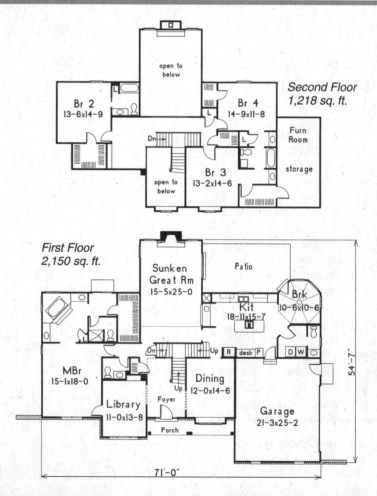

Second Floor 1,218 sq. ft.

open to below

Br 2 13-6x14-9

Br 4 14-9x11-8

Dn

Br 3 13-2x14-6

open to below

Furn Room

storage

First Floor 2,150 sq. ft.

Sunken Great Rm 15-5x25-0

Patio

Kit 18-11x15-7

Brk 10-6x10-6

MBr 15-1x18-0

Dn    Up

R  desk  P

D  W

Dining 12-0x14-6

Library 11-0x13-8

Foyer

Up

Garage 21-3x25-2

Porch

54'-7"

71'-0"

**1,040 total square feet of living area**

## Nostalgic Porch And Charming Interior

### Special features

- An island in the kitchen greatly simplifies your food preparation efforts

- A wide archway joins the formal living room to the dramatic angled kitchen and dining room

- Optional second floor has an additional 597 square feet of living area

- Optional first floor design has 2 bedrooms including a large master bedroom that enjoys a private luxury bath

- 3 bedrooms, 1 1/2 baths

- Basement, crawl space or slab foundation, please specify when ordering

**Price Code B**

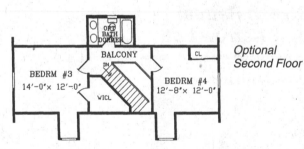

*Optional Second Floor*

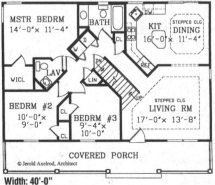

*First Floor 1,040 sq. ft.*

Width: 40'-0"
Depth: 26'-0"

**TO ORDER BLUEPRINTS USE THE FORM ON PAGE 15 OR CALL TOLL-FREE 1-877-671-6036**
View thousands more home plans online at www.familyhandyman.com/homeplans

107

**1,084 total square feet of living area**

## Stylish Retreat For A Narrow Lot

### Special features

- Delightful country porch for quiet evenings
- The living room offers a front feature window which invites the sun and includes a fireplace and dining area with private patio
- The U-shaped kitchen features lots of cabinets and bayed breakfast room with built-in pantry
- Both bedrooms have walk-in closets and access to their own bath
- 2 bedrooms, 2 baths
- Basement foundation

*Price Code AA*

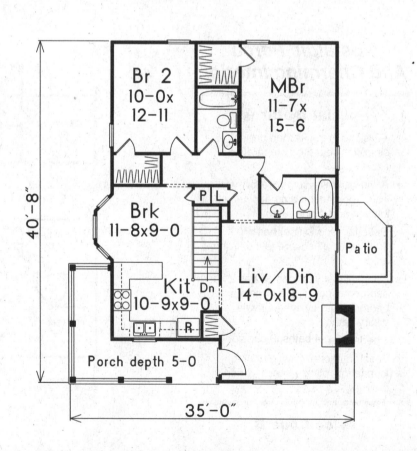

**108**

**TO ORDER BLUEPRINTS USE THE FORM ON PAGE 15 OR CALL TOLL-FREE 1-877-671-6036**
View thousands more home plans online at www.familyhandyman.com/homeplans

**3,098 total square feet of living area**

## Home Has A Contemporary Feel

### Special features

- Master bedroom is ultra luxurious with a private bath, enormous walk-in closet and sitting area leading to the lanai
- Vaulted family room has lots of windows and a corner fireplace
- Secluded study has double closets and built-ins
- Optional second floor has an additional 849 square feet of living area
- Framing - only concrete block available
- 4 bedrooms, 4 baths, 3-car side entry garage
- Slab foundation

**Price Code F**

Optional Second Floor

Bonus Rm. 18⁷ · 15⁵

Bath

Office 11⁸ · 13⁷

Study Niche 9⁵ · 7⁵

Mech.

78⁰

75⁴

Lanai

Stor.

Bedroom 12⁴ · 11¹⁰

Family Room 17⁹ · 15⁶

Bath

Bedroom 11¹⁰ · 12⁷

w.i.c.

Kitchen 15⁵ · 13⁷

Utility

Breakfast 12⁴ · 9¹⁰

Lanai

Living 14² · 13³

Bath

Sitting

Master Bedroom 15⁶ · 14⁰

Dining 12⁵ · 14⁰

Foyer

Study 10¹⁰ · 12³

Master Bath

3 Car Garage 20⁰ · 31⁹

Entry

w.i.c.

First Floor 3,098 sq. ft.

**TO ORDER BLUEPRINTS USE THE FORM ON PAGE 15 OR CALL TOLL-FREE 1-877-671-6036**
View thousands more home plans online at www.familyhandyman.com/homeplans

**109**

**1,979 total square feet of living area**

## Covered Front Porch Is A Special Touch

### Special features

- Striking corner fireplace is a stylish addition to the great room
- Open dining room allows the area to flow into the great room for added spaciousness
- Large pantry in the kitchen
- 3 bedrooms, 2 baths, 2-car side entry garage
- Slab foundation

*Price Code C*

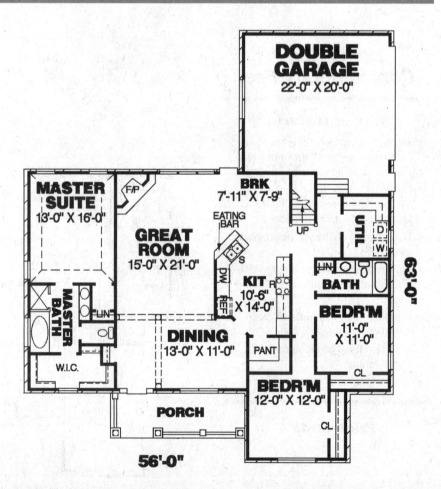

**840 total square feet of living area**

## Casual Open Living

### Special features

- Energy efficient home with 2" x 6" exterior walls
- Prominent gazebo located in the rear of the home for superb outdoor living
- Enormous bath has a corner oversized tub
- Lots of windows create a cheerful and sunny atmosphere throughout this home
- 1 bedroom, 1 bath
- Walk-out basement foundation

### Price Code AAA

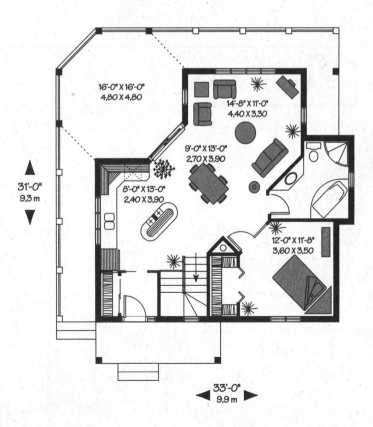

16'-0" X 16'-0"
4,80 X 4,80

14'-8" X 11'-0"
4,40 X 3,30

9'-0" X 13'-0"
2,70 X 3,90

8'-0" X 13'-0"
2,40 X 3,90

12'-0" X 11'-8"
3,60 X 3,50

31'-0"
9,3 m

33'-0"
9,9 m

**TO ORDER BLUEPRINTS USE THE FORM ON PAGE 15 OR CALL TOLL-FREE 1-877-671-6036**
View thousands more home plans online at www.familyhandyman.com/homeplans

111

**2,403 total square feet of living area**

## Two-Story With Elegant Appearance

### Special features

- The master bedroom has a 9' ceiling that raises to 11' in the octagon-shaped sitting area

- Kitchen is enhanced by a bar area, center island and extra-large pantry

- Multiple windows in the breakfast area create a cheerful environment

- 4 bedrooms, 3 1/2 baths, 2-car side entry garage

- Basement or slab foundation, please specify when ordering

### *Price Code D*

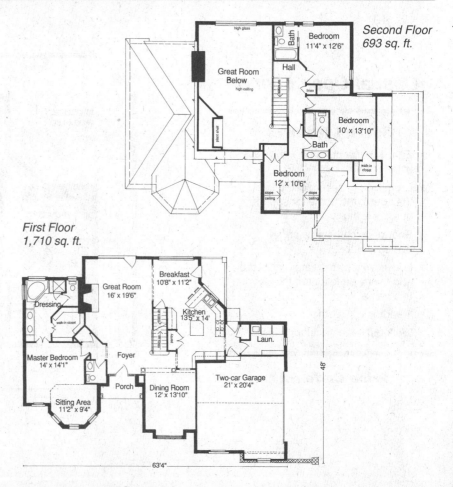

*Second Floor*
*693 sq. ft.*

Bath

Bedroom
11'4" x 12'6"

Great Room Below
high ceiling

Hall

linen

Bedroom
10' x 13'10"

Bath

walk-in closet

Bedroom
12' x 10'6"

slope ceiling    slope ceiling

plant shelf

high glass

*First Floor*
*1,710 sq. ft.*

Dressing

walk-in closet

Great Room
16' x 19'6"

Breakfast
10'8" x 11'2"

Kitchen
13'5" x 14'

pantry

Laun.

Master Bedroom
14' x 14'1"

Foyer

Porch

Dining Room
12' x 13'10"

Two-car Garage
21' x 20'4"

Sitting Area
11'2" x 9'4"

48'

63'4"

**TO ORDER BLUEPRINTS USE THE FORM ON PAGE 15 OR CALL TOLL-FREE 1-877-671-6036**
View thousands more home plans online at www.familyhandyman.com/homeplans

**1,674 total square feet of living area**

## Sculptured Roof Line And Facade Add Charm

### Special features

- Vaulted great room, dining area and kitchen all enjoy a central fireplace and log bin
- Convenient laundry/mud room is located between the garage and family area with handy stairs to the basement
- Easily expandable screened porch and adjacent patio access the dining area
- Master bedroom features a full bath with tub, separate shower and walk-in closet
- 3 bedrooms, 2 baths, 2-car garage
- Basement foundation, drawings also include crawl space and slab foundations

*Price Code B*

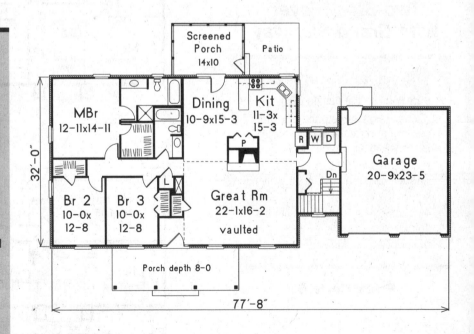

**TO ORDER BLUEPRINTS USE THE FORM ON PAGE 15 OR CALL TOLL-FREE 1-877-671-6036**
View thousands more home plans online at www.familyhandyman.com/homeplans

113

# Plan #717-001D-0038

**3,144 total square feet of living area**

## Two-Story Foyer With Grand Stairway

### Special features

- 9' ceilings on the first floor
- Kitchen offers large pantry, island cooktop and close proximity to laundry and dining rooms
- Expansive family room includes wet bar, fireplace and an attractive bay window
- 4 bedrooms, 4 1/2 baths, 3-car side entry garage
- Basement foundation

**Price Code E**

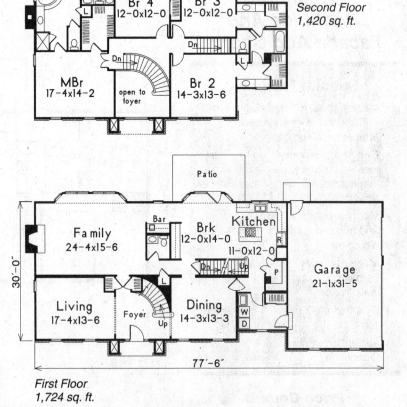

Second Floor
1,420 sq. ft.

Br 4
12-0x12-0

Br 3
12-0x12-0

MBr
17-4x14-2

open to foyer

Br 2
14-3x13-6

Patio

Family
24-4x15-6

Bar

Brk
12-0x14-0

Kitchen
11-0x12-0

Garage
21-1x31-5

Living
17-4x13-6

Foyer

Dining
14-3x13-3

30'-0"

77'-6"

First Floor
1,724 sq. ft.

**114**

**TO ORDER BLUEPRINTS USE THE FORM ON PAGE 15 OR CALL TOLL-FREE 1-877-671-6036**
View thousands more home plans online at www.familyhandyman.com/homeplans

**3,850 total square feet of living area**

**Interior View**

## Two-Story Solarium Welcomes The Sun

### Special features

- Entry, with balcony above, leads into a splendid great room with sunken solarium
- Kitchen layout boasts a half-circle bar and cooktop island
- Solarium features U-shaped stairs with balcony and arched window
- Master bedroom includes a luxurious bath and large study
- 5 bedrooms, 3 1/2 baths, 3-car garage
- Basement foundation

*Price Code F*

*Second Floor 1,544 sq. ft.*

Br 5
12-1x14-3

Sunken Solarium Below

Br 2
13-11x15-9

Loft

Dn

Br 4
12-1x12-0

Library
15-8x9-8

Br 3
15-5x12-0

open to below

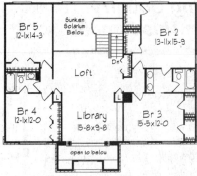

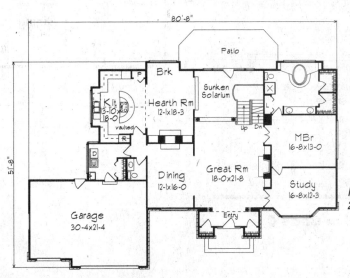

80'-8"

Patio

Brk

Kit
13-10x18-0
vaulted

Hearth Rm
12-1x18-3

Sunken Solarium

Up Dn

MBr
16-8x13-0

51'-8"

Dining
12-1x16-0

Great Rm
18-0x21-8

Study
16-8x12-3

Garage
30-4x21-4

Entry

*First Floor 2,306 sq. ft.*

**TO ORDER BLUEPRINTS USE THE FORM ON PAGE 15 OR CALL TOLL-FREE 1-877-671-6036**
View thousands more home plans online at www.familyhandyman.com/homeplans

115

**1,600 total square feet of living area**

## Charming Country Styling In This Ranch

### Special features

- Energy efficient home with 2" x 6" exterior walls

- Impressive sunken living room features a massive stone fireplace and 16' vaulted ceiling

- The dining room is conveniently located next to the kitchen and divided for privacy

- Special amenities include a sewing room, glass shelves in kitchen and master bath and a large utility area

- Sunken master bedroom features a distinctive sitting room

- 3 bedrooms, 2 baths, 2-car side entry garage

- Slab foundation, drawings also include crawl space and basement foundations

*Price Code C*

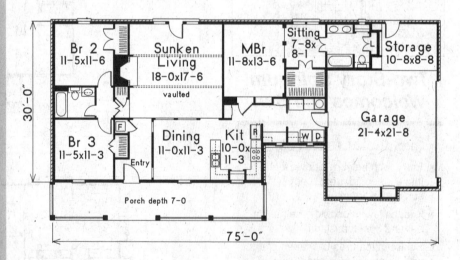

**2,850 total square feet of living area**

## A True Victorian Treasure

### Special features

- An enormous wrap-around porch surrounds the home on one side creating a lot of outdoor living area
- A double-door entry leads to the master bedroom which features a private bath with a spa tub
- Extra space in the garage allows for storage or work area
- Bonus room is included in the second floor square footage
- 3 bedrooms, 3 baths, 2-car side entry garage
- Crawl space foundation

**Price Code F**

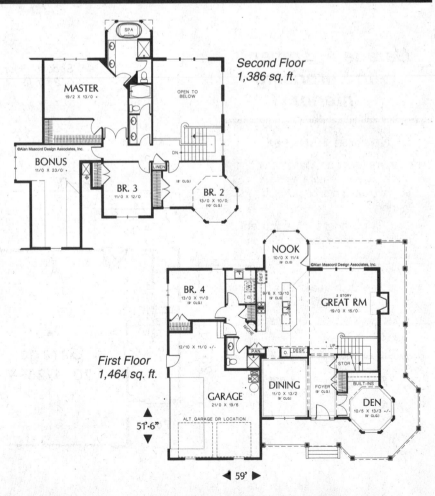

Second Floor
1,386 sq. ft.

SPA

MASTER
19/2 X 13/0

OPEN TO BELOW

BONUS
11/0 X 23/0

©Alan Mascord Design Associates, Inc.

DN

LINEN

BR. 3
11/0 X 12/0

18" CLG.

BR. 2
13/0 X 10/0
(10" CLG.)

NOOK
10/0 X 11/4
(9" CLG.)

©Alan Mascord Design Associates, Inc.

BR. 4
13/0 X 11/0
(9" CLG.)

REF.

9/6 X 13/10
(9" CLG.)

2 STORY
GREAT RM
19/0 X 15/0

12/10 X 11/0 +/-

NICHE

PAN.

DESK

UP

STOR

First Floor
1,464 sq. ft.

GARAGE
21/0 X 19/6

DINING
11/0 X 13/2
(9" CLG.)

FOYER
(9" CLG.)

BUILT-INS

DEN
10/5 X 13/3 +/-
(9" CLG.)

ALT GARAGE DR LOCATION

51'-6"

59'

**TO ORDER BLUEPRINTS USE THE FORM ON PAGE 15 OR CALL TOLL-FREE 1-877-671-6036**
View thousands more home plans online at www.familyhandyman.com/homeplans

117

**632 total square feet of living area**

## Garage Apartment With Surprising Interior

### Special features

- Porch leads to a vaulted entry and stair with feature window, coat closet and access to garage/laundry
- Cozy living room offers a vaulted ceiling, fireplace, large palladian window and pass-through to kitchen
- A garden tub with arched window is part of a very roomy bath
- 1 bedroom, 1 bath, 2-car garage
- Slab foundation

### Price Code AAA

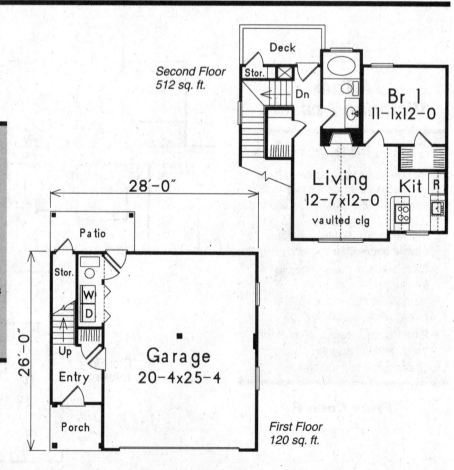

Second Floor
512 sq. ft.

Deck

Stor.

Dn

Br 1
11-1x12-0

Living
12-7x12-0
vaulted clg

Kit
R

28'-0"

Patio

Stor.

W
D

Up

Entry

Porch

26'-0"

Garage
20-4x25-4

First Floor
120 sq. ft.

118

**TO ORDER BLUEPRINTS USE THE FORM ON PAGE 15 OR CALL TOLL-FREE 1-877-671-6036**
View thousands more home plans online at www.familyhandyman.com/homeplans

**1,416 total square feet of living area**

## Attractive A-Frame

### Special features

- Second floor has a bedroom and bath secluded for privacy
- Efficiently designed kitchen accesses deck through sliding glass doors
- Wall of windows in dining/living area brightens interior
- Enormous wrap-around deck provides plenty of outdoor living area
- 3 bedrooms, 2 baths
- Basement or crawl space foundation, please specify when ordering

### Price Code A

*Second Floor*
*400 sq. ft.*

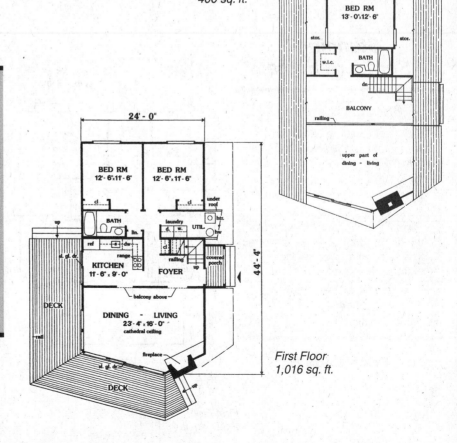

*First Floor*
*1,016 sq. ft.*

**TO ORDER BLUEPRINTS USE THE FORM ON PAGE 15 OR CALL TOLL-FREE 1-877-671-6036**
View thousands more home plans online at www.familyhandyman.com/homeplans

**119**

# Plan #717-024D-0034

**3,493 total square feet of living area**

## Stunning Southern Home

### Special features

- First floor master bedroom has an enormous walk-in closet and a lavish bath
- Cozy sitting nook on the second floor has access onto the covered second floor balcony
- Formal living room in the front of the home could easily be converted to a study with a double-door entrance for privacy
- 4 bedrooms, 3 1/2 baths, 3-car drive under garage
- Pier foundation

### Price Code H

Width: 46'-0"
Depth: 55'-0"

Porch 25'6"x 10'
Family 24'6"x 17'2"
Master Bedroom 20'2"x 16'10"
Breakfast 15'6"x 9'8"
Utility
Master Bath
Kitchen 15'6"x 14'2"
1/2 Bath
Walk-In Closet
Dining 11'x 13'8"
Foyer
Living 11'6"x 13'8"
Porch 46'x 8'

*First Floor*
*2,327 sq. ft.*

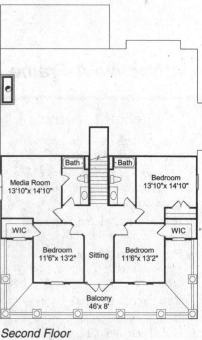

Bath     Bath
Media Room 13'10"x 14'10"
Bedroom 13'10"x 14'10"
WIC     WIC
Bedroom 11'6"x 13'2"     Sitting     Bedroom 11'6"x 13'2"
Balcony 46'x 8'

*Second Floor*
*1,166 sq. ft.*

**1,575 total square feet of living area**

## Stylish Living For A Narrow Lot

### Special features

- Inviting porch leads to spacious living and dining rooms
- Kitchen with corner windows features an island snack bar, attractive breakfast room bay, convenient laundry area and built-in pantry
- A luxury bath and walk-in closet adorn the master bedroom suite
- 3 bedrooms, 2 1/2 baths, 2-car garage
- Basement foundation, drawings also include crawl space and slab foundations

**Price Code B**

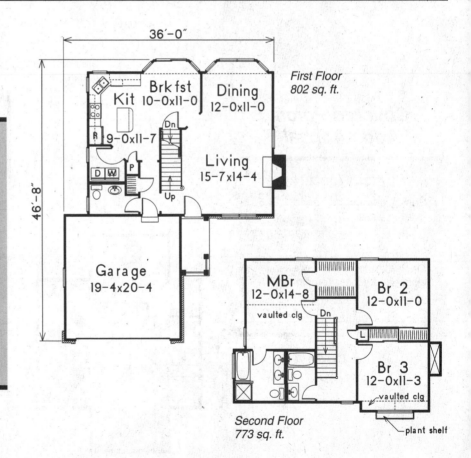

36'-0"

46'-8"

Kit
9-0x11-7

Brk fst
10-0x11-0

Dining
12-0x11-0

Living
15-7x14-4

*First Floor*
*802 sq. ft.*

DW

Dn

Up

P

Garage
19-4x20-4

MBr
12-0x14-8
vaulted clg

Br 2
12-0x11-0

Dn

L

Br 3
12-0x11-3
vaulted clg

*Second Floor*
*773 sq. ft.*

plant shelf

**TO ORDER BLUEPRINTS USE THE FORM ON PAGE 15 OR CALL TOLL-FREE 1-877-671-6036**
View thousands more home plans online at www.familyhandyman.com/homeplans

121

# Plan #717-032D-0040

**1,480 total square feet of living area**

## Covered Porch Adds Appeal

### Special features

- Energy efficient home with 2" x 6" exterior walls
- Cathedral ceilings in family and dining rooms
- Master bedroom has a walk-in closet and access to bath
- 2 bedrooms, 2 baths
- Basement foundation

### Price Code A

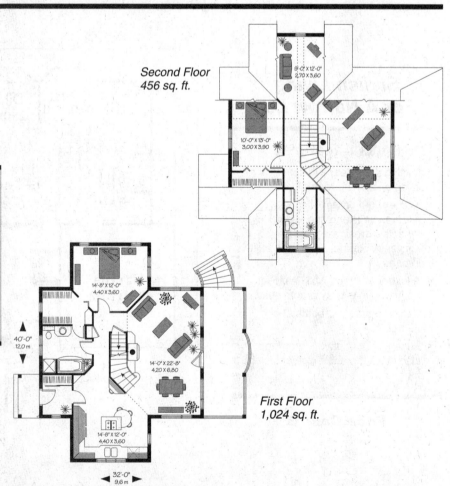

*Second Floor*
456 sq. ft.

9'-0" X 12'-0"
2,70 X 3,60

10'-0" X 13'-0"
3,00 X 3,90

14'-8" X 12'-0"
4,40 X 3,60

14'-0" X 22'-8"
4,20 X 6,80

14'-8" X 12'-0"
4,40 X 3,60

40'-0"
12,0 m

32'-0"
9,6 m

*First Floor*
1,024 sq. ft.

**TO ORDER BLUEPRINTS USE THE FORM ON PAGE 15 OR CALL TOLL-FREE 1-877-671-6036**
View thousands more home plans online at www.familyhandyman.com/homeplans

**1,660 total square feet of living area**

## Dramatic Expanse Of Windows

### Special features

- Convenient gear and equipment room
- Spacious living and dining rooms look even larger with the openness of the foyer and kitchen
- Large wrap-around deck is a great plus for outdoor living
- Broad balcony overlooks living and dining rooms
- 3 bedrooms, 3 baths
- Partial basement/crawl space foundation, drawings also include slab foundation

**Price Code C**

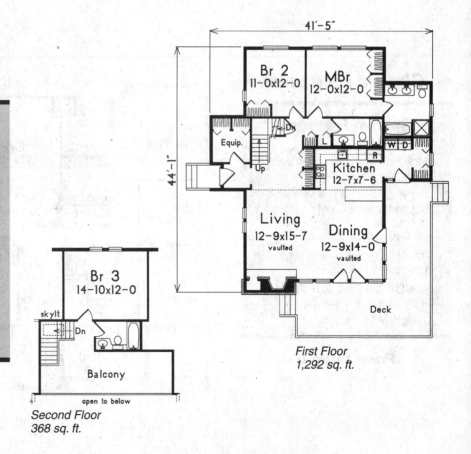

*Second Floor*
*368 sq. ft.*

*First Floor*
*1,292 sq. ft.*

**TO ORDER BLUEPRINTS USE THE FORM ON PAGE 15 OR CALL TOLL-FREE 1-877-671-6036**
View thousands more home plans online at www.familyhandyman.com/homeplans

**123**

**2,483 total square feet of living area**

## Classic Elegance

### Special features

- A large entry porch with open brick arches and palladian door welcomes guests
- The vaulted great room features an entertainment center alcove and the ideal layout for furniture placement
- The dining room is extra large with a stylish tray ceiling
- 4 bedrooms, 2 baths, 2-car side entry garage
- Basement foundation

*Price Code D*

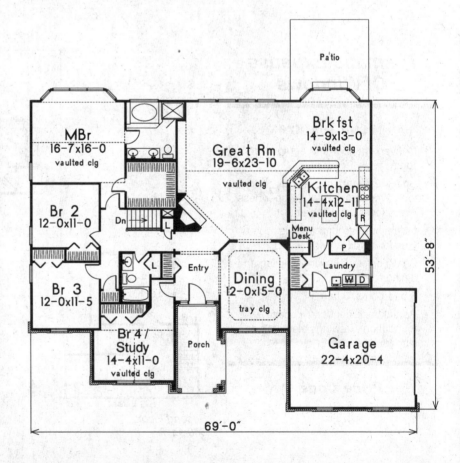

988 total square feet of living area

## Compact Ranch Is An Ideal Starter Home

### Special features

- Great room features corner fireplace
- Vaulted ceiling and corner windows add space and light in great room
- Eat-in kitchen with vaulted ceiling accesses deck for outdoor living
- Master bedroom features separate vanities and private access to the bath
- 2 bedrooms, 1 bath, 2-car garage
- Basement foundation

*Price Code AA*

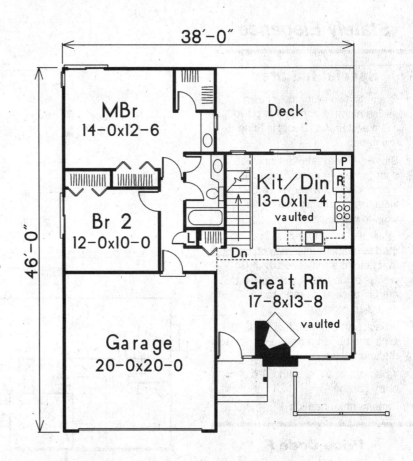

38'-0"

46'-0"

MBr
14-0x12-6

Deck

Br 2
12-0x10-0

Kit/Din
13-0x11-4
vaulted

Dn

Great Rm
17-8x13-8
vaulted

Garage
20-0x20-0

**TO ORDER BLUEPRINTS USE THE FORM ON PAGE 15 OR CALL TOLL-FREE 1-877-671-6036**
View thousands more home plans online at www.familyhandyman.com/HOMEPLANS

125

**3,657 total square feet of living area**

## Stately Elegance

### Special features

- Dramatic two-story foyer has a stylish niche, a convenient powder room and French doors leading to the parlor

- State-of-the-art kitchen includes a large walk-in pantry, breakfast island, computer center and 40' vista through family room with walk-in wet bar

- Vaulted master bath features marble steps and Roman columns that lead to a majestic-sized whirlpool tub with a surrounding marble deck and grand-scale palladian window

- A Jack and Jill bath, hall bath, loft area and huge bedrooms comprise the second floor

- 4 bedrooms, 3 1/2 baths, 3-car side entry garage

- Basement foundation

**Price Code F**

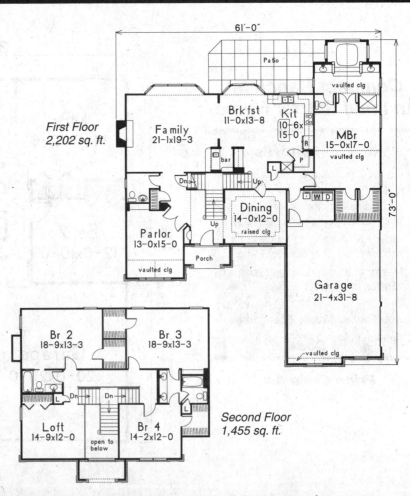

First Floor
2,202 sq. ft.

61'-0"

73'-0"

Patio

Family
21-1x19-3

Brk fst
11-0x13-8

Kit
10-6x
15-0

MBr
15-0x17-0
vaulted clg

bar

Dn

Up

Dining
14-0x12-0
raised clg

W D

Up

Parlor
13-0x15-0

Porch

vaulted clg

Garage
21-4x31-8

vaulted clg

Br 2
18-9x13-3

Br 3
18-9x13-3

Dn    Dn

Loft
14-9x12-0

Br 4
14-2x12-0

Second Floor
1,455 sq. ft.

open to below

**1,392 total square feet of living area**

## Simple And Cozy

### Special features

- Centralized great room welcomes guests with a warm fireplace
- Master bedroom has a separate entrance for added privacy
- Kitchen includes breakfast room, snack counter and laundry area
- 3 bedrooms, 2 baths, 2-car garage
- Basement foundation

### Price Code A

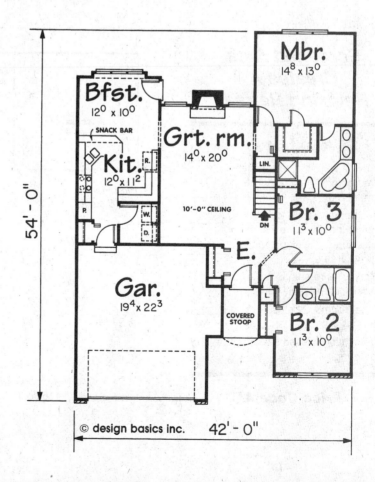

**TO ORDER BLUEPRINTS USE THE FORM ON PAGE 15 OR CALL TOLL-FREE 1-877-671-6036**
View thousands more home plans online at www.familyhandyman.com/homeplans

127

**1,434 total square feet of living area**

## Screened Area Creates A Relaxing Retreat

### Special features

- Private second floor master bedroom features a private bath and a roomy walk-in closet
- A country kitchen with peninsula counter adjoins the living room creating the feeling of a larger living area
- The living room has a warm fireplace and a tall ceiling
- 3 bedrooms, 2 baths, 2-car garage
- Basement, crawl space or slab foundation, please specify when ordering

### Price Code A

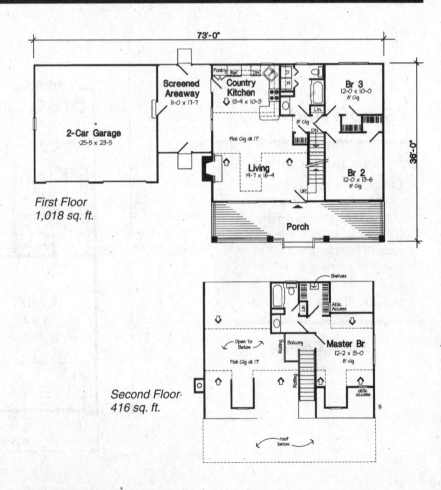

*First Floor*
*1,018 sq. ft.*

*Second Floor*
*416 sq. ft.*

**2,900 total square feet of living area**

## Classic Contemporary Wrapped In Brick

### Special features

- The grand-scale great room offers a vaulted ceiling and palladian windows flanking an 8' wide brick fireplace

- A smartly designed built-in-a-bay kitchen features a picture window above sink, huge pantry, cooktop island and is open to a large morning room with 12' of cabinetry

- All bedrooms include immense closet space

- 1,018 square feet of optional living area on the lower level with family room, walk-in bar and a fifth bedroom with a bath

- 4 bedrooms, 2 1/2 baths, 3-car side entry garage

- Walk-out basement foundation

**Price Code E**

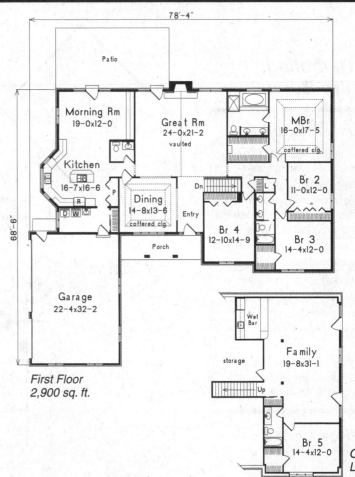

78'-4"

Patio

Morning Rm
19-0x12-0

Great Rm
24-0x21-2
vaulted

MBr
16-0x17-5
coffered clg.

Kitchen
16-7x16-6

Br 2
11-0x12-0

Dining
14-8x13-6
coffered clg.

Dn

Br 4
12-10x14-9

Entry

Br 3
14-4x12-0

68'-6"

Garage
22-4x32-2

Porch

*First Floor*
*2,900 sq. ft.*

Wet Bar

Family
19-8x31-1

storage

Up

Br 5
14-4x12-0

*Optional Lower Level*

**1,475 total square feet of living area**

## Rambling Country Bungalow

### Special features

- Family room features a high ceiling and prominent corner fireplace
- Kitchen with island counter and garden window makes a convenient connection between the family and dining rooms
- Hallway leads to three bedrooms all with large walk-in closets
- Covered breezeway joins main house and garage
- Full-width covered porch entry lends a country touch
- 3 bedrooms, 2 baths, 2-car detached side entry garage
- Slab foundation, drawings also include crawl space foundation

### *Price Code B*

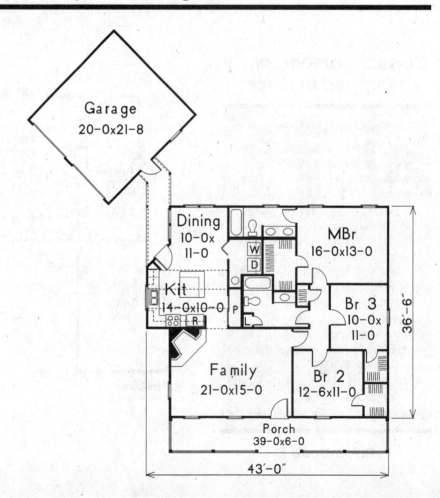

Garage
20-0x21-8

Dining
10-0x
11-0

W
D

MBr
16-0x13-0

Kit
14-0x10-0

P

Br 3
10-0x
11-0

36'-6"

Family
21-0x15-0

Br 2
12-6x11-0

Porch
39-0x6-0

43'-0"

**2,674 total square feet of living area**

## Impressive Gallery

### Special features

- First floor master bedroom has a convenient location
- Kitchen and breakfast area have an island and access to the covered front porch
- Second floor bedrooms have dormer window seats for added charm
- Optional future rooms on the second floor have an additional 520 square feet of living area
- 4 bedrooms, 3 baths, 3-car side entry garage
- Basement or slab foundation, please specify when ordering

**Price Code E**

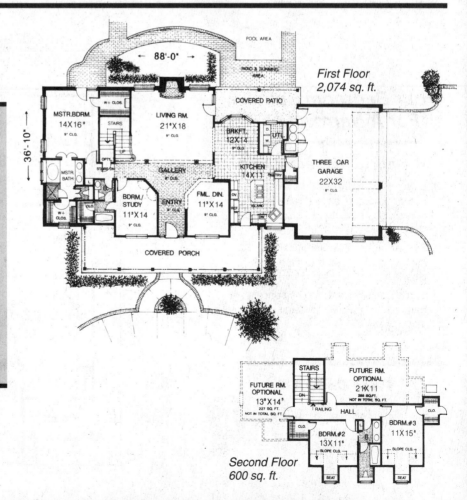

*First Floor*
2,074 sq. ft.

*Second Floor*
600 sq. ft.

**TO ORDER BLUEPRINTS USE THE FORM ON PAGE 15 OR CALL TOLL-FREE 1-877-671-6036**
View thousands more home plans online at www.familyhandyman.com/homeplans

131

**1,452 total square feet of living area**

## Four Bedroom Home For A Narrow Lot

### Special features

- Large living room features a cozy corner fireplace, bayed dining area and access from entry with guest closet
- Forward master bedroom enjoys having its own bath and linen closet
- Three additional bedrooms share a bath with a double-bowl vanity
- 4 bedrooms, 2 baths
- Basement foundation

### *Price Code A*

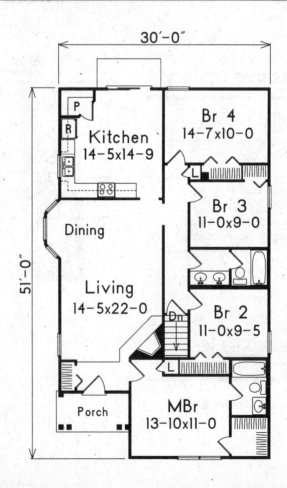

30'-0"

51'-0"

P

R

Kitchen
14-5x14-9

Br 4
14-7x10-0

L

Dining

Br 3
11-0x9-0

Living
14-5x22-0

Dn

Br 2
11-0x9-5

L

Porch

MBr
13-10x11-0

**TO ORDER BLUEPRINTS USE THE FORM ON PAGE 15 OR CALL TOLL-FREE 1-877-671-6036**
View thousands more home plans online at www.familyhandyman.com/homeplans

**2,880 total square feet of living area**

## Elegantly Styled Mediterranean Home

### Special features

- Varied ceiling heights throughout
- Charming master bedroom features a bayed sitting area, view to the courtyard and an exquisite master bath
- Interesting barrel vaulted living room
- 3 bedrooms, 2 1/2 baths, 3-car garage
- Crawl space foundation

*Price Code E*

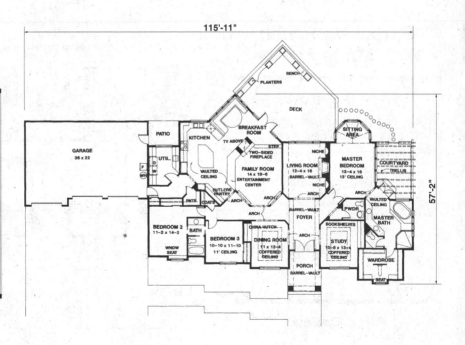

**TO ORDER BLUEPRINTS USE THE FORM ON PAGE 15 OR CALL TOLL-FREE 1-877-671-6036**
View thousands more home plans online at www.familyhandyman.com/homeplans

133

**2,991 total square feet of living area**

## Sprawling Ranch With Stone Facade

### Special features

- Two additional bedrooms share a full bath and each have a walk-in closet
- Separate dining area provides a formal atmosphere while entertaining
- Great room has built-in cabinets surrounding fireplace
- 3 bedrooms, 2 1/2 baths, 3-car side entry garage
- Basement foundation

### Price Code E

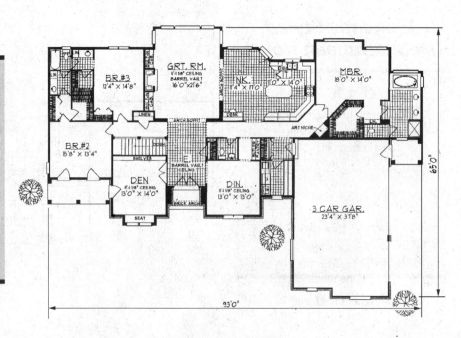

**1,944 total square feet of living area**

## Country Ranch Enjoys Large Great Room

### Special features

- Spacious surrounding porch, covered patio and stone fireplace create an expansive ponderosa appearance

- The large entry leads to a grand-sized great room featuring a vaulted ceiling, fireplace, wet bar and access to the porch through three patio doors

- The U-shaped kitchen is open to the hearth room and enjoys a snack bar, fireplace and patio access

- A luxury bath, walk-in closet and doors to the porch are a few of the amenities of the master bedroom

- 3 bedrooms, 2 baths, 3-car detached garage

- Basement foundation

*Price Code C*

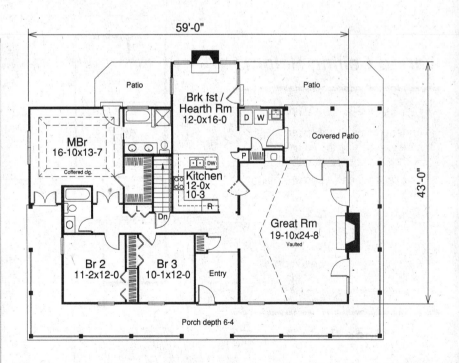

59'-0"

43'-0"

Patio

Brk fst / Hearth Rm
12-0x16-0

Patio

Covered Patio

MBr
16-10x13-7

Coffered clg.

Kitchen
12-0x
10-3

D W

P

Dn

Great Rm
19-10x24-8
Vaulted

Br 2
11-2x12-0

Br 3
10-1x12-0

Entry

Porch depth 6-4

**TO ORDER BLUEPRINTS USE THE FORM ON PAGE 15 OR CALL TOLL-FREE 1-877-671-6036**
View thousands more home plans online at www.familyhandyman.com/homeplans

135

**2,439 total square feet of living area**

## Varied Ceiling Heights

### Special features

- Enter columned gallery area just before reaching the family room with a see-through fireplace
- Master bath has a corner whirlpool tub
- Double-door entrance leads into the study
- 4 bedrooms, 3 baths, 2-car garage
- Slab, crawl space, basement or walk-out basement foundation, please specify when ordering

**Price Code D**

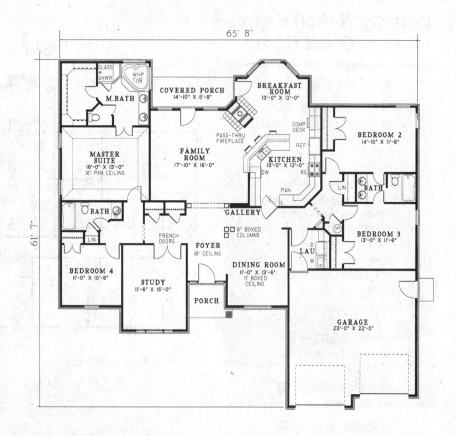

1,771 total square feet of living area

## Graceful Southern Hospitality

### Special features

- Efficient country kitchen shares space with a bayed eating area

- Two-story family/great room is warmed by a fireplace in winter and open to outdoor country comfort in the summer with double French doors

- First floor master suite offers a bay window and access to the porch through French doors

- 3 bedrooms, 2 1/2 baths, optional 2-car detached garage

- Basement foundation

**Price Code B**

Second Floor
600 sq. ft.

First Floor
1,171 sq. ft.

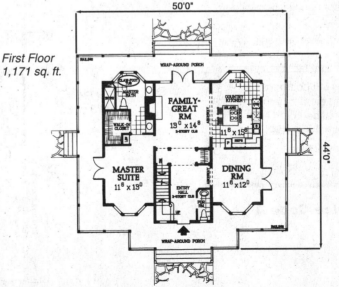

**TO ORDER BLUEPRINTS USE THE FORM ON PAGE 15 OR CALL TOLL-FREE 1-877-671-6036**
View thousands more home plans online at www.familyhandyman.com/homeplans

137

**1,428 total square feet of living area**

## Surrounding Porch For Country Views

### Special features

- Large vaulted family room opens to dining area and kitchen with breakfast bar
- First floor master bedroom offers large bath, walk-in closet and nearby laundry facilities
- A spacious loft/bedroom #3 overlooking the family room and an additional bedroom and bath complement the second floor
- 3 bedrooms, 2 baths
- Basement foundation

**Price Code A**

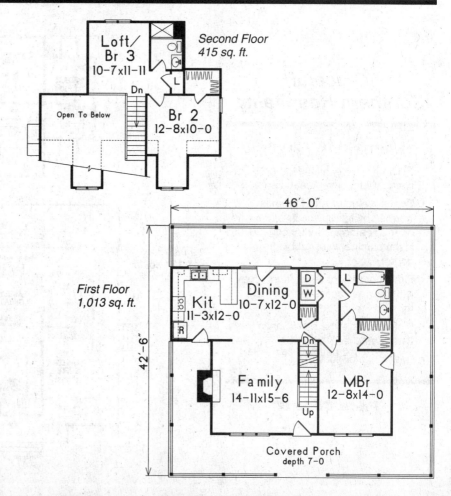

Second Floor
415 sq. ft.

Loft/ Br 3
10-7x11-11

Open To Below

Dn

Br 2
12-8x10-0

L

46'-0"

First Floor
1,013 sq. ft.

42'-6"

Kit
11-3x12-0

Dining
10-7x12-0

D
W

L

R

Dn

Family
14-11x15-6

Up

MBr
12-8x14-0

Covered Porch
depth 7-0

The Family **Handyman**

**1,220 total square feet of living area**

## Compact Home For Functional Living

### Special features

- Vaulted ceilings add luxury to the living room and master bedroom
- Spacious living room is accented with a large fireplace and hearth
- Gracious dining area is adjacent to the convenient wrap-around kitchen
- Washer and dryer are handy to the bedrooms
- Covered porch entry adds appeal
- Rear deck adjoins dining area
- 3 bedrooms, 2 baths, 2-car drive under garage
- Basement foundation

*Price Code A*

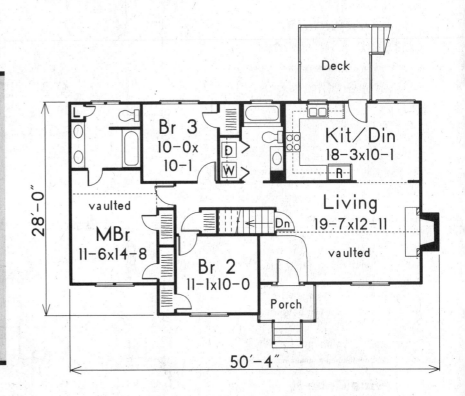

Deck

Br 3
10-0x
10-1

Kit/Din
18-3x10-1

vaulted

MBr
11-6x14-8

Living
19-7x12-11

vaulted

Br 2
11-1x10-0

Porch

28'-0"

50'-4"

**TO ORDER BLUEPRINTS USE THE FORM ON PAGE 15 OR CALL TOLL-FREE 1-877-671-6036**
View thousands more home plans online at www.familyhandyman.com/homeplans

139

**5,800 total square feet of living area**

## Extravagant Classic Traditional

### Special features

- Covered porch accesses several rooms and features a cozy fireplace for outdoor living
- A spectacular foyer leads directly to a central rotunda with a circular stair
- Luxury amenities on the first floor include a computer room, mud room and butler's pantry
- Bonus room on the second floor has an additional 500 square feet of living area
- 4 bedrooms, 5 1/2 baths, 2-car side entry garage and 2-car detached garage
- Crawl space foundation

*Price Code H*

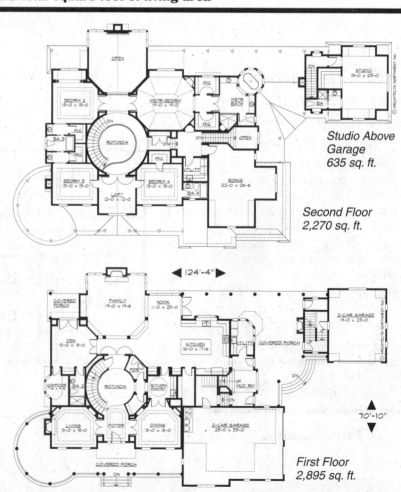

Studio Above Garage
635 sq. ft.

Second Floor
2,270 sq. ft.

First Floor
2,895 sq. ft.

**3,556 total square feet of living area**

## Wrap-Around Porch And Turret Accent Design

### Special features

- Jack and Jill bath is located between two of the bedrooms on the second floor
- Second floor features three bedrooms and overlooks the great room
- Formal entrance and additional family entrance from covered porch to laundry/mud room
- First floor master bedroom features a coffered ceiling, double walk-in closets, luxury bath and direct access to the study
- 4 bedrooms, 3 1/2 baths, 3-car side entry garage
- Basement foundation

**Price Code F**

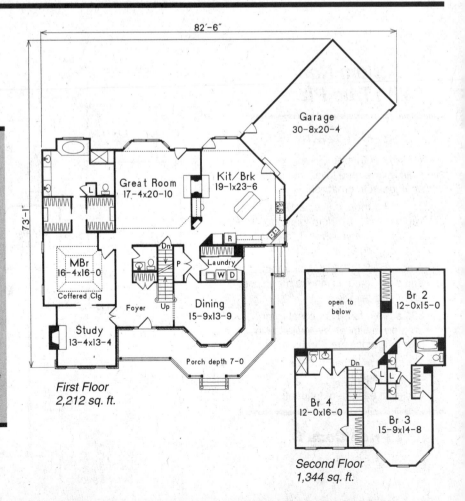

82'-6"

73'-1"

Garage
30-8x20-4

Great Room
17-4x20-10

Kit/Brk
19-1x23-6

MBr
16-4x16-0
Coffered Clg

Dn

Laundry
W D
R
P

Foyer
Up

Dining
15-9x13-9

Study
13-4x13-4

Porch depth 7-0

*First Floor*
*2,212 sq. ft.*

open to below

Br 2
12-0x15-0

Dn
L

Br 4
12-0x16-0

Br 3
15-9x14-8

*Second Floor*
*1,344 sq. ft.*

**TO ORDER BLUEPRINTS USE THE FORM ON PAGE 15 OR CALL TOLL-FREE 1-877-671-6036**
View thousands more home plans online at www.familyhandyman.com/homeplans

141

**2,397 total square feet of living area**

## Atrium Ranch With True Pizzazz

### Special features

- A grand entry porch leads to a dramatic vaulted foyer with plant shelf open to great room

- The great room enjoys a 12' vaulted ceiling, atrium featuring 2 1/2 story windows and fireplace with flanking bookshelves

- A conveniently located sunroom and side porch adjoin the breakfast room and garage

- 898 square feet of optional living area on the lower level with family room, bedroom #4 and bath

- 3 bedrooms, 2 baths, 3-car side entry garage

- Walk-out basement foundation

**Price Code D**

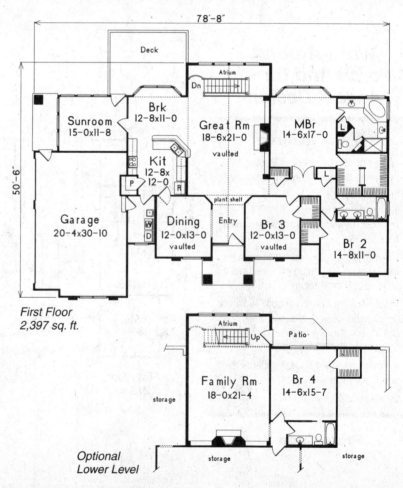

*First Floor 2,397 sq. ft.*

*Optional Lower Level*

**1,543 total square feet of living area**

## Expansive Glass Wall In Living Areas

### Special features

- Enormous sundeck makes this a popular vacation style
- A woodstove warms the vaulted living and dining rooms
- A vaulted kitchen has a prep island and breakfast bar
- Second floor vaulted master bedroom has a private bath and walk-in closet
- 3 bedrooms, 2 baths
- Crawl space foundation

**Price Code B**

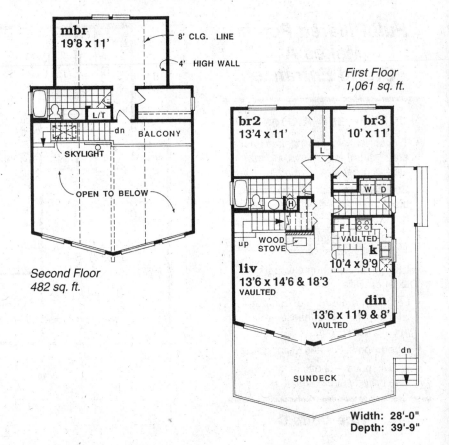

**mbr**
19'8 x 11'

8' CLG. LINE

4' HIGH WALL

L/T

dn

BALCONY

SKYLIGHT

OPEN TO BELOW

*Second Floor*
*482 sq. ft.*

*First Floor*
*1,061 sq. ft.*

**br2**
13'4 x 11'

**br3**
10' x 11'

L

W D

up

WOOD STOVE

H

F VAULTED

**k**
10'4 x 9'9

**liv**
13'6 x 14'6 & 18'3
VAULTED

**din**
13'6 x 11'9 & 8'
VAULTED

dn

SUNDECK

Width: 28'-0"
Depth: 39'-9"

**TO ORDER BLUEPRINTS USE THE FORM ON PAGE 15 OR CALL TOLL-FREE 1-877-671-6036**
View thousands more home plans online at www.familyhandyman.com/homeplans

143

**1,800 total square feet of living area**

## Full Pillared Porch Makes A Grand Entrance

### Special features

- The stylish kitchen and breakfast area feature large windows that allow a great view outdoors
- Covered front and rear porches provide an added dimension to this home's living space
- Generous storage areas and a large utility room
- Energy efficient home with 2" x 6" exterior walls
- Large separate master bedroom with adjoining bath has large tub and corner shower
- 3 bedrooms, 2 baths, 2-car garage
- Crawl space foundation, drawings also include slab foundation

**Price Code C**

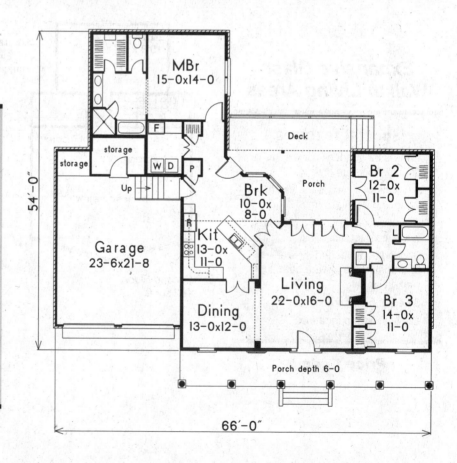

**1,849 total square feet of living area**

## Bedrooms Separate From Rest Of Home

### Special features

- Enormous laundry/mud room has many extras including a storage area and half bath
- Lavish master bath has a corner jacuzzi tub, double sinks, separate shower and walk-in closet
- Secondary bedrooms include walk-in closets
- Kitchen has a wrap-around eating counter and is positioned between the formal dining area and breakfast room for convenience
- 3 bedrooms, 2 1/2 baths, 2-car side entry garage
- Slab foundation, drawings also include crawl space foundation

### Price Code C

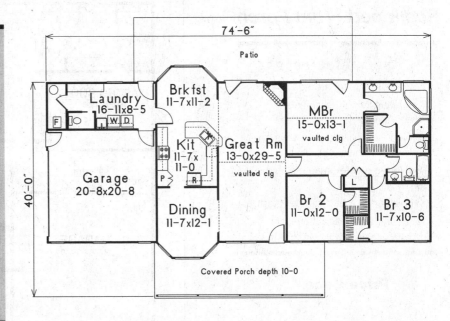

74'-6"

Patio

Laundry
16-11x8-5

Brkfst
11-7x11-2

MBr
15-0x13-1
vaulted clg

Garage
20-8x20-8

Kit
11-7x
11-0

Great Rm
13-0x29-5
vaulted clg

40'-0"

Dining
11-7x12-1

Br 2
11-0x12-0

Br 3
11-7x10-6

Covered Porch depth 10-0

**TO ORDER BLUEPRINTS USE THE FORM ON PAGE 15 OR CALL TOLL-FREE 1-877-671-6036**
View thousands more home plans online at www.familyhandyman.com/homeplans

**145**

**1,374 total square feet of living area**

## Scalloped Front Porch

### Special features

- Garage has extra storage space
- Spacious living room has a fireplace
- Well-designed kitchen enjoys an adjacent breakfast nook
- Secluded master suite maintains privacy
- 3 bedrooms, 2 baths, 2-car garage
- Slab or crawl space foundation, please specify when ordering

### Price Code A

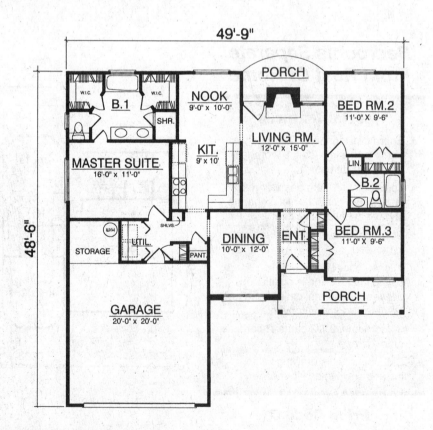

49'-9"

48'-6"

PORCH

NOOK
9'-0" x 10'-0"

BED RM.2
11'-0" X 9'-6"

W.I.C.    B.1    W.I.C.

SHR.

MASTER SUITE
16'-0" x 11'-0"

KIT.
9' x 10'

LIVING RM.
12'-0" x 15'-0"

LIN.

B.2

SHLVS.

STORAGE

UTIL.

PANT.

DINING
10'-0" x 12'-0"

ENT.

BED RM.3
11'-0" X 9'-6"

w/h

GARAGE
20'-0" x 20'-0"

PORCH

**1,779 total square feet of living area**

## Elaborate Dining Room

### Special features

- Well-designed floor plan has a vaulted family room with fireplace and access to the outdoors
- Decorative columns separate the dining area from the foyer
- A vaulted ceiling adds spaciousness in the master bath that also features a walk-in closet
- 3 bedrooms, 2 baths, 2-car garage
- Walk-out basement, slab or crawl space foundation, please specify when ordering

*Price Code B*

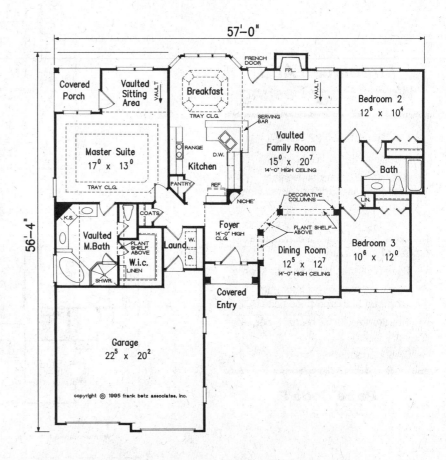

57'-0"

56'-4"

Covered Porch

Vaulted Sitting Area

VAULT

Breakfast
TRAY CLG.

FRENCH DOOR
FPL.

VAULT

Bedroom 2
12⁶ x 10⁴

Master Suite
17⁰ x 13⁰
TRAY CLG.

RANGE
D.W.
Kitchen

SERVING BAR

Vaulted Family Room
15⁰ x 20⁷
14'-0" HIGH CEILING

Bath

PANTRY
REF.
NICHE'

DECORATIVE COLUMNS

LIN.

K.S.

COATS

Foyer
14'-0" HIGH CLG.

PLANT SHELF ABOVE

Vaulted M.Bath
PLANT SHELF ABOVE

Laund.
W.
D.

Dining Room
12⁵ x 12⁷
14'-0" HIGH CEILING

Bedroom 3
10⁶ x 12⁰

W.i.c.
LINEN
SHWR.

Covered Entry

Garage
22⁵ x 20²

copyright © 1995 frank betz associates, inc.

**TO ORDER BLUEPRINTS USE THE FORM ON PAGE 15 OR CALL TOLL-FREE 1-877-671-6036**
View thousands more home plans online at www.familyhandyman.com/homeplans

147

**2,932 total square feet of living area**

## Fireplaces Add Warm Cozy Feeling

### Special features

- 9' ceilings throughout home
- Rear stairs create convenient access to second floor from living area
- Spacious kitchen has pass-through to the family room, a convenient island and pantry
- Cozy built-in table in breakfast area
- Secluded master bedroom has a luxurious bath and patio access
- 4 bedrooms, 3 1/2 baths, 2-car side entry garage
- Slab foundation

### Price Code F

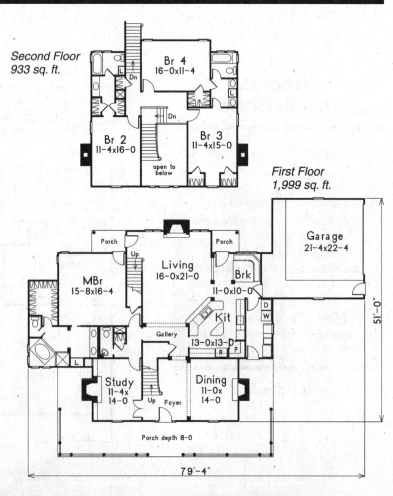

Second Floor
933 sq. ft.

Br 4
16-0x11-4

Br 2
11-4x16-0

Br 3
11-4x15-0

open to below

First Floor
1,999 sq. ft.

Garage
21-4x22-4

Porch

Living
16-0x21-0

Porch

Brk
11-0x10-0

MBr
15-8x16-4

Kit
13-0x13-0

Gallery

Study
11-4x 14-0

Dining
11-0x 14-0

Foyer

Porch depth 8-0

79'-4"

51'-0"

**2,311 total square feet of living area**

## Comfortable Living

### Special features

• Fireplaces warm the master suite and family room

• Vaulted breakfast room is near the kitchen

• Formal living room is near the dining room

• Optional bonus room on the second floor has an additional 425 square feet of living area

• 3 bedrooms, 2 1/2 baths, 2-car side entry garage

• Walk-out basement, slab or crawl space foundation, please specify when ordering

**Price Code D**

*First Floor*
*2,311 sq. ft.*

*Optional*
*Second Floor*

149

2,962 total square feet of living area

## Luxurious Bayed Master Bath

### Special features

- Vaulted breakfast nook is adjacent to the kitchen for convenience
- Bedroom #4 is an ideal guest suite with private bath
- ...ster bedroom includes see-...h fireplace, bayed vanity and ... walk-in closet
- ...ns, 3 baths, 3-car side ...ge
- ...tion

*Code E*

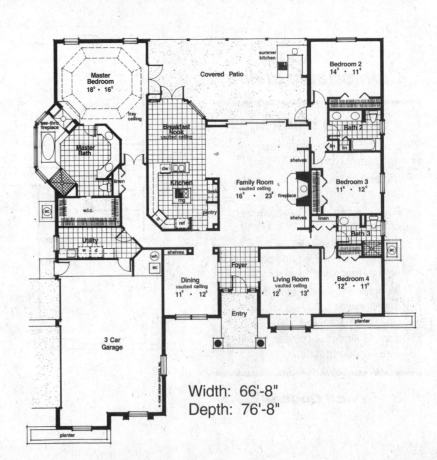

Width: 66'-8"
Depth: 76'-8"

TO ORDE...

BLUEPRINTS USE THE FORM ON PAGE 15 OR CALL TOLL-FREE 1-877-671-6036
...thousands more home plans online at www.familyhandyman.com/homeplans

**1,404 total square feet of living area**

## Compact Home Is Charming And Functional

### Special features

- Split-foyer entrance
- Bayed living area features a unique vaulted ceiling and fireplace
- Wrap-around kitchen has corner windows for added sunlight and a bar that overlooks dining area
- Master bath features a garden tub with separate shower
- Rear deck provides handy access to dining room and kitchen
- 3 bedrooms, 2 baths, 2-car drive under garage
- Basement foundation, drawings also include partial crawl space foundation

*Price Code A*

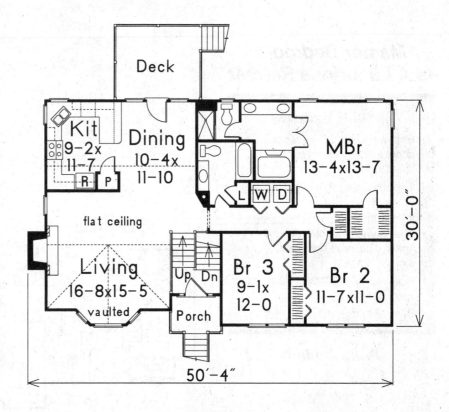

Deck

Kit
9-2x
11-7

Dining
10-4x
11-10

MBr
13-4x13-7

flat ceiling

L W D

Living
16-8x15-5

Up Dn

Br 3
9-1x
12-0

Br 2
11-7x11-0

vaulted

Porch

30'-0"

50'-4"

**TO ORDER BLUEPRINTS USE THE FORM ON PAGE 15 OR CALL TOLL-FREE 1-877-671-6036**
View thousands more home plans online at www.familyhandyman.com/homeplans

151

**2,587 total square feet of living area**

## Master Bedroom Is A Luxurious Retreat

### Special features

- High windows above French doors in the great room create a spectacular view
- The spacious kitchen serves the breakfast and dining rooms with ease
- The second floor offers plenty of space with three bedrooms and a storage area
- 4 bedrooms, 3 1/2 baths, 2-car side entry garage
- Basement foundation

### Price Code D

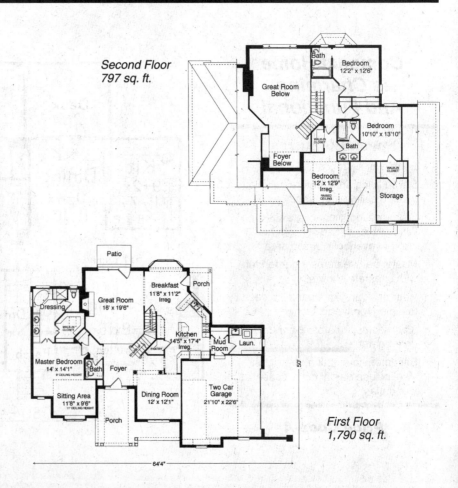

*Second Floor 797 sq. ft.*

*First Floor 1,790 sq. ft.*

**152**

**TO ORDER BLUEPRINTS USE THE FORM ON PAGE 15 OR CALL TOLL-FREE 1-877-671-6036**
View thousands more home plans online at www.familyhandyman.com/homeplans

© 2003, Garrell Associates, Inc.

**1,985 total square feet of living area**

## Ranch With Traditional Feel

### Special features

- 9' ceilings throughout home
- Master suite has direct access into the sunroom
- Sunny breakfast room features a bay window
- Bonus room on the second floor has an additional 191 square feet of living area
- 3 bedrooms, 3 baths, 2-car side entry garage
- Slab foundation

*Price Code G*

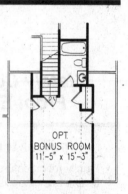

*Optional Second Floor*

OPT. BONUS ROOM 11'-5" x 15'-3"

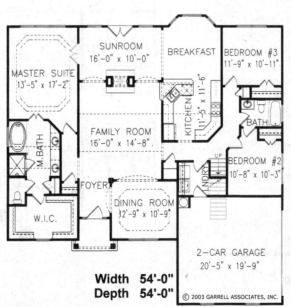

SUNROOM 16'-0" x 10'-0"
BREAKFAST
BEDROOM #3 11'-9" x 10'-11"
MASTER SUITE 13'-5" x 17'-2"
KITCHEN 11'-5" x 11'-6"
BATH
FAMILY ROOM 16'-0" x 14'-8"
M. BATH
BEDROOM #2 10'-8" x 10'-3"
FOYER
DINING ROOM 12'-9" x 10'-9"
W.I.C.
2-CAR GARAGE 20'-5" x 19'-9"

*First Floor 1,985 sq. ft.*

Width 54'-0"
Depth 54'-0"

© 2003 GARRELL ASSOCIATES, INC.

**2,089 total square feet of living area**

## Stately Covered Front Entry

### Special features

- Family room features a fireplace, built-in bookshelves and triple sliders opening to the covered patio
- Kitchen overlooks the family room and features a pantry and desk
- Separated from the three secondary bedrooms, the master bedroom becomes a quiet retreat with patio access
- Master bedroom features an oversized bath with walk-in closet and corner tub
- 4 bedrooms, 3 baths, 2-car garage
- Slab foundation

### *Price Code C*

Floor plan labels:

- Br 2 10-0x11-10
- Br 3 12-0x11-0
- Br 4 12-0x11-0
- Covered Patio
- MBr 16-10x13-0
- Nook 9-0x9-0
- Family 19-4x15-10
- Kit 10-0x11-8
- Living 11-10x12-8
- Foyer
- Dining 11-10x12-8
- Garage 20-0x20-0
- Entry
- plant shelf
- 45'-8"
- 61'-8"

**1,491 total square feet of living area**

## Southern Styling With Covered Porch

### Special features

- Two-story family room has a vaulted ceiling
- Well-organized kitchen has serving bar which overlooks the family and dining rooms
- First floor master suite has a tray ceiling, walk-in closet and private bath
- 3 bedrooms, 2 1/2 baths, 2-car drive under garage
- Walk-out basement foundation

**Price Code A**

*First Floor*
*1,061 sq. ft.*

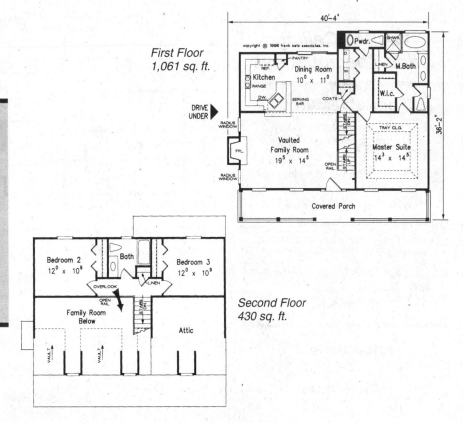

*Second Floor*
*430 sq. ft.*

**TO ORDER BLUEPRINTS USE THE FORM ON PAGE 15 OR CALL TOLL-FREE 1-877-671-6036**
View thousands more home plans online at www.familyhandyman.com/homeplans

155

**1,854 total square feet of living area**

## Vaulted Ceiling Adds Spaciousness

### Special features

- Front entrance is enhanced by arched transom windows and rustic stone
- Isolated master bedroom includes a dressing area and walk-in closet
- Family room features a high sloped ceiling and large fireplace
- Breakfast area accesses covered rear porch
- 3 bedrooms, 2 1/2 baths, 2-car side entry garage
- Basement foundation

**Price Code D**

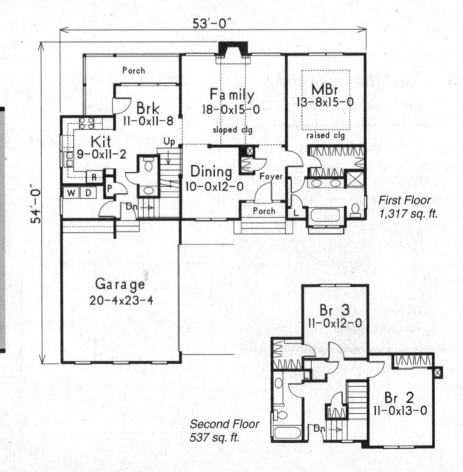

*First Floor 1,317 sq. ft.*

*Second Floor 537 sq. ft.*

**TO ORDER BLUEPRINTS USE THE FORM ON PAGE 15 OR CALL TOLL-FREE 1-877-671-6036**
View thousands more home plans online at www.familyhandyman.com/homeplans

156

**2,322 total square feet of living area**

## *Bounty Of Bay Windows*

### Special features

- Vaulted family room has a fireplace and access to the kitchen
- Decorative columns and arched openings surround dining area
- Master suite has a sitting room and grand-scale bath
- Kitchen includes an island with serving bar
- 3 bedrooms, 2 1/2 baths, 2-car side entry garage
- Walk-out basement, crawl space or slab foundation, please specify when ordering

### *Price Code D*

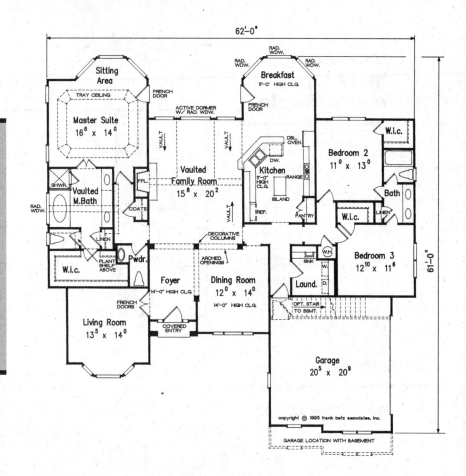

**TO ORDER BLUEPRINTS USE THE FORM ON PAGE 15 OR CALL TOLL-FREE 1-877-671-6036**
View thousands more home plans online at www.familyhandyman.com/homeplans

157

**1,546 total square feet of living area**

## Central Living Area Keeps Bedrooms Private

### Special features

- Spacious, open rooms create a casual atmosphere
- Master bedroom is secluded for privacy
- Dining room features a large bay window
- Kitchen and dinette combine for added space and include access to the outdoors
- Large laundry room includes a convenient sink
- 3 bedrooms, 2 baths, 2-car garage
- Basement foundation

**Price Code C**

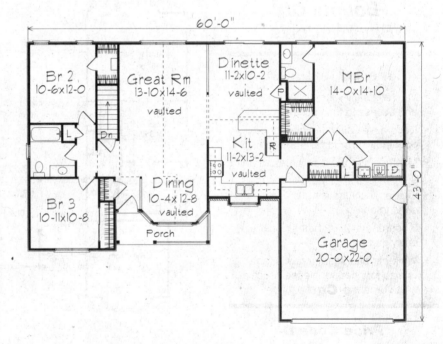

60'-0"

43'-0"

Br 2
10-6x12-0

Great Rm
13-10x14-6
vaulted

Dn

Dinette
11-2x10-2
vaulted

MBr
14-0x14-10

Kit
11-2x13-2
vaulted

Br 3
10-11x10-8

Dining
10-4x12-8
vaulted

Porch

Garage
20-0x22-0

**1,850 total square feet of living area**

## Convenient Wet Bar

### Special features

- Oversized rooms throughout
- Great room spotlights fireplace with sunny windows on both sides
- Master bedroom has a private skylighted bath
- Interesting wet bar between kitchen and dining area is an added bonus when entertaining
- 3 bedrooms, 2 baths, 2-car garage
- Basement foundation

*Price Code C*

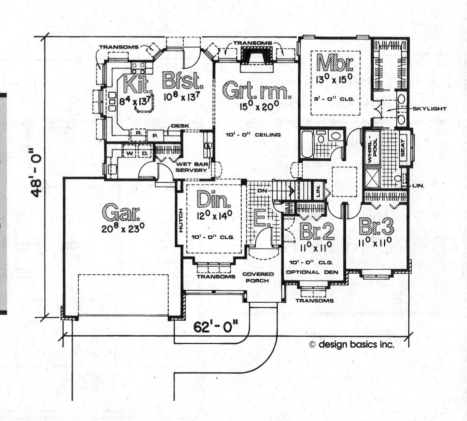

© design basics inc.

**TO ORDER BLUEPRINTS USE THE FORM ON PAGE 15 OR CALL TOLL-FREE 1-877-671-6036**
View thousands more home plans online at www.familyhandyman.com/homeplans

159

**1,993 total square feet of living area**

## Country Farmhouse Appeal

### Special features

- Charming front and rear porches
- 12' ceiling enhances the living room
- Exquisite master bath enjoys a large walk-in closet
- 3 bedrooms, 2 baths, 2-car side entry garage
- Crawl space foundation, drawings also include slab foundation

**Price Code C**

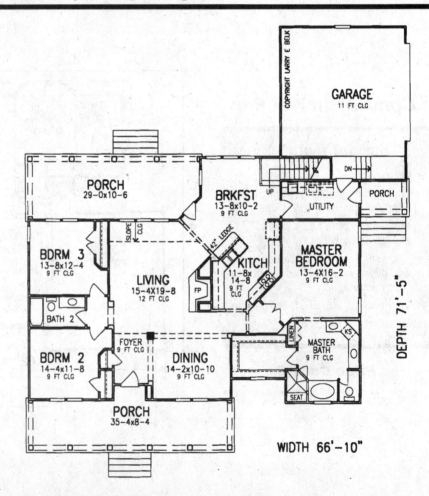

COPYRIGHT LARRY E. BELK

GARAGE
11 FT CLG

PORCH
29-0x10-6

BRKFST
13-8x10-2
9 FT CLG

UTILITY

UP  DN

PORCH

BDRM 3
13-8x12-4
9 FT CLG

SLOPE CLG

42" LEDGE

KITCH
11-8x
14-8
9 FT CLG

MASTER BEDROOM
13-4x16-2
9 FT CLG

LIVING
15-4x19-8
12 FT CLG

FP

BATH 2

LINEN

MASTER BATH
9 FT CLG

KS

FOYER
9 FT CLG

DINING
14-2x10-10
9 FT CLG

SEAT

BDRM 2
14-4x11-8
9 FT CLG

PORCH
35-4x8-4

DEPTH 71'-5"

WIDTH 66'-10"

**2,805 total square feet of living area**

## Luxurious Master Bedroom

### Special features

- Wrap-around counter in kitchen opens to bayed breakfast area
- Great room features a grand fireplace flanked by doors that access the rear covered porch
- Secondary bedrooms enjoy walk-in closets
- The extra-large utility room offers an abundance of workspace
- 4 bedrooms, 3 baths, 2-car side entry garage
- Basement, crawl space or slab foundation, please specify when ordering

*Price Code E*

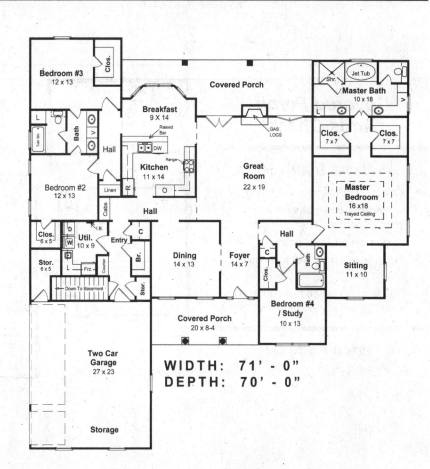

WIDTH: 71' - 0"
DEPTH: 70' - 0"

**TO ORDER BLUEPRINTS USE THE FORM ON PAGE 15 OR CALL TOLL-FREE 1-877-671-6036**
View thousands more home plans online at www.familyhandyman.com/homeplans

**161**

**2,069 total square feet of living area**

## Covered Porch Adds Charm

### Special features

- 9' ceilings throughout this home
- Kitchen has many amenities including a snack bar
- Large front and rear porches
- 3 bedrooms, 2 1/2 baths, 2-car garage
- Slab or crawl space foundation, please specify when ordering

### *Price Code C*

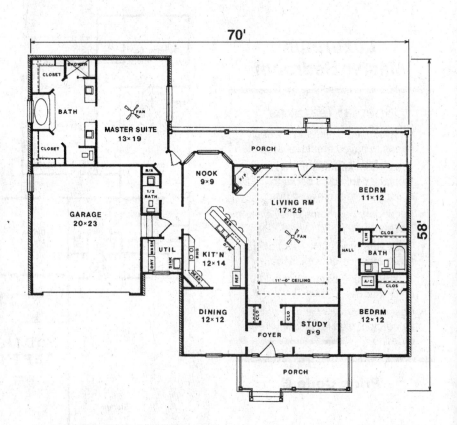

**TO ORDER BLUEPRINTS USE THE FORM ON PAGE 15 OR CALL TOLL-FREE 1-877-671-6036**

View thousands more home plans online at www.familyhandyman.com/homeplans

**2,217 total square feet of living area**

## Modest-Sized Home With Much To Offer

### Special features

- Great room features a fireplace and is open to the foyer, breakfast and dining rooms
- Laundry room and storage closet are located off the garage
- Secluded master suite includes a bath with a corner whirlpool tub, split vanities, corner shower and a large walk-in closet
- 4 bedrooms, 2 baths, 2-car garage
- Crawl space or slab foundation, please specify when ordering

### Price Code C

GLASS BLOCKS

61'-2"

M. BATH
15'-9" X 14'-4"

K.S.

BREAKFAST ROOM
11'-4" X 12'-4"

GRILLING PORCH
17'-6" X 8'-0"

BEDROOM 4
14'-10" X 12'-6"

MASTER SUITE
15'-8" X 14'-0"
10' BOXED CEILING

KITCHEN
11'-4" X 12'-6"

RG    DW

REF.

GREAT ROOM
17'-6" X 20'-8"
10' CEILING

BEDROOM 3
11'-0" X 10'-8"

55'-6"

10' CEILING

LIN.

STORAGE
12'-0" X 5'-6"

D.  LAU.
8'-5" X 5'-6"
W.

8" COLUMNS

FOYER
6'-4" X 7'-8"
10' CEILING

BEDROOM 2
11'-0" X 13'-6"

DN

OPTIONAL BASEMENT PLAN

DINING ROOM
11'-4" X 14'-10"
10' CEILING

ENTRY

BATH

© 1993 NELSON DESIGN GROUP, LLC.

GARAGE
20'-10" X 20'-0"

**TO ORDER BLUEPRINTS USE THE FORM ON PAGE 15 OR CALL TOLL-FREE 1-877-671-6036**
View thousands more home plans online at www.familyhandyman.com/homeplans

163

**1,455 total square feet of living area**

## Decorative Accents Featured On Front Porch

### Special features

- Spacious mud room has a large pantry, space for a freezer, sink/counter area and bath with shower
- Bedroom #2 can easily be converted to a study or office area
- Optional second floor bedroom and playroom have an additional 744 square feet of living area
- 2 bedrooms, 2 baths
- Slab or crawl space foundation, please specify when ordering

**Price Code A**

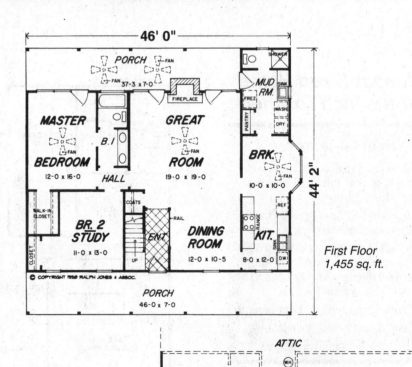

First Floor
1,455 sq. ft.

Optional Second Floor

**1,784 total square feet of living area**

## Outdoor Living Area Created By Wrap-Around Porch

### Special features

- Spacious living area with corner fireplace offers a cheerful atmosphere with large windows
- Large second floor gathering room is great for kid's play area
- Secluded master bedroom has separate porch entrances and a large master bath with walk-in closet
- 3 bedrooms, 2 1/2 baths, 1-car garage
- Basement foundation, drawings also include crawl space foundation

**Price Code B**

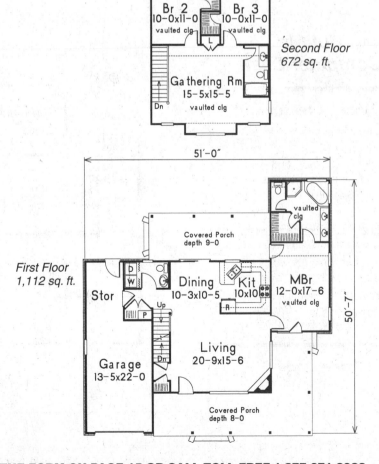

Second Floor 672 sq. ft.

First Floor 1,112 sq. ft.

**TO ORDER BLUEPRINTS USE THE FORM ON PAGE 15 OR CALL TOLL-FREE 1-877-671-6036**
View thousands more home plans online at www.familyhandyman.com/homeplans

165

**1,525 total square feet of living area**

## Built-In Computer Desk

### Special features

- Corner fireplace is highlighted in the great room
- Unique glass block window over the whirlpool tub in the master bath brightens the interior
- Open bar overlooks both the kitchen and great room
- Breakfast room leads to an outdoor grilling and covered porch
- 3 bedrooms, 2 baths, 2-car garage
- Basement, walk-out basement, crawl space or slab foundation, please specify when ordering

**Price Code B**

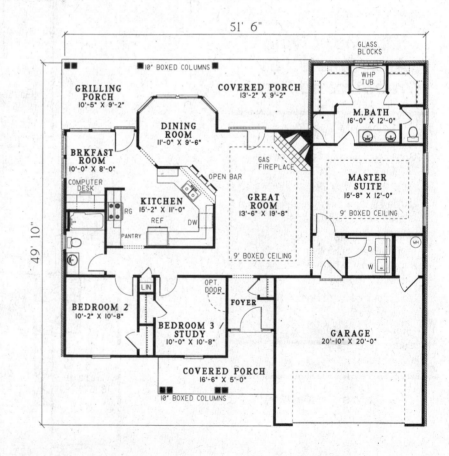

**TO ORDER BLUEPRINTS USE THE FORM ON PAGE 15 OR CALL TOLL-FREE 1-877-671-6036**
View thousands more home plans online at www.familyhandyman.com/homeplans

**1,819 total square feet of living area**

## Secluded Master Bedroom

### Special features

- Master bedroom features access to the outdoors, large walk-in closet and private bath
- 9' ceilings throughout
- Formal foyer with coat closet opens into the vaulted great room with fireplace and formal dining room
- Kitchen and breakfast room create a cozy and casual area
- 3 bedrooms, 2 baths, 2-car side entry garage
- Basement foundation

*Price Code C*

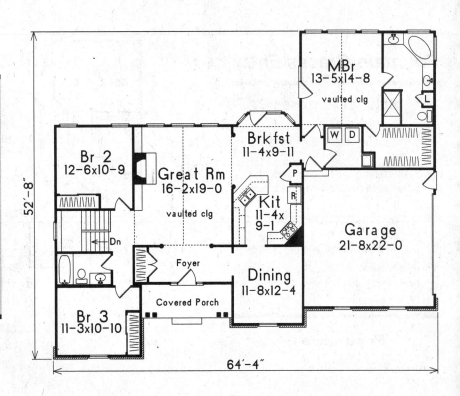

MBr
13-5x14-8
vaulted clg

Br 2
12-6x10-9

Great Rm
16-2x19-0
vaulted clg

Brkfst
11-4x9-11

Kit
11-4x
9-1

W D

P

R

Garage
21-8x22-0

Dn

Foyer

Dining
11-8x12-4

Br 3
11-3x10-10

Covered Porch

52'-8"

64'-4"

**TO ORDER BLUEPRINTS USE THE FORM ON PAGE 15 OR CALL TOLL-FREE 1-877-671-6036**
View thousands more home plans online at www.familyhandyman.com/HOMEPLANS

167

J.K. HANSEN

**2,397 total square feet of living area**

## Fountain Graces Entry

### Special features

- Covered entrance with fountain leads to the double-door entry and foyer
- Kitchen features two pantries and opens into the breakfast and family rooms
- Master bath features a huge walk-in closet, electric clothes carousel, double-bowl vanity and corner tub
- 3 bedrooms, 2 1/2 baths, 2-car garage
- Slab foundation

*Price Code E*

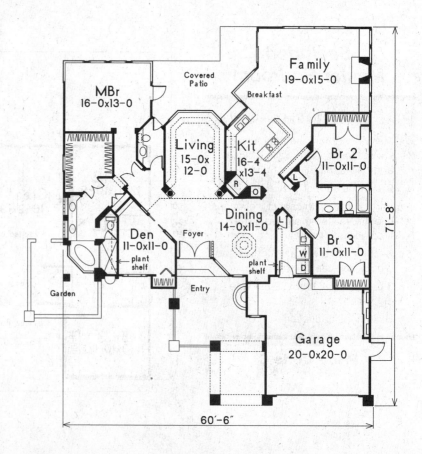

**3,470 total square feet of living area**

## Grand Features Enhance Home

### Special features

- Two-story entry showcases grand staircase
- The family room features a fireplace flanked by built-in cabinets and a two-story ceiling
- The bayed nook enjoys a double-door entry to the sun room and access onto the courtyard
- The spacious master bedroom boasts a bayed sitting area, walk-in closet and deluxe bath with whirlpool tub
- 4 bedrooms, 3 full baths, 2 half baths, 4-car side entry garage
- Basement foundation

*Price Code G*

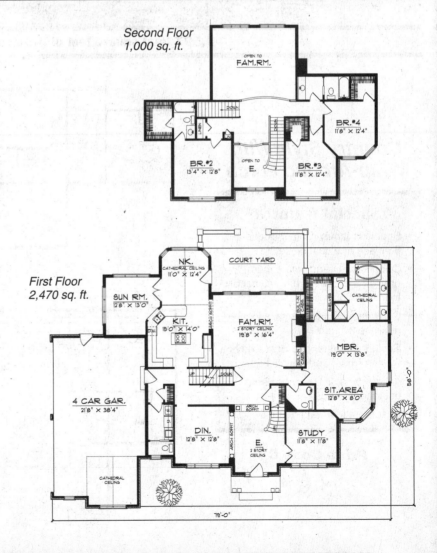

Second Floor
1,000 sq. ft.

First Floor
2,470 sq. ft.

**TO ORDER BLUEPRINTS USE THE FORM ON PAGE 15 OR CALL TOLL-FREE 1-877-671-6036**
View thousands more home plans online at www.familyhandyman.com/homeplans

169

**1,597 total square feet of living area**

## Country Style With Wrap-Around Porch

### Special features

- Spacious family room includes a fireplace and coat closet
- Open kitchen and dining room provide a breakfast bar and access to the outdoors
- Convenient laundry area is located near the kitchen
- Secluded master bedroom enjoys a walk-in closet and private bath
- 4 bedrooms, 2 1/2 baths, 2-car detached garage
- Basement foundation

*Price Code C*

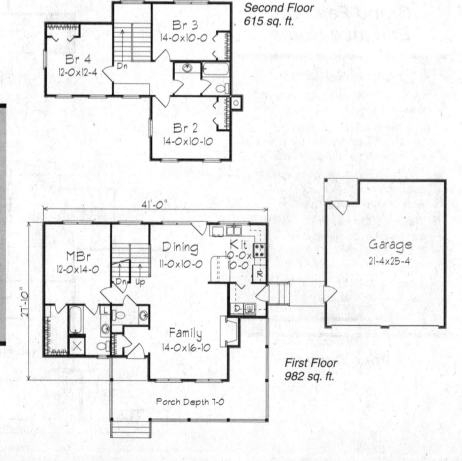

Second Floor
615 sq. ft.

Br 4
12-0x12-4

Br 3
14-0x10-0

Br 2
14-0x10-10

41'-0"

MBr
12-0x14-0

Dining
11-0x10-0

Kit
10-0x10-0

Garage
21-4x25-4

Family
14-0x16-10

27'-10"

Porch Depth 7-0

First Floor
982 sq. ft.

**1,673 total square feet of living area**

## Casual Country Home With Unique Loft

### Special features

- Great room flows into the breakfast nook with outdoor access and beyond to an efficient kitchen
- Master bedroom on the second floor has access to loft/study, private balcony and bath
- Covered porch surrounds the entire home for outdoor living area
- 3 bedrooms, 2 baths
- Crawl space foundation

**Price Code B**

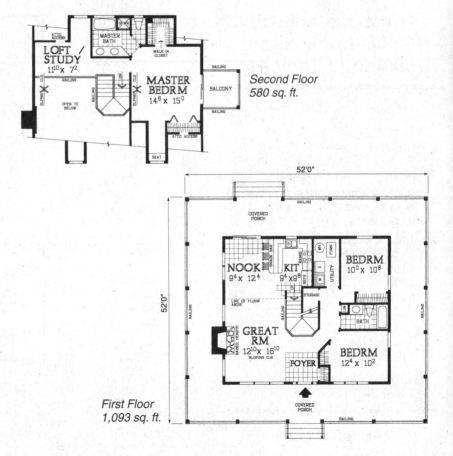

*Second Floor*
*580 sq. ft.*

*First Floor*
*1,093 sq. ft.*

**TO ORDER BLUEPRINTS USE THE FORM ON PAGE 15 OR CALL TOLL-FREE 1-877-671-6036**
View thousands more home plans online at www.familyhandyman.com/homeplans

171

**5,321 total square feet of living area**

## Timeless Appeal, This Home Has Luxurious Comforts

### Special features

- The combination of stone, brick, multiple gables and roof dormers creates an exciting and sophisticated structure
- A two-story foyer and wide, finely crafted staircase with niche is inviting and elegant
- The kitchen includes a bayed breakfast room, hearth room with fireplace and is convenient to a large dining room with butler's pantry
- The master bedroom with sitting room and sumptuous bath is unsurpassed in luxury
- 5 bedrooms, 5 1/2 baths, 3-car rear entry garage
- Basement foundation

**Second Floor 1,784 sq. ft.**

**First Floor 3,537 sq. ft.**

*Price Code H*

**2,059 total square feet of living area**

## Country Charm
## Wrapped In A Veranda

### Special features

- Octagon-shaped breakfast room offers plenty of windows and creates a view to the veranda

- First floor master bedroom has a large walk-in closet and deluxe bath

- 9' ceilings throughout the home

- Secondary bedrooms and bath feature dormers and are adjacent to the cozy sitting area

- 3 bedrooms, 2 1/2 baths, 2-car detached garage

- Slab foundation, drawings also include basement and crawl space foundations

*Price Code C*

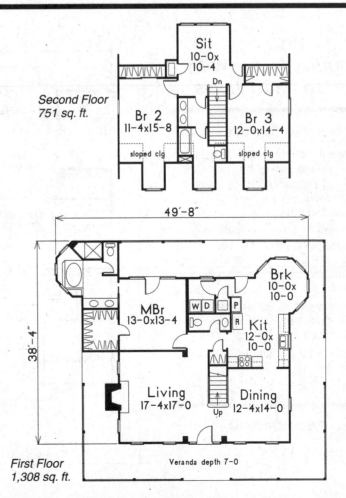

Second Floor
751 sq. ft.

Sit
10-0x
10-4

Br 2
11-4x15-8

Dn

Br 3
12-0x14-4

sloped clg          sloped clg

49'-8"

38'-4"

Brk
10-0x
10-0

MBr
13-0x13-4

W D   P
R

Kit
12-0x
10-0

Living
17-4x17-0

Up

Dining
12-4x14-0

First Floor
1,308 sq. ft.

Veranda depth 7-0

**TO ORDER BLUEPRINTS USE THE FORM ON PAGE 15 OR CALL TOLL-FREE 1-877-671-6036**
View thousands more home plans online at www.familyhandyman.com/homeplans

173

# Plan #717-007D-0113

## 2,547 total square feet of living area

## Country Home With Grand Patio Views

### Special features

- Grand-sized great room features a 12' volume ceiling, fireplace with built-in wrap-around shelving and patio doors with sidelights and transom windows
- The walk-in pantry, computer desk, large breakfast island for seven and bayed breakfast area are the many features of this outstanding kitchen
- The master bedroom suite enjoys a luxurious bath, large walk-in closets and patio access
- 4 bedrooms, 2 1/2 baths, 3-car side entry garage
- Basement foundation

**Price Code D**

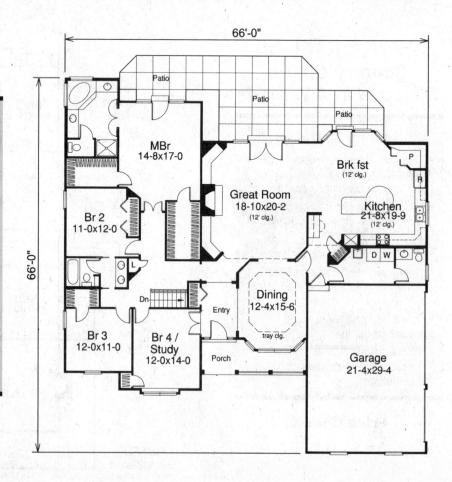

**2,558 total square feet of living area**

## Full Windows Grace Elegant Family Room

### Special features

- 9' ceilings throughout the home
- Angled counter in the kitchen serves breakfast and family rooms
- The entry foyer is flanked by formal living and dining rooms
- Garage includes storage space
- 4 bedrooms, 3 baths, 2-car side entry garage
- Slab foundation, drawings also include crawl space foundation

*Price Code D*

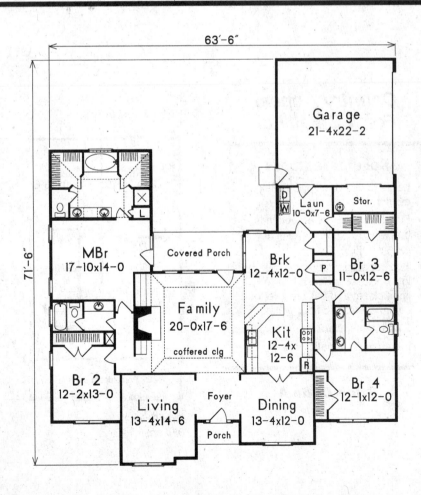

**TO ORDER BLUEPRINTS USE THE FORM ON PAGE 15 OR CALL TOLL-FREE 1-877-671-6036**
View thousands more home plans online at www.familyhandyman.com/HOMEPLANS

**175**

**1,299 total square feet of living area**

## Country Appeal For A Small Lot

### Special features

- Large porch for enjoying relaxing evenings
- First floor master bedroom has a bay window, walk-in closet and roomy bath
- Two generous bedrooms with lots of closet space, a hall bath, linen closet and balcony overlook comprise second floor
- 3 bedrooms, 2 1/2 baths
- Basement foundation

**Price Code A**

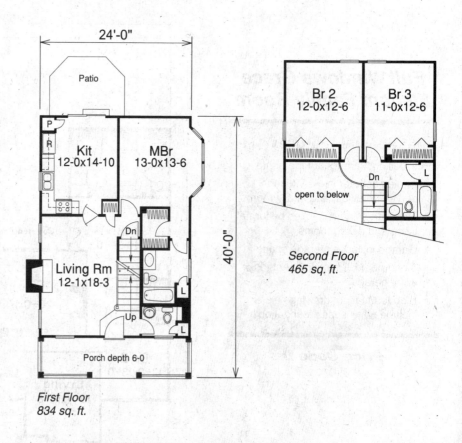

24'-0"

Patio

Kit
12-0x14-10

MBr
13-0x13-6

Living Rm
12-1x18-3

40'-0"

Dn

Up

Porch depth 6-0

*First Floor*
*834 sq. ft.*

Br 2
12-0x12-6

Br 3
11-0x12-6

Dn

open to below

*Second Floor*
*465 sq. ft.*

**3,369 total square feet of living area**

## Grand Covered Entry

### Special features

- Large playroom overlooks to great room below and makes a great casual family area
- Extra storage is located in garage
- Well-planned hearth room and kitchen are open and airy
- Foyer flows into unique diagonal gallery area creating a dramatic entrance into the great room
- 3 bedrooms, 2 1/2 baths, 2-car side entry garage
- Slab foundation

**Price Code F**

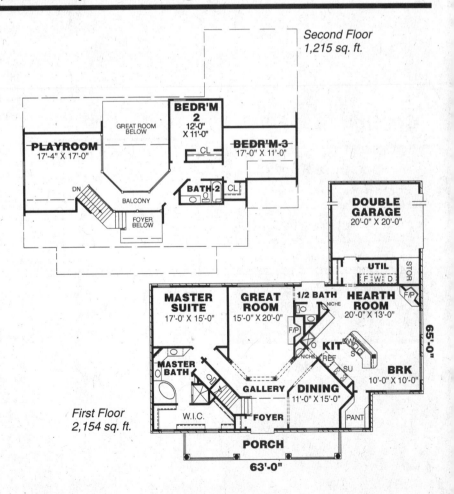

Second Floor 1,215 sq. ft.

PLAYROOM 17'-4" X 17'-0"

GREAT ROOM BELOW

BEDR'M 2 12'-0" X 11'-0"

BEDR'M-3 17'-0" X 11'-0"

CL

DN

BALCONY

FOYER BELOW

BATH-2

CL

DOUBLE GARAGE 20'-0" X 20'-0"

UTIL
F W D

STOR

MASTER SUITE 17'-0" X 15'-0"

GREAT ROOM 15'-0" X 20'-0"

1/2 BATH
NICHE

HEARTH ROOM 20'-0" X 13'-0"

F/P

MASTER BATH

KIT

BRK 10'-0" X 10'-0"

NICHE REF

W.I.C.

GALLERY

DINING 11'-0" X 15'-0"

FOYER

PANT

First Floor 2,154 sq. ft.

PORCH

63'-0"

65'-0"

**TO ORDER BLUEPRINTS USE THE FORM ON PAGE 15 OR CALL TOLL-FREE 1-877-671-6036**
View thousands more home plans online at www.familyhandyman.com/homeplans

177

**1,253 total square feet of living area**

## Covered Rear Porch

### Special features

- Sloped ceiling and fireplace in family room add drama
- U-shaped kitchen is efficiently designed
- Large walk-in closets are found in all the bedrooms
- 3 bedrooms, 2 baths, 2-car garage
- Crawl space or slab foundation, please specify when ordering

*Price Code A*

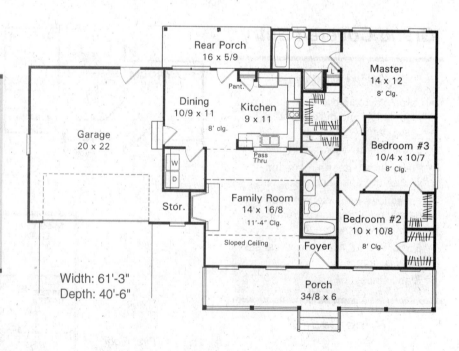

Rear Porch 16 x 5/9

Master 14 x 12 8' Clg.

Pant.

Dining 10/9 x 11 8' clg.

Kitchen 9 x 11

Garage 20 x 22

Bedroom #3 10/4 x 10/7 8' Clg.

Pass Thru

W D

Stor.

Family Room 14 x 16/8 11'-4" Clg.

Bedroom #2 10 x 10/8 8' Clg.

Sloped Ceiling

Foyer

Width: 61'-3"
Depth: 40'-6"

Porch 34/8 x 6

**The Family Handyman**

**1,977 total square feet of living area**

## Classic Atrium Ranch With Rooms To Spare

### Special features

- Classic traditional exterior is always in style
- Spacious great room boasts a vaulted ceiling, dining area, atrium with elegant staircase and feature windows
- Atrium opens to 1,416 square feet of optional living area below which consists of a family room, two bedrooms, two baths and a study
- 4 bedrooms, 2 1/2 baths, 3-car side entry garage
- Walk-out basement foundation

**Price Code C**

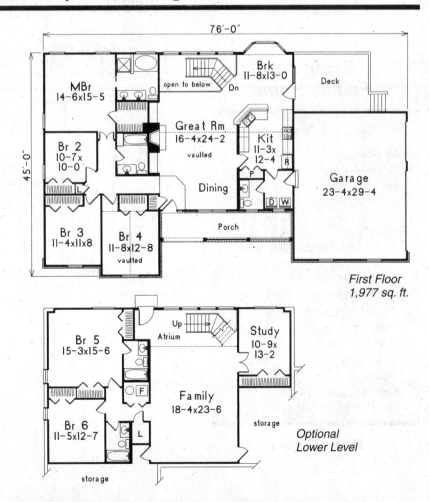

First Floor
1,977 sq. ft.

Optional
Lower Level

**TO ORDER BLUEPRINTS USE THE FORM ON PAGE 15 OR CALL TOLL-FREE 1-877-671-6036**
View thousands more home plans online at www.familyhandyman.com/HOMEPLANS

179

**3,870 total square feet of living area**

## Exquisite Family Home

### Special features

- 10' ceiling on the first floor
- The formal living and dining rooms are convenient to the kitchen and provide plenty of room for entertaining
- The master bedroom is a wonderful retreat with a double-door entry, immense bath and private access to the study
- All bedrooms enjoy walk-in closets
- Future playroom on the second floor has an additional 421 square feet of living area
- 4 bedrooms, 3 1/2 baths, 3-car garage
- Slab or basement foundation, please specify when ordering

**Price Code F**

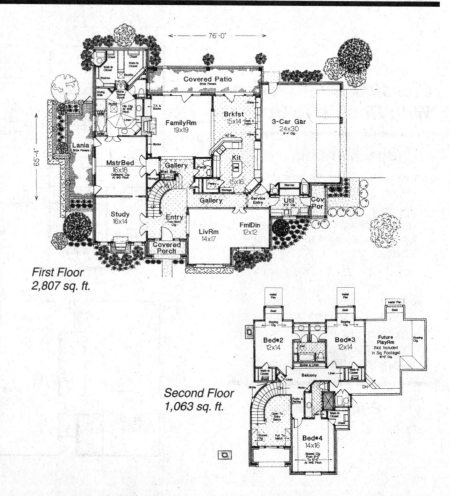

*First Floor*
*2,807 sq. ft.*

*Second Floor*
*1,063 sq. ft.*

**2,408 total square feet of living area**

## Floridian Architecture With Mother-In-Law Suite

### Special features

- Large vaulted great room overlooks atrium and window wall, adjoins dining room, spacious breakfast room with bay and pass-through kitchen

- A special private bedroom with bath, separate from other bedrooms, is perfect for mother-in-law suite or children home from college

- Atrium opens to 1,100 square feet of optional living area below

- 4 bedrooms, 3 baths, 3-car side entry garage

- Walk-out basement foundation

### *Price Code D*

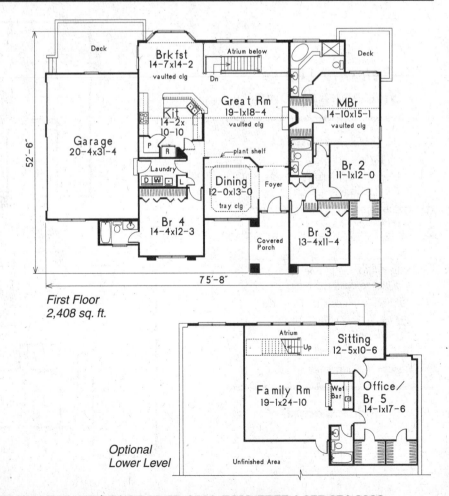

*First Floor*
*2,408 sq. ft.*

*Optional Lower Level*

**TO ORDER BLUEPRINTS USE THE FORM ON PAGE 15 OR CALL TOLL-FREE 1-877-671-6036**
View thousands more home plans online at www.familyhandyman.com/homeplans

181

**2,444 total square feet of living area**

## Balcony Offers Sweeping Views

### Special features

- Laundry room with workspace, pantry and coat closet is adjacent to the kitchen
- Two bedrooms, a study, full bath and plenty of closets are on the second floor
- Large walk-in closet and private bath make this master bedroom one you're sure to enjoy
- Kitchen with cooktop island and easy access to living area
- 3 bedrooms, 2 1/2 baths, 2-car side entry garage
- Basement foundation

**Price Code D**

Study
12-0x12-3

open to below

Dn

Br 2
10-10x14-1

open to below

Br 3
10-11x14-1

*Second Floor*
*772 sq. ft.*

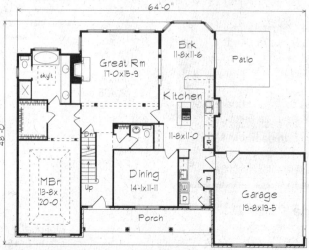

64'-0"

48'-0"

skylt

Great Rm
17-0x15-9

Brk
11-8x11-6

Patio

Kitchen
11-8x11-0

Dn

MBr
13-8x 20-0

up

Dining
14-1x11-11

Porch

Garage
19-8x19-5

*First Floor*
*1,672 sq. ft.*

**2,808 total square feet of living area**

## Sophisticated Ranch With Split Bedrooms

### Special features

- An impressive front exterior showcases three porches for quiet times
- Large living and dining rooms flank an elegant entry
- Bedroom #3 shares a porch with the living room and a spacious bath with bedroom #2
- Vaulted master bedroom enjoys a secluded screened porch and sumptuous bath with corner tub, double vanities and huge walk-in closet
- Living room can easily convert to an optional fourth bedroom
- 3 bedrooms, 2 1/2 baths, 3-car side entry garage
- Basement foundation

*Price Code F*

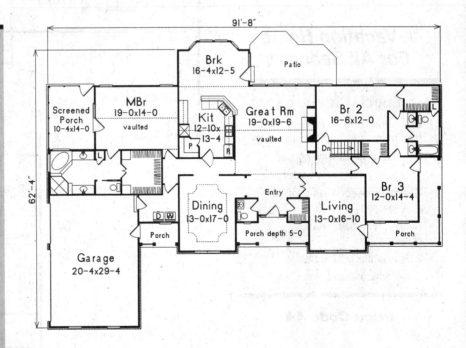

**TO ORDER BLUEPRINTS USE THE FORM ON PAGE 15 OR CALL TOLL-FREE 1-877-671-6036**
View thousands more home plans online at www.familyhandyman.com/homeplans

183

**1,039 total square feet of living area**

## A Vacation Home For All Seasons

### Special features

- Cathedral construction provides the maximum in living area openness
- Expansive glass viewing walls
- Two decks, front and back
- Charming second story loft arrangement
- Simple, low-maintenance construction
- 2 bedrooms, 1 1/2 baths
- Crawl space foundation

**Price Code AA**

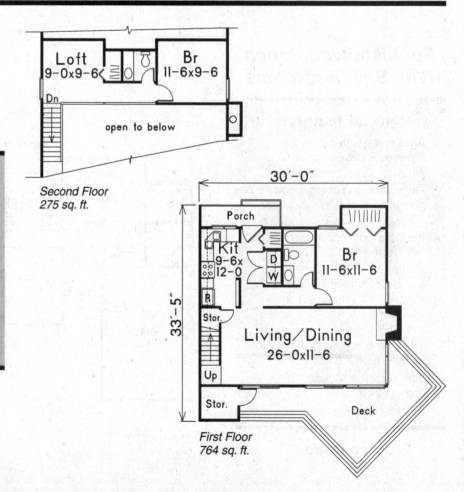

*Second Floor*
*275 sq. ft.*

*First Floor*
*764 sq. ft.*

**2,838 total square feet of living area**

## Step Into An Elegant Foyer

### Special features

- Elegant foyer is enormous and spotlights a grand staircase to the second floor
- A cozy study is tucked away for privacy
- Sunny kitchen and breakfast area have cathedral ceilings
- 4 bedrooms, 3 baths, 2-car garage
- Basement foundation, drawings also include crawl space and slab foundations

*Price Code E*

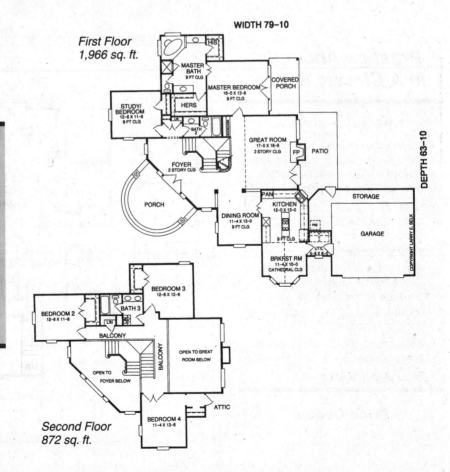

WIDTH 79-10

*First Floor*
*1,966 sq. ft.*

HIS

MASTER BATH
9 FT CLG

MASTER BEDROOM
16-0 X 13-6
9 FT CLG

COVERED PORCH

STUDY/ BEDROOM
12-6 X 11-6
9 FT CLG

HERS

BATH 2

GREAT ROOM
17-0 X 18-6
2 STORY CLG

FP

PATIO

FOYER
2 STORY CLG

PORCH

PAN

KITCHEN
12-0 X 13-0

STORAGE

DINING ROOM
11-4 X 13-0
9 FT CLG

UTIL

GARAGE

BRKFST RM
11-4 X 10-0
CATHEDRAL CLG

DEPTH 63-10

COPYRIGHT LARRY E. BELK

BEDROOM 2
12-6 X 11-6

BEDROOM 3
12-6 X 12-6

BATH 3

LIN

BALCONY

BALCONY

OPEN TO GREAT ROOM BELOW

OPEN TO FOYER BELOW

ATTIC

BEDROOM 4
11-4 X 13-6

*Second Floor*
*872 sq. ft.*

**TO ORDER BLUEPRINTS USE THE FORM ON PAGE 15 OR CALL TOLL-FREE 1-877-671-6036**
View thousands more home plans online at www.familyhandyman.com/homeplans

185

**2,723 total square feet of living area**

## Prestige Abounds In A Classic Ranch

### Special features

- Large porch invites you into an elegant foyer which accesses a vaulted bedroom #4/study with private hall and coat closet
- Great room is second to none, comprised of a fireplace, built-in shelves, vaulted ceiling and a 1 1/2 story window wall
- A spectacular hearth room with vaulted ceiling and masonry fireplace opens to an elaborate kitchen featuring two snack bars, a cooking island and walk-in pantry
- 4 bedrooms, 2 1/2 baths, 3-car side entry garage
- Basement foundation

*Price Code E*

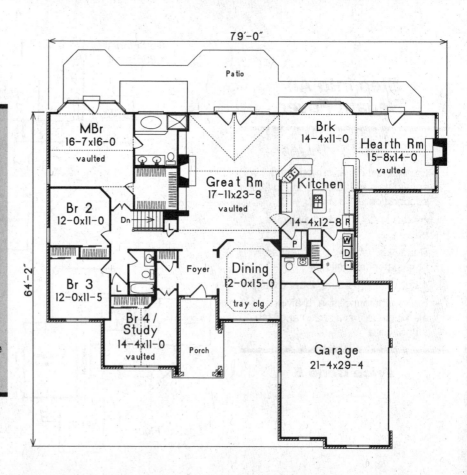

79'-0"

64'-2"

Patio

MBr
16-7x16-0
vaulted

Brk
14-4x11-0

Hearth Rm
15-8x14-0
vaulted

Br 2
12-0x11-0

Great Rm
17-11x23-8
vaulted

Kitchen
14-4x12-8

Br 3
12-0x11-5

Foyer

Dining
12-0x15-0
tray clg

Br 4/
Study
14-4x11-0
vaulted

Porch

Garage
21-4x29-4

**2,874 total square feet of living area**

## Spacious Country Charmer

### Special features

- Openness characterizes the casual areas
- The kitchen is separated from the bayed breakfast nook by an island workspace
- Stunning great room has dramatic vaulted ceiling and a corner fireplace
- Unfinished loft on the second floor has an additional 300 square feet of living area
- 4 bedrooms, 3 baths, 3-car side entry garage
- Basement, crawl space or slab foundation, please specify when ordering

### Price Code G

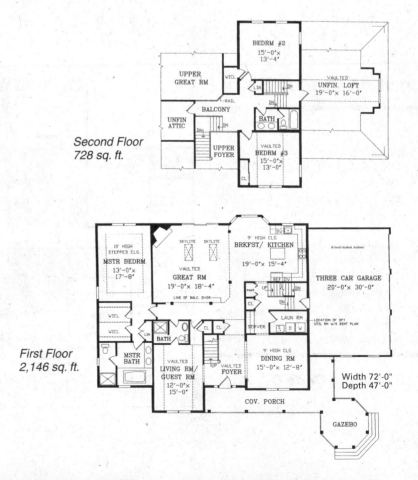

*Second Floor*
*728 sq. ft.*

*First Floor*
*2,146 sq. ft.*

Width 72'-0"
Depth 47'-0"

**TO ORDER BLUEPRINTS USE THE FORM ON PAGE 15 OR CALL TOLL-FREE 1-877-671-6036**
View thousands more home plans online at www.familyhandyman.com/homeplans

187

**2,097 total square feet of living area**

## Inviting Vaulted Entry

### Special features

- Angled kitchen, family room and eating area adds interest to this home
- Family room includes a TV niche making this a cozy place to relax
- Sumptuous master bedroom includes a sitting area, double walk-in closet and a full bath with double vanities
- 3 bedrooms, 3 baths, 3-car side entry garage
- Crawl space or slab foundation, please specify when ordering

*Price Code C*

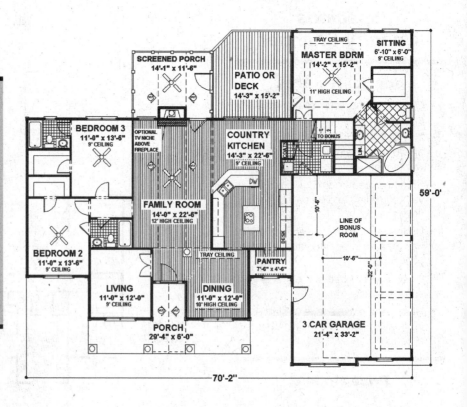

**1,092 total square feet of living area**

## Innovative Ranch Has A Cozy Corner Patio

### Special features

- Box window and inviting porch with dormers create a charming facade
- Eat-in kitchen offers a pass-through breakfast bar, corner window wall to patio, pantry and convenient laundry with half bath
- Master bedroom features a double-door entry and walk-in closet
- 3 bedrooms, 1 1/2 baths, 1-car garage
- Basement foundation

*Price Code AA*

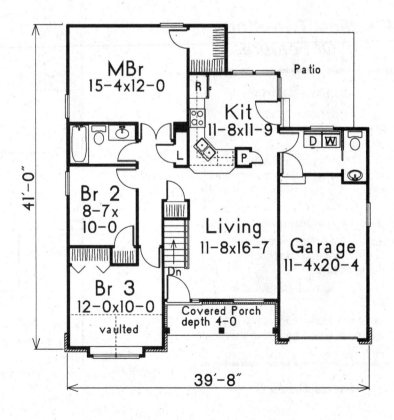

**TO ORDER BLUEPRINTS USE THE FORM ON PAGE 15 OR CALL TOLL-FREE 1-877-671-6036**
View thousands more home plans online at www.familyhandyman.com/homeplans

**189**

# Plan #717-003D-0001

**2,058 total square feet of living area**

## Practical Two-Story, Full Of Features

### Special features

- Handsome two-story foyer with balcony creates a spacious entrance area
- Vaulted ceiling in the master bedroom with private dressing area and large walk-in closet
- Skylights furnish natural lighting in the hall and master bath
- Laundry closet is conveniently located on the second floor near the bedrooms
- 3 bedrooms, 2 1/2 baths, 2-car garage
- Basement foundation, drawings also include slab and crawl space foundations

**Price Code C**

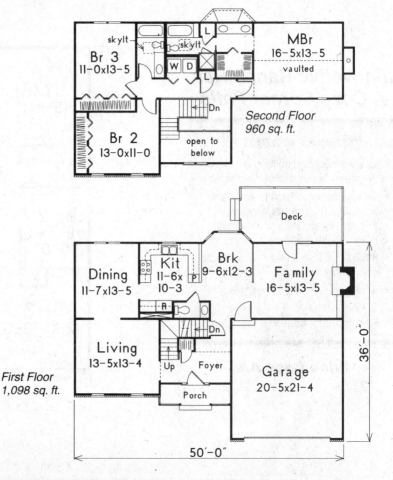

Br 3
11-0x13-5

skylt          skylt

W D

MBr
16-5x13-5
vaulted

Dn

Br 2
13-0x11-0

open to below

*Second Floor
960 sq. ft.*

Deck

Dining
11-7x13-5

Kit
11-6x
10-3

Brk
9-6x12-3

Family
16-5x13-5

Living
13-5x13-4

Dn

Up      Foyer

Garage
20-5x21-4

Porch

36'-0"

50'-0"

*First Floor
1,098 sq. ft.*

**1,721 total square feet of living area**

*Rear View*

## Atrium's Dramatic Ambiance

### Special features

- Roof dormers add great curb appeal
- Vaulted dining and great rooms are immersed in light from the atrium window wall
- Breakfast room opens onto the covered porch
- Functionally designed kitchen
- 3 bedrooms, 2 baths, 3-car garage
- Walk-out basement foundation, drawings also include crawl space and slab foundations
- 1,604 square feet on the first floor and 117 square feet on the lower level

**Price Code C**

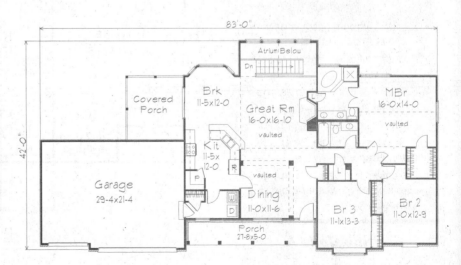

**TO ORDER BLUEPRINTS USE THE FORM ON PAGE 15 OR CALL TOLL-FREE 1-877-671-6036**
View thousands more home plans online at www.familyhandyman.com/homeplans

191

# Plan #717-001D-0024

**1,360 total square feet of living area**

## Functional Layout For Comfortable Living

### Special features

- Kitchen/dining room features island workspace and plenty of dining area
- Master bedroom has a large walk-in closet and private bath
- Laundry room is adjacent to the kitchen for easy access
- Convenient workshop in garage
- Large closets in secondary bedrooms maintain organization
- 3 bedrooms, 2 baths, 2-car side entry garage
- Basement foundation, drawings also include crawl space and slab foundations

**Price Code A**

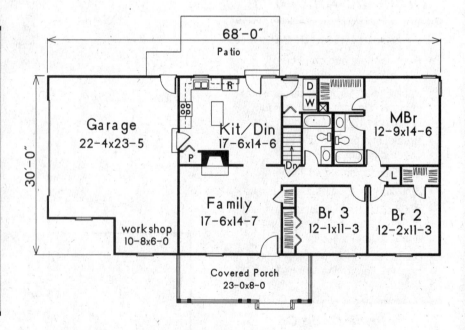

# Plan #717-007D-0006

**2,624 total square feet of living area**

## Irresistible Grandeur

### Special features

- Dramatic two-story entry opens to a bayed dining room through a classic colonnade
- Magnificent great room with 18' ceiling is brightly lit with three palladian windows
- Master bedroom includes a bay window, walk-in closets, plant shelves and sunken bath
- 4 bedrooms, 2 1/2 baths, 2-car side entry garage
- Basement foundation

### *Price Code E*

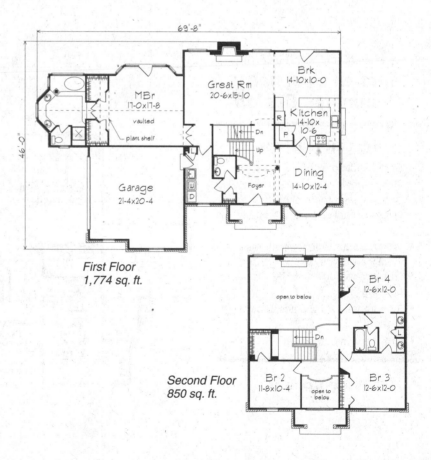

*First Floor*
*1,774 sq. ft.*

*Second Floor*
*850 sq. ft.*

**TO ORDER BLUEPRINTS USE THE FORM ON PAGE 15 OR CALL TOLL-FREE 1-877-671-6036**
View thousands more home plans online at www.familyhandyman.com/homeplans

193

**1,712 total square feet of living area**

## *Great Room And Kitchen Symmetry Dominates Design*

### Special features

- Stylish stucco exterior enhances curb appeal
- Sunken great room offers corner fireplace flanked by 9' wide patio doors
- Well-designed kitchen features ideal view of the great room and fireplace through breakfast bar opening
- 3 bedrooms, 2 1/2 baths, 2-car garage
- Crawl space foundation

*Price Code B*

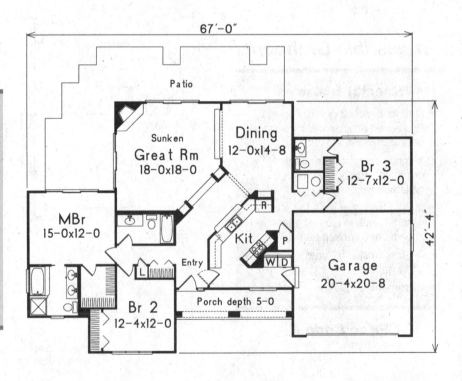

67'-0"

42'-4"

Patio

Sunken
**Great Rm**
18-0x18-0

**Dining**
12-0x14-8

**Br 3**
12-7x12-0

R

**MBr**
15-0x12-0

**Kit**

P

Entry

W D

**Garage**
20-4x20-8

L

**Br 2**
12-4x12-0

Porch depth 5-0

**2,505 total square feet of living area**

## Charming House, Spacious And Functional

### Special features

- The garage features extra storage area and ample workspace
- Laundry room is accessible from the garage and the outdoors
- Deluxe raised tub and immense walk-in closet grace master bath
- 3 bedrooms, 2 1/2 baths, 2-car side entry garage
- Basement foundation, drawings also include crawl space foundation

*Price Code D*

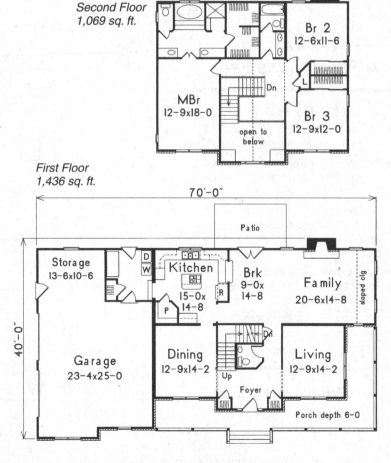

*Second Floor 1,069 sq. ft.*

Br 2 12-6x11-6
MBr 12-9x18-0
Br 3 12-9x12-0
Dn
open to below

*First Floor 1,436 sq. ft.*

70'-0"
40'-0"
Patio
Storage 13-6x10-6
Kitchen 15-0x 14-8
Brk 9-0x 14-8
Family 20-6x14-8
sloped clg
Garage 23-4x25-0
Dining 12-9x14-2
Living 12-9x14-2
Foyer
Up Dn
Porch depth 6-0

**TO ORDER BLUEPRINTS USE THE FORM ON PAGE 15 OR CALL TOLL-FREE 1-877-671-6036**
View thousands more home plans online at www.familyhandyman.com/homeplans

195

**3,444 total square feet of living area**

## Two-Story Has A Farmhouse Feel

### Special features

- Lavish master bath has double vanities and walk-in closets
- Kitchen has a wonderful food preparation island that doubles as extra dining space
- Computer/library area on the second floor has double-door access onto the second floor balcony
- Future gameroom on the second floor has an additional 318 square feet of living area
- 5 bedrooms, 4 baths, 2-car detached garage
- Crawl space foundation

**Price Code G**

First Floor
2,236 sq. ft.

Width: 42'-6"
Depth: 71'-4"

Porch

Master Bath

Family 17'8" x 21'2"

Master Bedroom 14'4" x 16'10"

Kitchen

Breakfast

Hall

Utility

Bath

Dining 14'2" x 12'3"

Porch

Study 14'4" x 14'6"

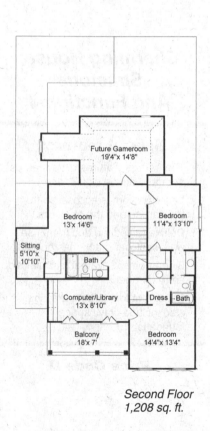

Future Gameroom 19'4" x 14'8"

Bedroom 13'x 14'6"

Bedroom 11'4" x 13'10"

Sitting 5'10"x 10'10"

Bath

Computer/Library 13'x 8'10"

Dress Bath

Balcony 18'x 7'

Bedroom 14'4" x 13'4"

Second Floor
1,208 sq. ft.

**196**

**TO ORDER BLUEPRINTS USE THE FORM ON PAGE 15 OR CALL TOLL-FREE 1-877-671-6036**
View thousands more home plans online at www.familyhandyman.com/homeplans

**2,449 total square feet of living area**

## Wrap-Around Country-Style Home

### Special features

- Striking living area features fireplace flanked with windows, cathedral ceiling and balcony
- First floor master bedroom has twin walk-in closets and large linen storage
- Dormers add space for desks or seats
- 3 bedrooms, 2 1/2 baths, 2-car detached garage
- Slab foundation, drawings also include crawl space foundation

**Price Code E**

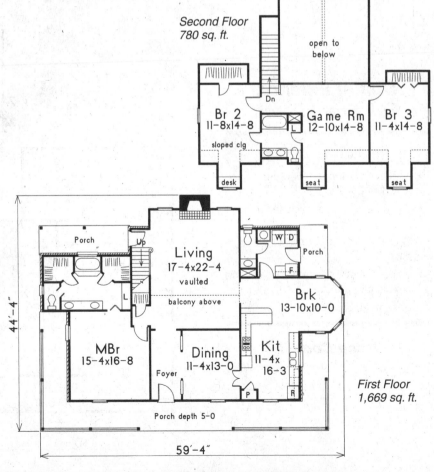

Second Floor
780 sq. ft.

open to below

Dn

Br 2
11-8x14-8

Game Rm
12-10x14-8

Br 3
11-4x14-8

sloped clg

desk

seat

seat

L

Up

Porch

Living
17-4x22-4
vaulted

balcony above

W/D

Porch

F

L

MBr
15-4x16-8

Dining
11-4x13-0

Kit
11-4x
16-3

Brk
13-10x10-0

Foyer

P

R

44'-4"

59'-4"

Porch depth 5-0

First Floor
1,669 sq. ft.

**TO ORDER BLUEPRINTS USE THE FORM ON PAGE 15 OR CALL TOLL-FREE 1-877-671-6036**
View thousands more home plans online at www.familyhandyman.com/homeplans

197

# Plan #717-053D-0030

**1,657 total square feet of living area**

## Quaint Exterior, Full Front Porch

### Special features

- Stylish pass-through between living and dining areas
- Master bedroom is secluded from living area for privacy
- Large windows in breakfast and dining areas
- 3 bedrooms, 2 1/2 baths, 2-car drive under garage
- Basement foundation

**Price Code B**

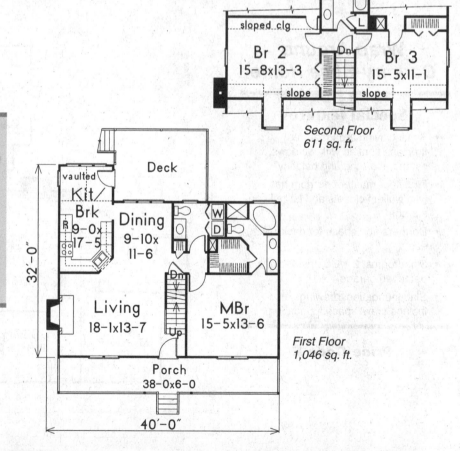

Br 2
15-8x13-3

Br 3
15-5x11-1

sloped clg

slope        slope

Dn

*Second Floor*
*611 sq. ft.*

Deck

vaulted

Kit/
Brk
9-0x
17-5

Dining
9-10x
11-6

W
D

Living
18-1x13-7

MBr
15-5x13-6

Dn

Up

Porch
38-0x6-0

32'-0"

40'-0"

*First Floor*
*1,046 sq. ft.*

**198**

**TO ORDER BLUEPRINTS USE THE FORM ON PAGE 15 OR CALL TOLL-FREE 1-877-671-6036**
View thousands more home plans online at www.familyhandyman.com/homeplans

**3,746 total square feet of living area**

## Vaulted Ceiling Adds Spaciousness

### Special features

- Upon entering a large foyer guests are greeted by a beautiful central two-story rotunda with circular staircase
- An oval tray ceiling in the formal dining room creates a Victorian feel
- Two-story family room is sunny and bright with windows on two floors
- Bonus room on the second floor has an additional 314 square feet of living area
- 4 bedrooms, 3 1/2 baths, 3-car garage
- Crawl space foundation

### *Price Code G*

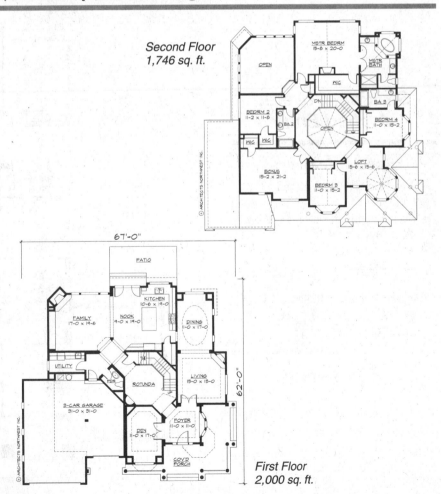

*Second Floor*
*1,746 sq. ft.*

*First Floor*
*2,000 sq. ft.*

**TO ORDER BLUEPRINTS USE THE FORM ON PAGE 15 OR CALL TOLL-FREE 1-877-671-6036**
View thousands more home plans online at www.familyhandyman.com/homeplans

**199**

**1,859 total square feet of living area**

## Striking, Covered Arched Entry

### Special features

- Fireplace highlights vaulted great room
- Master bedroom includes a large closet and private bath
- Kitchen adjoins breakfast room providing easy access to the outdoors
- 3 bedrooms, 2 1/2 baths, 2-car garage
- Basement foundation

**Price Code D**

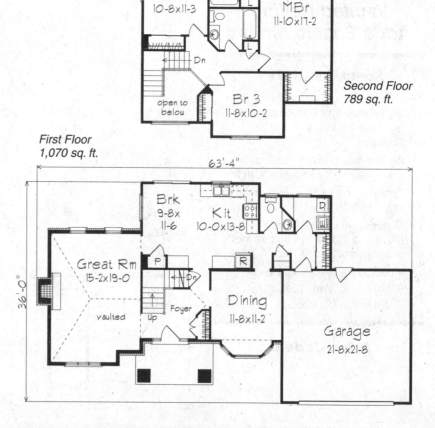

First Floor
1,070 sq. ft.

Second Floor
789 sq. ft.

**2,789 total square feet of living area**

## Spacious Design With A Luxurious Appeal

### Special features

- Master bedroom with large walk-in closets has a glass shower and whirlpool tub
- Great room has a sunny wall of windows creating a cheerful atmosphere
- Second floor includes bonus room with 286 square feet of living area
- 4 bedrooms, 3 baths, 2-car side entry garage
- Walk-out basement, basement, crawl space or slab foundation, please specify when ordering

### *Price Code E*

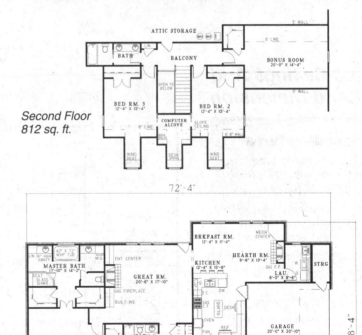

*Second Floor 812 sq. ft.*

*First Floor 1,977 sq. ft.*

**TO ORDER BLUEPRINTS USE THE FORM ON PAGE 15 OR CALL TOLL-FREE 1-877-671-6036**
View thousands more home plans online at www.familyhandyman.com/homeplans

201

**1,676 total square feet of living area**

## Vaulted Ceilings Add Light And Dimension

### Special features

- The living area skylights and large breakfast room with bay window provide plenty of sunlight

- The master bedroom has a walk-in closet and both the secondary bedrooms have large closets

- Vaulted ceilings, plant shelving and a fireplace provide a quality living area

- 3 bedrooms, 2 baths, 2-car garage

- Basement foundation, drawings also include crawl space and slab foundations

*Price Code B*

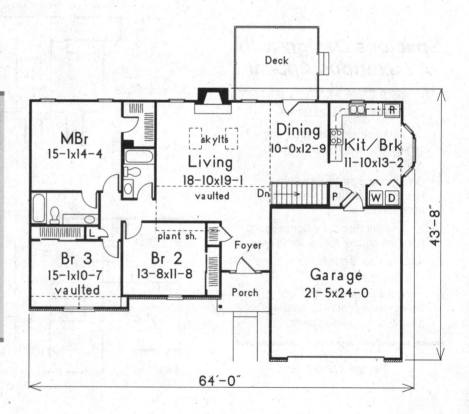

202

**TO ORDER BLUEPRINTS USE THE FORM ON PAGE 15 OR CALL TOLL-FREE 1-877-671-6036**
View thousands more home plans online at www.familyhandyman.com/homeplans

**1,771 total square feet of living area**

## Traditional Ranch With Extras

### Special features

- Den has a sloped ceiling and charming window seat
- Private master bedroom has access to the outdoors
- Central kitchen allows for convenient access when entertaining
- 2 bedrooms, 2 baths, 2-car garage
- Basement, crawl space or slab foundation, please specify when ordering

*Price Code B*

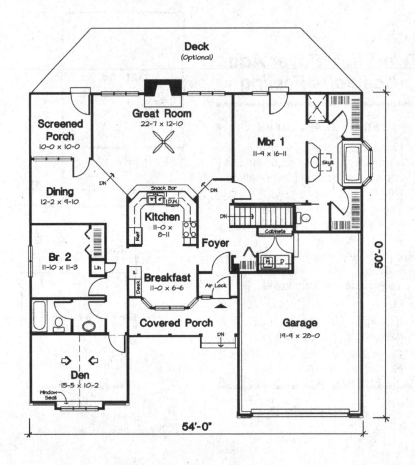

**TO ORDER BLUEPRINTS USE THE FORM ON PAGE 15 OR CALL TOLL-FREE 1-877-671-6036**
View thousands more home plans online at www.familyhandyman.com/homeplans

203

**1,814 total square feet of living area**

## Two-Story Foyer Adds Spacious Feeling

### Special features

- Large master bedroom includes a spacious bath with garden tub, separate shower and large walk-in closet

- The spacious kitchen and dining area is brightened by large windows and patio access

- Detached two-car garage with walkway leading to house adds charm to this country home

- Large front porch

- 3 bedrooms, 2 1/2 baths, 2-car detached side entry garage

- Crawl space foundation, drawings also include slab foundation

### Price Code D

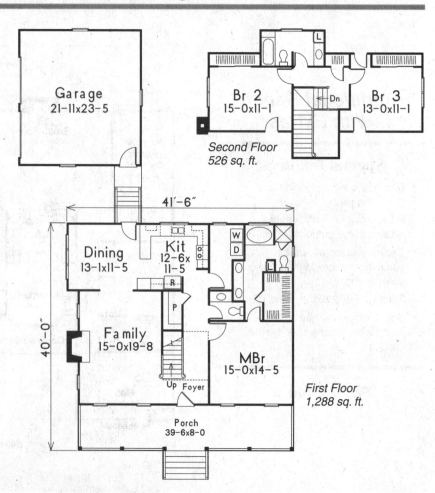

Garage
21-11x23-5

Br 2
15-0x11-1

Br 3
13-0x11-1

*Second Floor
526 sq. ft.*

41'-6"

Dining
13-1x11-5

Kit
12-6x11-5

W D

Family
15-0x19-8

40'-0"

MBr
15-0x14-5

Up Foyer

*First Floor
1,288 sq. ft.*

Porch
39-6x8-0

**204**

**TO ORDER BLUEPRINTS USE THE FORM ON PAGE 15 OR CALL TOLL-FREE 1-877-671-6036**
View thousands more home plans online at www.familyhandyman.com/homeplans

# Plan #717-065D-0024

**4,652 total square feet of living area**

## Stately Colonial Entry

### Special features

- A grand foyer introduces a formal dining room and library with beamed ceiling and built-ins
- Covered porches at the rear of the home offer splendid views
- A magnificent master bedroom has a 10' ceiling, a private sitting area and a luxurious dressing room with walk-in closet
- Secondary bedrooms have window seats, large closets and private bath access
- 4 bedrooms, 3 1/2 baths, 3-car side entry garage
- Walk-out basement foundation

**Price Code G**

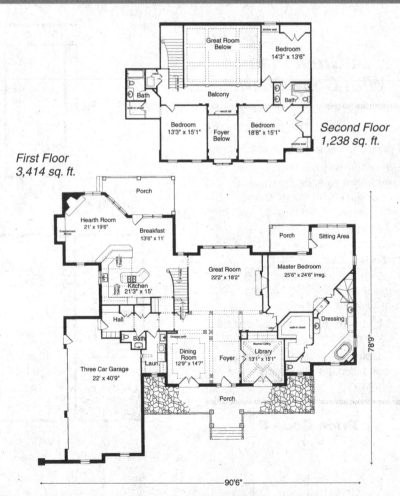

*First Floor 3,414 sq. ft.*

*Second Floor 1,238 sq. ft.*

**TO ORDER BLUEPRINTS USE THE FORM ON PAGE 15 OR CALL TOLL-FREE 1-877-671-6036**
View thousands more home plans online at www.familyhandyman.com/homeplans

205

**1,892 total square feet of living area**

## A Great Plan With Cozy Charm

### Special features

- Victorian home includes folk charm
- This split bedroom plan places a lovely master bedroom on the opposite end of the other two bedrooms for privacy
- Central living and dining areas combine creating a great place for entertaining
- Bonus room on the second floor has an additional 285 square feet of living area
- 3 bedrooms, 2 1/2 baths, 2-car side entry garage
- Basement, crawl space or slab foundation, please specify when ordering

### Price Code D

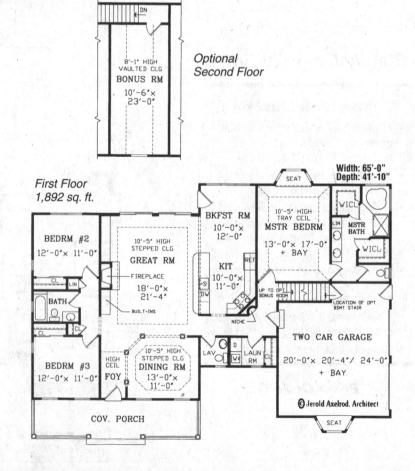

*Optional Second Floor*

8'-1" HIGH VAULTED CLG
**BONUS RM**
10'-6" x 23'-0"

*First Floor 1,892 sq. ft.*

Width: 65'-0"
Depth: 41'-10"

SEAT

**BEDRM #2**
12'-0" x 11'-0"

10'-5" HIGH STEPPED CLG
**GREAT RM**
FIREPLACE
18'-0" x 21'-4"
BUILT-INS

**BKFST RM**
10'-0" x 12'-0"

**KIT**
10'-0" x 11'-0"

10'-5" HIGH TRAY CEIL
**MSTR BEDRM**
13'-0" x 17'-0" + BAY

WICL
LIN
**MSTR BATH**
WICL

CL LIN
**BATH**
CL CL

UP TO OPT BONUS ROOM

LOCATION OF OPT BSMT STAIR

NICHE

**BEDRM #3**
12'-0" x 11'-0"

HIGH CEIL
**FOY**

10'-5" HIGH STEPPED CLG
**DINING RM**
13'-0" x 11'-0"

LAV
**LAUN RM**
D W

**TWO CAR GARAGE**
20'-0" x 20'-4" / 24'-0" + BAY

© Jerold Axelrod, Architect

**COV. PORCH**

SEAT

**3,144 total square feet of living area**

## Brick And Stucco Facade Add Charm

### Special features

- Angled walls and different floor levels give home interior interest
- Master suite has lots of privacy with a double-door entry and seclusion from other bedrooms
- Enormous outdoor covered patio creates another entire living area for entertaining
- Framing - only concrete block available
- 4 bedrooms, 3 baths, 3-car side entry garage
- Slab foundation

*Price Code F*

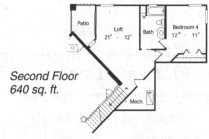

*Second Floor*
*640 sq. ft.*

*First Floor*
*2,504 sq. ft.*

**TO ORDER BLUEPRINTS USE THE FORM ON PAGE 15 OR CALL TOLL-FREE 1-877-671-6036**
View thousands more home plans online at www.familyhandyman.com/homeplans

**207**

**5,250 total square feet of living area**

## Gorgeous Award-Winning Victorian Design

### Special features

- Spacious wrap-around covered porch features an outdoor fireplace and built-in barbecue grill perfect for entertaining
- Each bedroom has its own bath and walk-in closet
- Dramatic circular staircase is highlighted in rotunda with 27' ceiling
- Master bath showcases an octagon-shaped space featuring a whirlpool tub
- 4 bedrooms, 4 1/2 baths, 4-car side entry garage
- Crawl space foundation

*Price Code H*

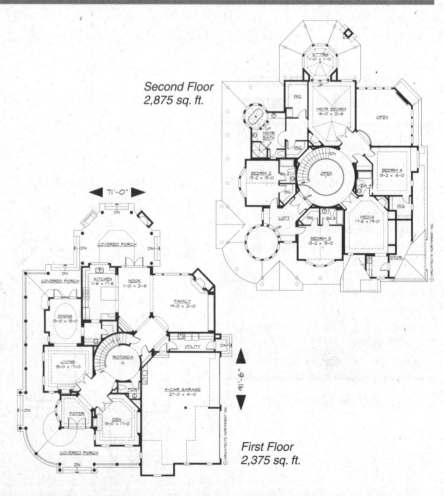

Second Floor
2,875 sq. ft.

First Floor
2,375 sq. ft.

**TO ORDER BLUEPRINTS USE THE FORM ON PAGE 15 OR CALL TOLL-FREE 1-877-671-6036**
View thousands more home plans online at www.familyhandyman.com/homeplans

**1,996 total square feet of living area**

## Blends Open And Private Living Areas

### Special features

- Dining area features an octagon-shaped coffered ceiling and built-in china cabinet

- Both the master bath and second floor bath have cheerful skylights

- Family room includes a wet bar and fireplace flanked by attractive quarter round windows

- 9' ceilings throughout the first floor with plant shelving in foyer and dining area

- 3 bedrooms, 2 1/2 baths, 2-car side entry garage

- Basement foundation, drawings also include crawl space and slab foundations

*Price Code C*

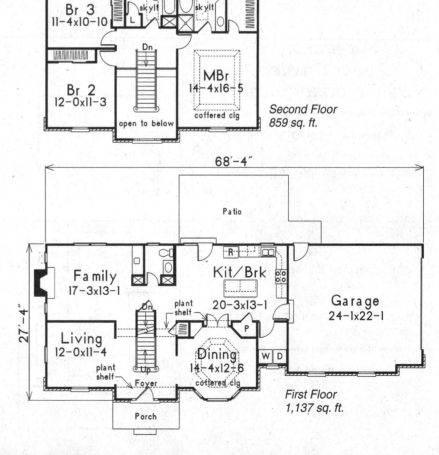

Br 3
11-4x10-10

skylt

skylt

Br 2
12-0x11-3

Dn

MBr
14-4x16-5

open to below

coffered clg

*Second Floor
859 sq. ft.*

68'-4"

Patio

Family
17-3x13-1

Kit/Brk
20-3x13-1

Garage
24-1x22-1

27'-4"

Dn

plant shelf

Living
12-0x11-4

Up

Dining
14-4x12-6

plant shelf

P

W  D

plant shelf

Foyer

coffered clg

*First Floor
1,137 sq. ft.*

Porch

**TO ORDER BLUEPRINTS USE THE FORM ON PAGE 15 OR CALL TOLL-FREE 1-877-671-6036**
View thousands more home plans online at www.familyhandyman.com/homeplans

**209**

**2,050 total square feet of living area**

## Dramatic Layout Created By Victorian Turret

### Special features

- Large kitchen and dining area have access to garage and porch
- Master bedroom features a unique turret design, private bath and large walk-in closet
- Laundry facilities are conveniently located near the bedrooms
- 3 bedrooms, 2 1/2 baths, 2-car side entry garage
- Basement foundation, drawings also include crawl space and slab foundations

**Price Code C**

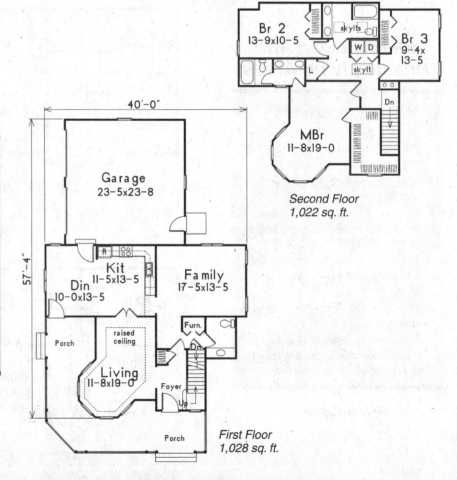

Second Floor
1,022 sq. ft.

First Floor
1,028 sq. ft.

**1,787 total square feet of living area**

## Uncommonly Styled Ranch

### Special features

- Skylights brighten screen porch which connects to the family room and deck outdoors
- Master bedroom features a comfortable sitting area, large private bath and direct access to screen porch
- Kitchen has a serving bar which extends dining into the family room
- 3 bedrooms, 2 baths, 2-car side entry garage
- Basement, crawl space or slab foundation, please specify when ordering

*Price Code B*

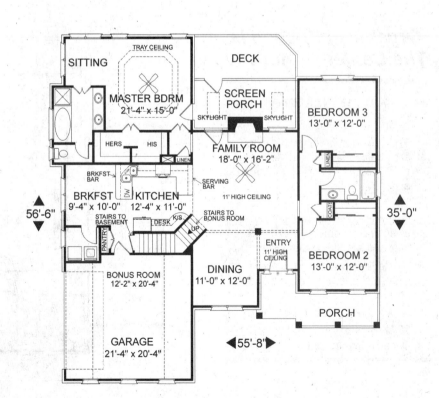

**TO ORDER BLUEPRINTS USE THE FORM ON PAGE 15 OR CALL TOLL-FREE 1-877-671-6036**
View thousands more home plans online at www.familyhandyman.com/homeplans

211

**1,882 total square feet of living area**

## Organized Kitchen Is The Center Of Activity

### Special features

- Handsome brick facade
- Spacious great room and dining area combination is brightened by unique corner windows and patio access
- Well-designed kitchen incorporates a breakfast bar peninsula, sweeping casement window above sink and a walk-in pantry island
- Master bedroom features a large walk-in closet and private bath with bay window
- 4 bedrooms, 2 baths, 2-car side entry garage
- Basement foundation

*Price Code C*

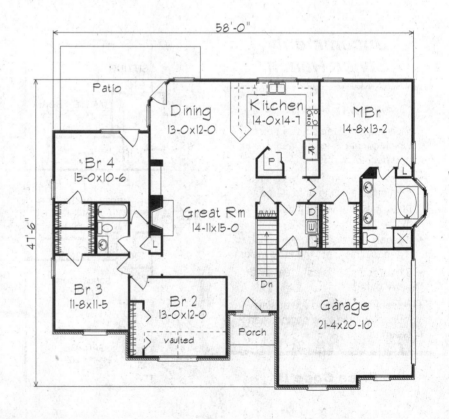

58'-0"

41'-6"

Patio

Dining
13-0x12-0

Kitchen
14-0x14-7

MBr
14-8x13-2

Br 4
15-0x10-6

Great Rm
14-11x15-0

Br 3
11-8x11-5

Br 2
13-0x12-0

vaulted

Porch

Dn

Garage
21-4x20-10

**2,567 total square feet of living area**

## Country-Style Home With Inviting Porch

### Special features

- Breakfast room has a 12' cathedral ceiling and a bayed area full of windows

- Great room has a stepped ceiling, built-in media center and a corner fireplace

- Bonus room on the second floor has an additional 300 square feet of living area

- 4 bedrooms, 3 baths, 2-car side entry garage

- Basement, crawl space or slab foundation, please specify when ordering

### Price Code F

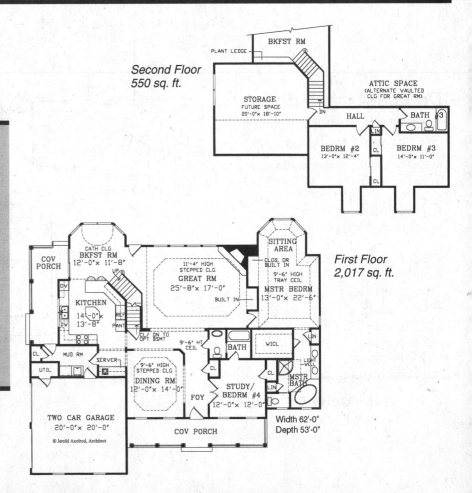

Second Floor
550 sq. ft.

First Floor
2,017 sq. ft.

Width 62'-0"
Depth 53'-0"

**TO ORDER BLUEPRINTS USE THE FORM ON PAGE 15 OR CALL TOLL-FREE 1-877-671-6036**
View thousands more home plans online at www.familyhandyman.com/homeplans

213

**3,494 total square feet of living area**

## Striking Double-Arched Entry

### Special features

- Majestic two-story foyer opens into the living and dining rooms, both framed by arched columns
- Balcony overlooks the large living area featuring French doors to a covered porch
- Luxurious master bedroom
- Convenient game room supports lots of activities
- 4 bedrooms, 3 1/2 baths, 3-car side entry garage
- Slab foundation, drawings also include crawl space foundation

**Price Code F**

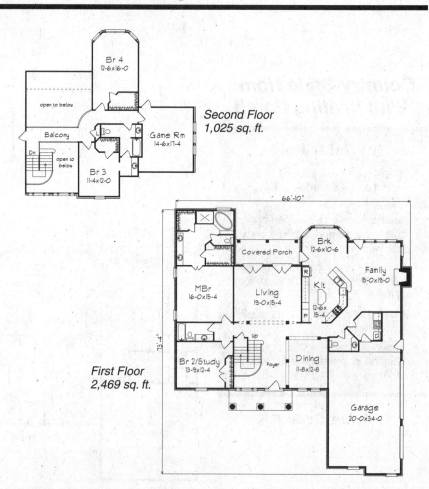

Second Floor 1,025 sq. ft.

First Floor 2,469 sq. ft.

**2,758 total square feet of living area**

## Excellent Ranch For Country Setting

### Special features

- Vaulted great room excels with fireplace, wet bar, plant shelves and skylights
- Fabulous master bedroom enjoys a fireplace, large bath, walk-in closet and vaulted ceiling
- Trendsetting kitchen and breakfast area adjoins the spacious screened porch
- Convenient office near kitchen is perfect for computer room, hobby enthusiast or fifth bedroom
- 4 bedrooms, 2 1/2 baths, 3-car side entry garage
- Basement foundation

**Price Code E**

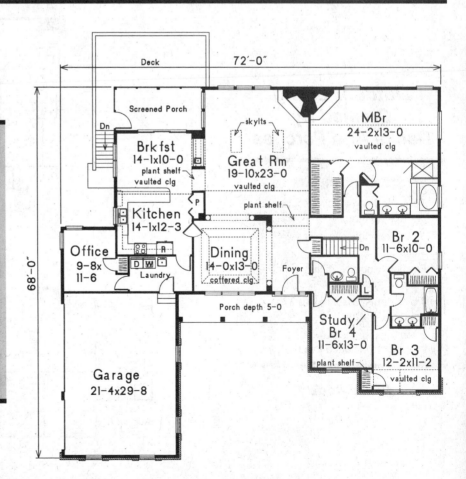

**TO ORDER BLUEPRINTS USE THE FORM ON PAGE 15 OR CALL TOLL-FREE 1-877-671-6036**
View thousands more home plans online at www.familyhandyman.com/homeplans

215

**3,149 total square feet of living area**

## Outdoor Living Created By Decks And Porches

### Special features

- 10' ceilings on the first floor and 9' ceilings on the second floor
- All bedrooms include walk-in closets
- Formal living and dining rooms flank two-story foyer
- 4 bedrooms, 3 1/2 baths, 2-car detached garage
- Slab foundation, drawings also include crawl space foundation

**Price Code E**

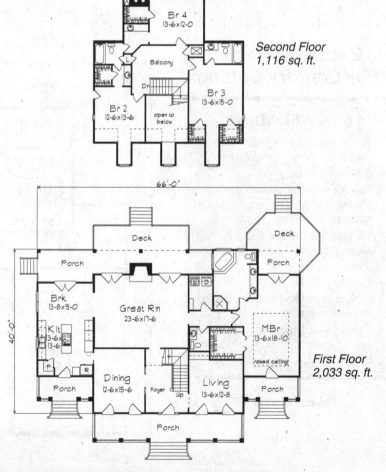

Second Floor
1,116 sq. ft.

Br 4
13-6x12-0

Balcony

Br 2
12-6x13-6

Dn

open to below

Br 3
13-6x15-0

First Floor
2,033 sq. ft.

66'-0"

40'-0"

Deck

Deck

Porch

Porch

Brk
13-8x9-0

Great Rm
23-6x17-6

Kit
13-6x
13-6

MBr
13-6x18-10

raised ceiling

Porch

Dining
12-6x15-6

Foyer

up

Living
13-6x12-8

Porch

Porch

**2,029 total square feet of living area**

## Country Home
## With Front Orientation

### Special features

- Stonework, gables, roof dormer and double porches create a country flavor

- Kitchen enjoys extravagant cabinetry and counterspace in a bay, island snack bar, built-in pantry and cheery dining area with multiple tall windows

- Angled stair descends from large entry with wood columns and is open to vaulted great room with corner fireplace

- Master bedroom boasts two walk-in closets, a private bath with double-door entry and a secluded porch

- 4 bedrooms, 2 baths, 2-car side entry garage

- Basement foundation, drawings also include crawl space and slab foundations

**Price Code D**

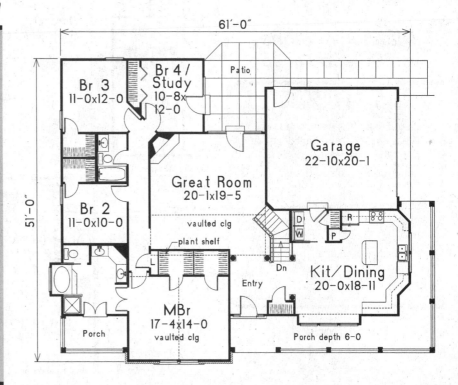

**TO ORDER BLUEPRINTS USE THE FORM ON PAGE 15 OR CALL TOLL-FREE 1-877-671-6036**
View thousands more home plans online at www.familyhandyman.com/homeplans

217

**1,677 total square feet of living area**

## Distinctive Stone And Stucco Facade

### Special features

- Master suite has a secluded feel with a private and remote location from other bedrooms
- Great room is complete with fireplace and beautiful windows
- Optional second floor has an additional 350 square feet of living area
- 3 bedrooms, 2 baths, 2-car side entry garage
- Slab foundation

*Price Code B*

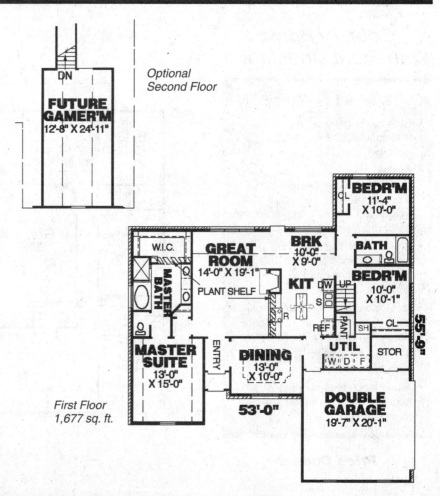

*Optional Second Floor*

**FUTURE GAMER'M**
12'-8" X 24'-11"

*First Floor*
*1,677 sq. ft.*

BEDR'M 11'-4" X 10'-0"

GREAT ROOM 14'-0" X 19'-1"

BRK 10'-0" X 9'-0"

BATH

BEDR'M 10'-0" X 10'-1"

PLANT SHELF

MASTER BATH

KIT

W.I.C.

UTIL

STOR

MASTER SUITE 13'-0" X 15'-0"

ENTRY

DINING 13'-0" X 10'-0"

DOUBLE GARAGE 19'-7" X 20'-1"

55'-9"

53'-0"

**1,672 total square feet of living area**

## Circle-Top Windows Grace The Facade Of This Home

### Special features

- Vaulted master bedroom features a walk-in closet and adjoining bath with separate tub and shower
- Energy efficient home with 2" x 6" exterior walls
- Covered front and rear porches
- 12' ceilings in the living room, kitchen and bedroom #2
- Kitchen is complete with a pantry, angled bar and adjacent eating area
- Sloped ceiling in the dining room
- 3 bedrooms, 2 baths, 2-car side entry garage
- Crawl space foundation, drawings also include basement and slab foundations

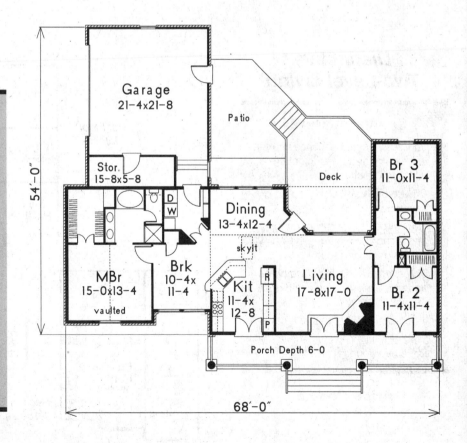

*Price Code C*

**TO ORDER BLUEPRINTS USE THE FORM ON PAGE 15 OR CALL TOLL-FREE 1-877-671-6036**
View thousands more home plans online at www.familyhandyman.com/homeplans

219

**3,138 total square feet of living area**

## Distinctive Two-Level Living

### Special features

- Impressive stair descends into the large entry and through double doors to the study
- Private dining is spacious and secluded
- Family room, master bedroom and laundry are among the many generously sized rooms
- Three large bedrooms, two baths and four walk-in closets compose the second floor
- 4 bedrooms, 3 1/2 baths, 2-car side entry garage
- Basement foundation

**Price Code E**

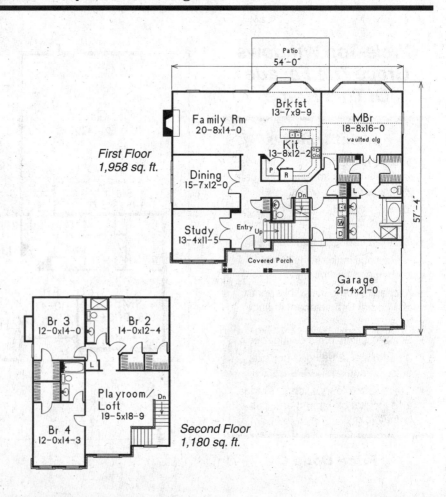

*First Floor*
*1,958 sq. ft.*

Patio
54'-0"

Brkfst
13-7x9-9

Family Rm
20-8x14-0

MBr
18-8x16-0
vaulted clg

Kit
13-8x12-2

Dining
15-7x12-0

Study
13-4x11-5

Entry
Up

Covered Porch

Garage
21-4x21-0

57'-4"

Br 3
12-0x14-0

Br 2
14-0x12-4

Playroom/
Loft
19-5x18-9

Br 4
12-0x14-3

*Second Floor*
*1,180 sq. ft.*

**TO ORDER BLUEPRINTS USE THE FORM ON PAGE 15 OR CALL TOLL-FREE 1-877-671-6036**
View thousands more home plans online at www.familyhandyman.com/homeplans

220

**2,135 total square feet of living area**

## Open Breakfast/Family Room Combination

### Special features

- Family room features extra space, an impressive fireplace and full wall of windows that joins the breakfast room creating a spacious entertainment area
- Washer and dryer are conveniently located on the second floor near the bedrooms
- The kitchen features an island counter and pantry
- 4 bedrooms, 2 1/2 baths, 2-car garage
- Basement foundation

*Price Code D*

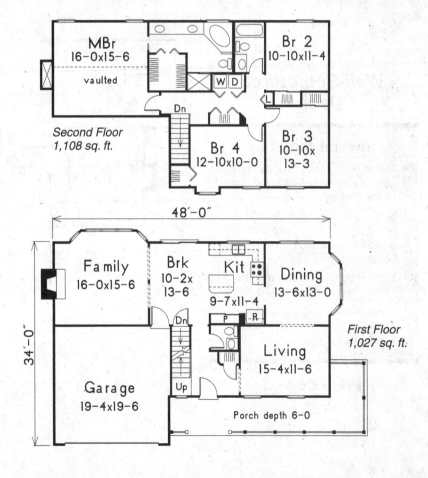

MBr
16-0x15-6
vaulted

Br 2
10-10x11-4

W D

Br 4
12-10x10-0

Br 3
10-10x
13-3

*Second Floor
1,108 sq. ft.*

48'-0"

Family
16-0x15-6

Brk
10-2x
13-6

Kit
9-7x11-4

Dining
13-6x13-0

34'-0"

Dn

P R

Garage
19-4x19-6

Living
15-4x11-6

Up

Porch depth 6-0

*First Floor
1,027 sq. ft.*

**TO ORDER BLUEPRINTS USE THE FORM ON PAGE 15 OR CALL TOLL-FREE 1-877-671-6036**
View thousands more home plans online at www.familyhandyman.com/homeplans

221

**1,759 total square feet of living area**

## Well-Sculptured Design

### Special features

- The striking entry is created by a unique stair layout, an open high ceiling and a fireplace
- Bonus area over garage, which is included in the square footage, could easily convert to a fourth bedroom or activity center
- Second floor bedrooms share a private dressing area and bath
- 3 bedrooms, 2 1/2 baths, 2-car garage
- Basement foundation

*Price Code B*

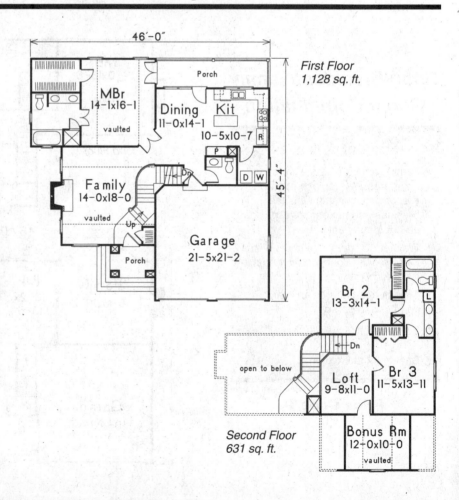

46'-0"

*First Floor*
*1,128 sq. ft.*

MBr
14-1x16-1
vaulted

Dining
11-0x14-1

Kit
10-5x10-7

Porch

Family
14-0x18-0
vaulted

Dn

Up

Garage
21-5x21-2

Porch

45'-4"

*Second Floor*
*631 sq. ft.*

Br 2
13-3x14-1

Dn

open to below

Loft
9-8x11-0

Br 3
11-5x13-11

Bonus Rm
12-0x10-0
vaulted

**2,900 total square feet of living area**

## Two-Story Atrium For Great Views

### Special features

- Elegant entry foyer leads to the second floor balcony overlook of the vaulted two-story atrium
- Spacious kitchen features an island breakfast bar, walk-in pantry, bayed breakfast room and adjoining screened porch
- Two large second floor bedrooms and stair balconies overlook a sun-drenched two-story vaulted atrium
- 4 bedrooms, 3 1/2 baths, 2-car side entry garage
- Basement foundation

**Price Code E**

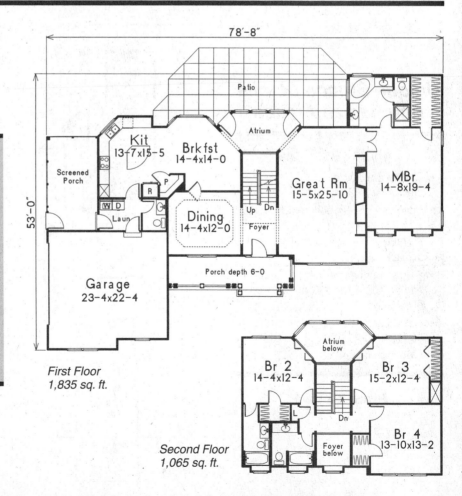

*First Floor*
*1,835 sq. ft.*

*Second Floor*
*1,065 sq. ft.*

**TO ORDER BLUEPRINTS USE THE FORM ON PAGE 15 OR CALL TOLL-FREE 1-877-671-6036**
View thousands more home plans online at www.familyhandyman.com/homeplans

223

**3,570 total square feet of living area**

## Unique Stucco Details Emphasize Arches

### Special features

- Casual living areas combine creating lots of space for living
- Spacious master bedroom includes sitting area and an oversized bath
- Framing - only concrete block available
- Bonus room on the second floor has an additional 430 square feet of living area
- 4 bedrooms, 4 baths, 3-car side entry garage
- Slab foundation

***Price Code F***

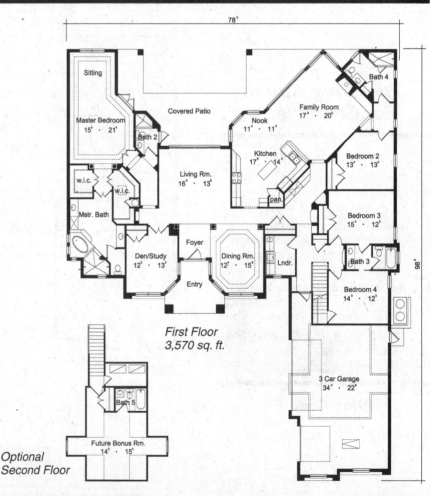

*First Floor*
*3,570 sq. ft.*

*Optional*
*Second Floor*

**1,749 total square feet of living area**

## Cozy Covered Front Porch

### Special features

- Tray ceiling in master suite
- A breakfast bar overlooks the vaulted great room
- Additional bedrooms are located away from master suite for privacy
- Optional bonus room above the garage has an additional 308 square feet of living area
- 3 bedrooms, 2 baths, 2-car garage
- Walk-out basement, slab or crawl space foundation, please specify when ordering

*Price Code B*

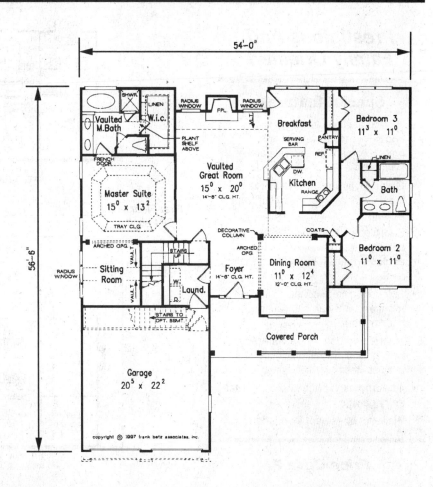

**TO ORDER BLUEPRINTS USE THE FORM ON PAGE 15 OR CALL TOLL-FREE 1-877-671-6036**
View thousands more home plans online at www.familyhandyman.com/homeplans

225

**3,420 total square feet of living area**

## Prestigious And Family Oriented

### Special features

- Hip roofs, elliptical windows and brick facade with quoins emphasize stylish sophisticated living

- Grand foyer has flared staircase in addition to secondary stair from kitchen

- Enormous kitchen features a cooktop island, walk-in pantry, angled breakfast bar and computer desk

- Splendid gallery connects family room and wet bar with vaulted hearth room

- Master bedroom has a coffered ceiling, double walk-in closets and a lavish bath

- 4 bedrooms, 3 1/2 baths, 3-car rear entry garage

- Walk-out basement foundation

*Price Code F*

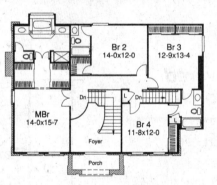

*Second Floor 1,526 sq. ft.*

Br 2 14-0x12-0

Br 3 12-9x13-4

MBr 14-0x15-7

Dn

Dn

Br 4 11-8x12-0

Foyer

Porch

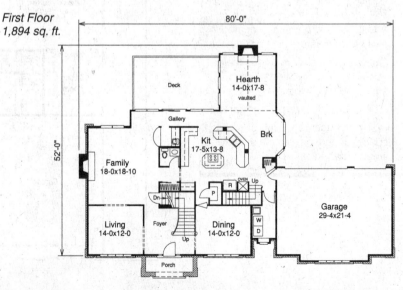

*First Floor 1,894 sq. ft.*

80'-0"

52'-0"

Deck

Hearth 14-0x17-8 vaulted

Gallery

Kit 17-5x13-8

Brk

Family 18-0x18-10

Dn

Living 14-0x12-0

Foyer

Dining 14-0x12-0

Garage 29-4x21-4

P

R

OVEN

Up

W

D

Up

Porch

# Plan #717-036D-0060

**1,760 total square feet of living area**

## Study Off Main Entrance

### Special features

- Stone and brick exterior has old-world charm
- Master bedroom includes a sitting area and is situated away from other bedrooms for privacy
- Kitchen and dinette access the outdoors
- Great room includes fireplace, built-in bookshelves and an entertainment center
- 3 bedrooms, 2 baths, 2-car side entry garage
- Slab foundation

***Price Code B***

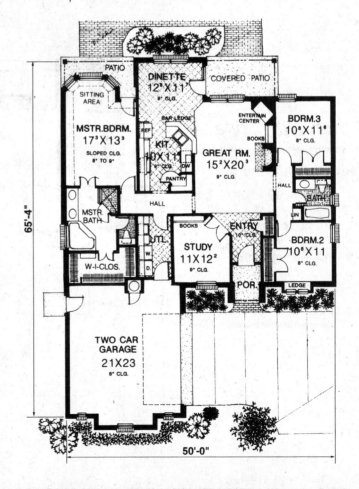

**TO ORDER BLUEPRINTS USE THE FORM ON PAGE 15 OR CALL TOLL-FREE 1-877-671-6036**
View thousands more home plans online at www.familyhandyman.com/homeplans

227

**1,591 total square feet of living area**

## Ranch With Style

### Special features

- Fireplace in great room is accented by windows on both sides
- Practical kitchen is splendidly designed for organization
- Large screen porch for three-season entertaining
- 3 bedrooms, 2 baths, 3-car garage
- Basement foundation

### Price Code B

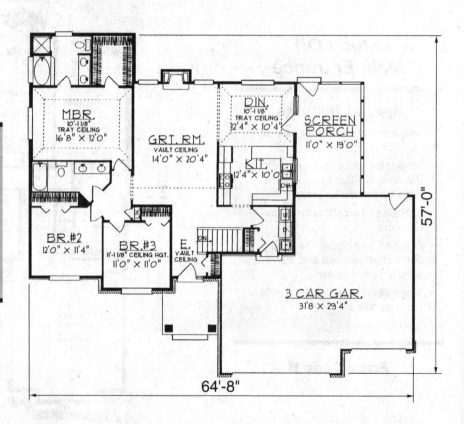

**1,231 total square feet of living area**

## Atrium Living For Views On A Narrow Lot

### Special features

- Dutch gables and stone accents provide an enchanting appearance
- The spacious living room offers a masonry fireplace, atrium with window wall and is open to a dining area with bay window
- Kitchen has a breakfast counter, lots of cabinet space and glass sliding doors to a balcony
- 380 square feet of optional living area on the lower level
- 2 bedrooms, 2 baths, 1-car drive under garage
- Walk-out basement foundation

### Price Code A

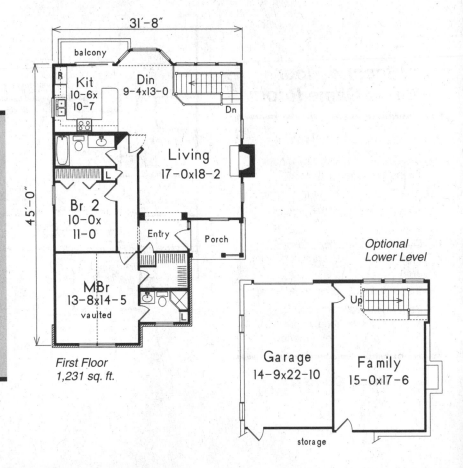

31'-8"

balcony

Kit
10-6x
10-7

Din
9-4x13-0

Dn

Living
17-0x18-2

45'-0"

Br 2
10-0x
11-0

Entry

Porch

MBr
13-8x14-5
vaulted

L

*First Floor*
*1,231 sq. ft.*

*Optional Lower Level*

Up

Garage
14-9x22-10

Family
15-0x17-6

storage

**TO ORDER BLUEPRINTS USE THE FORM ON PAGE 15 OR CALL TOLL-FREE 1-877-671-6036**
View thousands more home plans online at www.familyhandyman.com/homeplans

**229**

**1,957 total square feet of living area**

## Second Floor Bonus Game Room

### Special features

- Breakfast room with bay window opens to kitchen with bar
- 9' ceilings throughout this home
- Master suite has 10' boxed ceiling and atrium doors to rear porch
- Optional second floor has an additional 479 square feet of living area
- 3 bedrooms, 2 baths, 2-car garage
- Basement, walk-out basement, slab or crawl space foundation, please specify when ordering

**Price Code C**

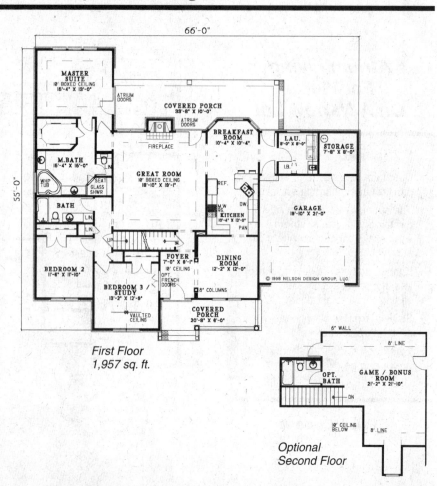

First Floor
1,957 sq. ft.

Optional
Second Floor

**1,982 total square feet of living area**

## Two-Story With Victorian Feel

### Special features

- Spacious master bedroom has bath with corner whirlpool tub and sunny skylight above
- Breakfast area overlooks into the great room
- Screened porch with skylight above extends the home outdoors and allows for another entertainment area
- 4 bedrooms, 2 1/2 baths
- Crawl space or slab foundation, please specify when ordering

*Price Code C*

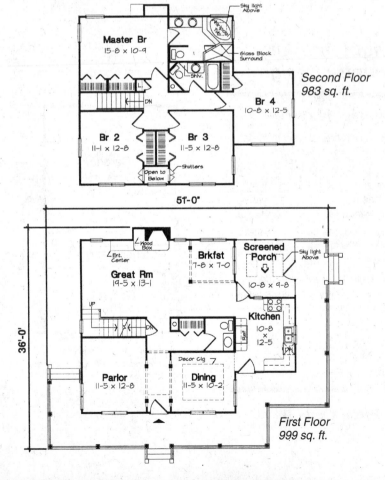

Master Br 15-8 x 10-9

Sky light Above

Glass Block Surround

Shlv.

Br 4 10-8 x 12-5

Second Floor 983 sq. ft.

DN

Br 2 11-1 x 12-8

Br 3 11-5 x 12-8

Open to Below

Shutters

51'-0"

Wood Box

Ent. Center

Brkfst 7-8 x 7-0

Screened Porch 10-8 x 9-8

Sky light Above

Great Rm 19-5 x 13-1

36'-0"

UP   DN

Kitchen 10-8 x 12-5

Ref.

Decor Clg 7

Parlor 11-5 x 12-8

Dining 11-5 x 10-2

First Floor 999 sq. ft.

**TO ORDER BLUEPRINTS USE THE FORM ON PAGE 15 OR CALL TOLL-FREE 1-877-671-6036**
View thousands more home plans online at www.familyhandyman.com/homeplans

231

# Plan #717-007D-0140

**1,591 total square feet of living area**

## Bright And Airy Country Design

### Special features

- Spacious porch and patio provide outdoor enjoyment
- Large entry foyer leads to a cheery kitchen and breakfast room which welcomes the sun through a wide array of windows
- The great room features a vaulted ceiling, corner fireplace, wet bar and access to the rear patio
- Double walk-in closets, private porch and a luxury bath are special highlights of the vaulted master bedroom suite
- 3 bedrooms, 2 baths, 2-car side entry garage
- Basement foundation

*Price Code B*

57'-0"

44'-8"

Patio

Garage
21-4x19-8

Br 3
11-4x10-0

Br 2
10-0x10-9

Great Rm
17-3x16-4
vaulted

Kitchen
11-5x15-8

Dn

Brk fst
13-6x11-0

Entry

MBr
15-4x12-0
vaulted

Porch

Covered Porch depth 5-0

**1,118 total square feet of living area**

## Modern Rustic Design

### Special features

- Convenient kitchen has direct access into garage and looks out onto front covered porch

- The covered patio is enjoyed by both the living room and master suite

- Octagon-shaped dining room adds interest to the front exterior while the interior is sunny and bright

- 2 bedrooms, 2 baths, 2-car garage

- Slab foundation

*Price Code AA*

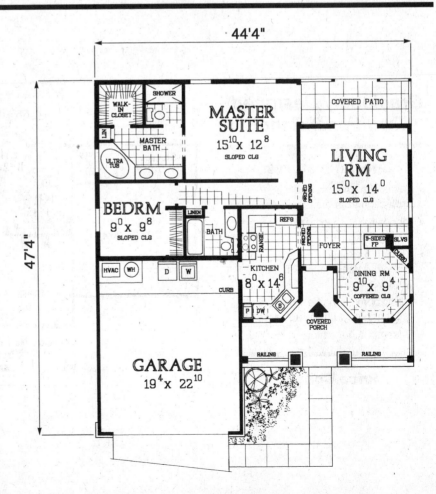

**1,477 total square feet of living area**

## Graciously Designed Traditional Ranch

### Special features

- Oversized porch provides protection from the elements
- Innovative kitchen employs step-saving design
- Kitchen has snack bar which opens to the breakfast room with bay window
- 3 bedrooms, 2 baths, 2-car side entry garage with storage area
- Basement foundation

*Price Code A*

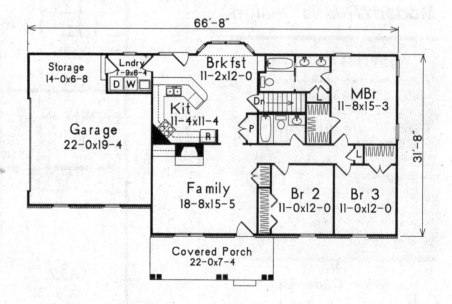

Storage
14-0x6-8

Lndry
7-9x6-4

D  W

Brk fst
11-2x12-0

MBr
11-8x15-3

Kit
11-4x11-4

R

Dn

P

Garage
22-0x19-4

66'-8"

31'-8"

Family
18-8x15-5

Br 2
11-0x12-0

Br 3
11-0x12-0

Covered Porch
22-0x7-4

**2,718 total square feet of living area**

## Striking Front Facade With Arched Entry

### Special features

- Master bedroom has a tray ceiling, access to the rear deck, walk-in closet and an impressive private bath
- Dining and living rooms flank the foyer and both feature tray ceilings
- Spacious family room features a 12' ceiling, fireplace and access to the rear deck
- Kitchen has a 9' ceiling, large pantry and bar overlooking the breakfast room
- 4 bedrooms, 2 1/2 baths, 2-car side entry garage
- Basement foundation

**Price Code E**

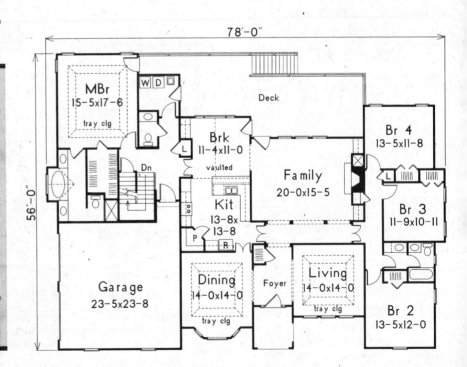

**TO ORDER BLUEPRINTS USE THE FORM ON PAGE 15 OR CALL TOLL-FREE 1-877-671-6036**
View thousands more home plans online at www.familyhandyman.com/homeplans

235

**2,079 total square feet of living area**

## Great Room Atrium Door Accesses Covered Deck

### Special features

- Large formal entry foyer with openings to formal dining and great rooms
- Great room has built-in bookshelves, a fireplace, and a coffered ceiling
- Unique angled morning room with bay windows overlooks the covered deck
- Master bath enjoys double walk-in closets, a step-up tub, separate shower and a coffered ceiling
- 3 bedrooms, 2 baths, 2-car garage
- Slab or crawl space foundation, please specify when ordering

**Price Code C**

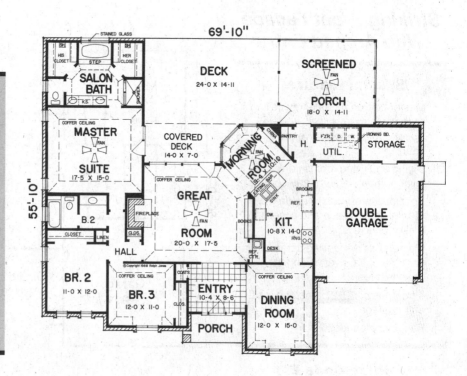

236

**TO ORDER BLUEPRINTS USE THE FORM ON PAGE 15 OR CALL TOLL-FREE 1-877-671-6036**
View thousands more home plans online at www.familyhandyman.com/homeplans

**1,795 total square feet of living area**

## Expansive Deck Enhances Outdoor Living Areas

### Special features

- Window wall in living and dining areas brings the outdoors in
- Master bedroom has a full bath and walk-in closet
- Vaulted loft on the second floor is a unique feature
- 3 bedrooms, 2 1/2 baths
- Basement or crawl space foundation, please specify when ordering

*Price Code B*

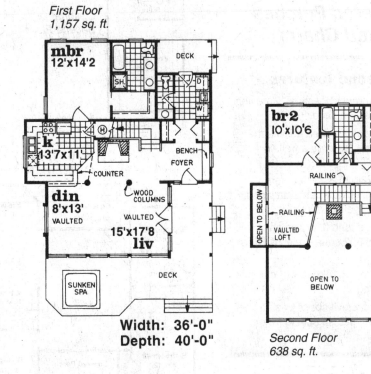

First Floor
1,157 sq. ft.

**mbr** 12'x14'2

DECK

SH.

D

k 13'7"x11'

COUNTER

H

BENCH FOYER

W

WOOD COLUMNS

**din** 8'x13' VAULTED

VAULTED

15'x17'8 **liv**

SUNKEN SPA

DECK

**Width: 36'-0"**
**Depth: 40'-0"**

br2 10'x10'6

br3 10'x14' VAULTED

RAILING

OPEN TO BELOW

RAILING

VAULTED LOFT

PLANT LEDGE

OPEN TO BELOW

Second Floor
638 sq. ft.

**TO ORDER BLUEPRINTS USE THE FORM ON PAGE 15 OR CALL TOLL-FREE 1-877-671-6036**
View thousands more home plans online at www.familyhandyman.com/homeplans

237

**1,855 total square feet of living area**

## Front And Rear Covered Porches Add Charm

### Special features

- The great room boasts a 12' ceiling and corner fireplace
- Bayed breakfast area adjoins the kitchen that features a walk-in pantry
- The relaxing master bedroom includes a private bath with walk-in closet and garden tub
- Optional second floor has an additional 352 square feet of living area
- 3 bedrooms, 2 1/2 baths, 2-car side entry garage
- Basement, crawl space or slab foundation, please specify when ordering

**Price Code D**

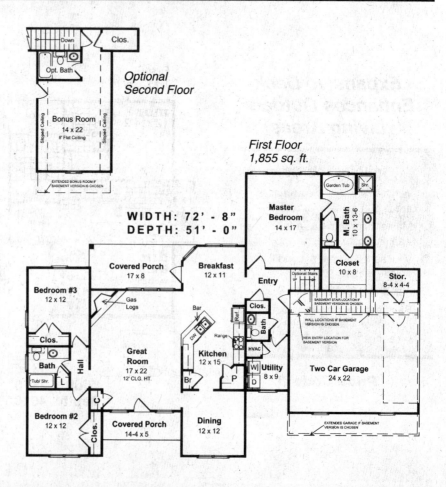

Optional Second Floor

First Floor
1,855 sq. ft.

WIDTH: 72' - 8"
DEPTH: 51' - 0"

238

**TO ORDER BLUEPRINTS USE THE FORM ON PAGE 15 OR CALL TOLL-FREE 1-877-671-6036**
View thousands more home plans online at www.familyhandyman.com/homeplans

**4,370 total square feet of living area**

## Elegant, Stylish And Sophisticated

### Special features

- Detailed brickwork surrounding the arched windows and quoined corners create a timeless exterior

- Two-story great room has a large fireplace, flanking bookshelves, massive window wall and balcony overlook

- The state-of-the-art kitchen has an island cooktop, built-in oven/ microwave oven, large pantry, menu desk and opens to the breakfast and hearth rooms

- A coffered ceiling, bay window, two walk-in closets and a huge bath adorn the master bedroom

- 4 bedrooms, 3 1/2 baths, 3-car side entry garage

- Walk-out basement foundation

**Price Code G**

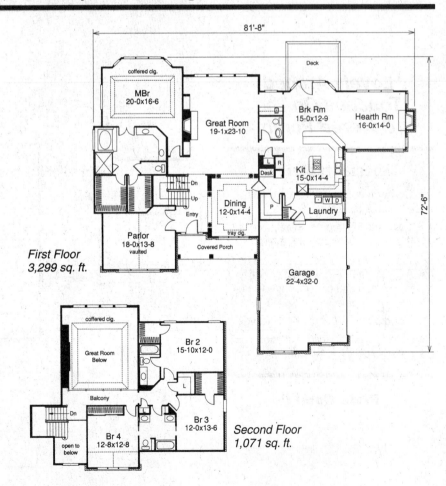

81'-8"

*coffered clg.*

MBr
20-0x16-6

Great Room
19-1x23-10

Deck

Brk Rm
15-0x12-9

Hearth Rm
16-0x14-0

Desk

Kit
15-0x14-4

Dn

Up

Dining
12-0x14-4
tray clg.

P

Laundry
W D

Entry

Parlor
18-0x13-8
vaulted

Covered Porch

Garage
22-4x32-0

*First Floor
3,299 sq. ft.*

72'-6"

*coffered clg.*

Great Room
Below

Br 2
15-10x12-0

Balcony

L

Dn

Br 3
12-0x13-6

Br 4
12-8x12-8

open to
below

*Second Floor
1,071 sq. ft.*

**TO ORDER BLUEPRINTS USE THE FORM ON PAGE 15 OR CALL TOLL-FREE 1-877-671-6036**
View thousands more home plans online at www.familyhandyman.com/homeplans

239

**1,594 total square feet of living area**

## Lovely Arched Touches On The Covered Porch

### Special features

- Corner fireplace in the great room creates a cozy feel
- Spacious kitchen combines with the dining room creating a terrific gathering place
- A handy family and guest entrance is a casual and convenient way to enter the home
- 3 bedrooms, 2 baths, 2-car garage
- Slab or crawl space foundation, please specify when ordering

*Price Code B*

# Plan #717-021D-0021

**3,153 total square feet of living area**

## Large Porches Bring In The Outdoors

### Special features

- Energy efficient home with 2" x 6" exterior walls
- Master bedroom has full amenities
- Covered breezeway and front and rear porches
- Full-sized workshop and storage with garage below is a unique combination
- 4 bedrooms, 3 1/2 baths, 2-car drive under garage
- Basement foundation, drawings also include crawl space and slab foundations

*Price Code E*

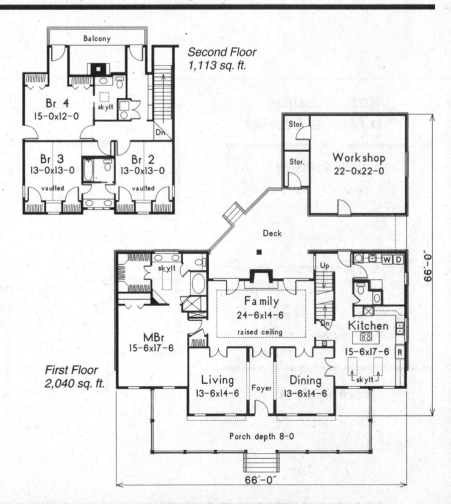

*Second Floor 1,113 sq. ft.*

Balcony

Br 4
15-0x12-0

Br 3
13-0x13-0
vaulted

Br 2
13-0x13-0
vaulted

skylt

Dn

Stor.

Stor.

Workshop
22-0x22-0

Deck

*First Floor 2,040 sq. ft.*

MBr
15-6x17-6

skylt

Family
24-6x14-6
raised ceiling

Up

Dn

W D

Kitchen
15-6x17-6

R

skylt

Living
13-6x14-6

Foyer

Dining
13-6x14-6

Porch depth 8-0

66'-0"

66'-0"

**TO ORDER BLUEPRINTS USE THE FORM ON PAGE 15 OR CALL TOLL-FREE 1-877-671-6036**
View thousands more home plans online at www.familyhandyman.com/homeplans

241

**1,429 total square feet of living area**

## Master Suite With Media Center

### Special features

- Master suite includes a sitting area and private bath with two walk-in closets
- Kitchen and dining area overlook the living room
- Living room has a fireplace, media center and access to the covered porch
- 3 bedrooms, 2 baths, 2-car garage
- Slab or crawl space foundation, please specify when ordering

**Price Code A**

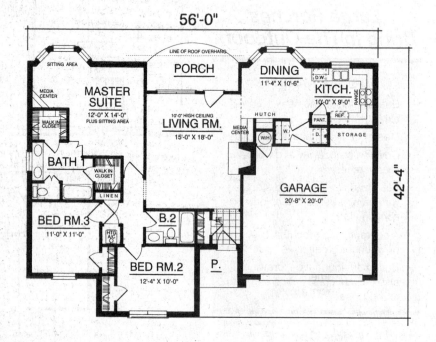

**2,349 total square feet of living area**

## Bright And Beautiful

### Special features

- Open and airy with two-story foyer and family room
- Den is secluded from the rest of the home and is ideal as an office space
- Second floor bedrooms have walk-in closets and share a bath
- Optional bonus room has an additional 276 square feet of living area
- 4 bedrooms, 3 baths, 2-car garage
- Walk-out basement, slab or crawl space foundation, please specify when ordering

**Price Code D**

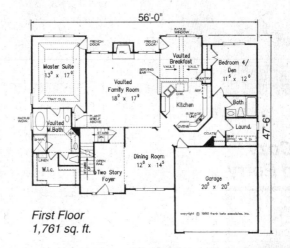

*First Floor*
*1,761 sq. ft.*

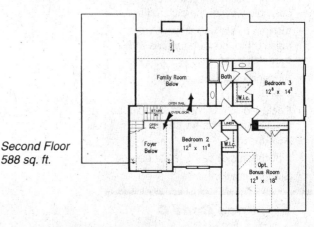

*Second Floor*
*588 sq. ft.*

**TO ORDER BLUEPRINTS USE THE FORM ON PAGE 15 OR CALL TOLL-FREE 1-877-671-6036**
View thousands more home plans online at www.familyhandyman.com/homeplans

243

**1,923 total square feet of living area**

*Rear View*

## Inviting And Cozy Covered Arched Entry

### Special features

- The foyer opens into a spacious living room with fireplace and splendid view of the covered porch
- Kitchen has a walk-in pantry adjacent to the laundry area and breakfast room
- All bedrooms feature walk-in closets
- Secluded master bedroom includes unique angled bath with spacious walk-in closet
- 3 bedrooms, 2 baths, 2-car garage
- Slab foundation

*Floor plan labels:*

61'-0"

56'-4"

raised ceiling
MBr
14-4x16-0

Covered Patio

Br 2
11-4x12-0

Living
16-4x17-0

Breakfast
10-4x10-0

4" step

Kitchen
10-4x12-0

plant shelf

Garage
20-4x22-4

Foyer

Dining
11-4x13-4

Br 3
11-4x12-0

sloped clg

sloped clg

### Price Code C

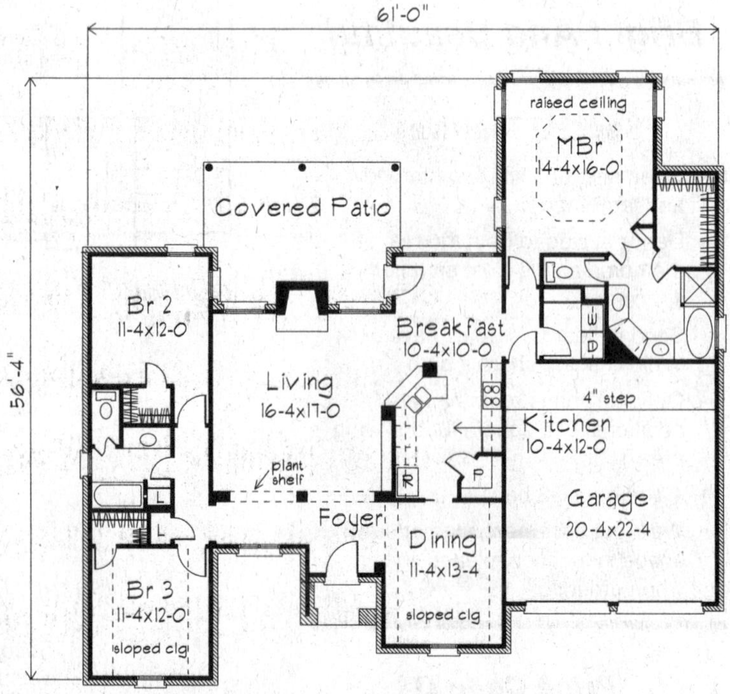

**TO ORDER BLUEPRINTS USE THE FORM ON PAGE 15 OR CALL TOLL-FREE 1-877-671-6036**
View thousands more home plans online at www.familyhandyman.com/homeplans

**1,915 total square feet of living area**

## Bayed Breakfast Room

### Special features

- Large breakfast area overlooks the vaulted great room
- Master suite has a cheerful sitting room and private bath
- Plan features a unique in-law suite with private bath and walk-in closet
- 4 bedrooms, 3 baths, 2-car garage
- Walk-out basement, slab or crawl space foundation, please specify when ordering

*Price Code C*

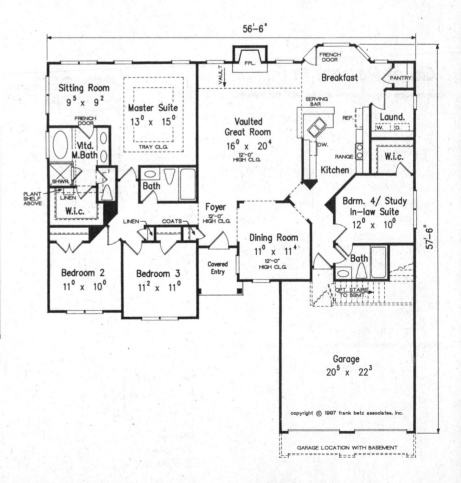

**TO ORDER BLUEPRINTS USE THE FORM ON PAGE 15 OR CALL TOLL-FREE 1-877-671-6036**
View thousands more home plans online at www.familyhandyman.com/homeplans

245

**3,106 total square feet of living area**

## Quiet Retreat In Parlor

### Special features

- Unique angled rooms create an exciting feel
- Well-organized kitchen with island is adjacent to family room
- Beautiful sculptured ceilings in master suite
- The guest house provides an additional 330 square feet of living area with 1 bedroom, 1 bath and 1-car garage
- 3 bedrooms, 3 full baths, 2 half baths, 2-car garage
- Slab foundation

*Price Code E*

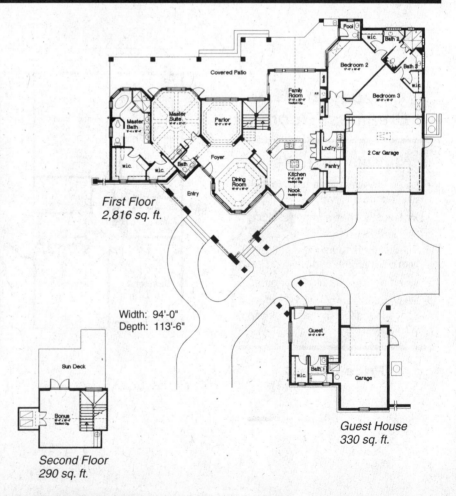

*First Floor*
*2,816 sq. ft.*

Width: 94'-0"
Depth: 113'-6"

*Second Floor*
*290 sq. ft.*

*Guest House*
*330 sq. ft.*

**TO ORDER BLUEPRINTS USE THE FORM ON PAGE 15 OR CALL TOLL-FREE 1-877-671-6036**
View thousands more home plans online at www.familyhandyman.com/homeplans

**2,513 total square feet of living area**

## Stylish And Practical Plan

### Special features

- Coffered ceilings in master bedroom, living and dining rooms
- Kitchen features island cooktop and built-in desk
- Dramatic vaulted ceiling in the breakfast room is framed by plenty of windows
- Covered entry porch leads into spacious foyer
- Family room features an impressive fireplace and vaulted ceiling that joins the breakfast room creating a spacious entertainment area
- 4 bedrooms, 2 full baths, 2 half baths, 2-car side entry garage
- Basement foundation

*Price Code D*

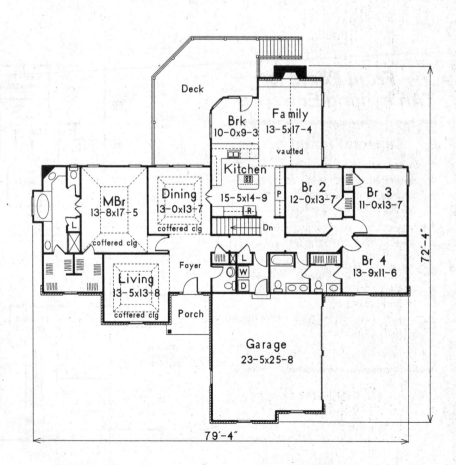

Deck

Brk
10-0x9-3

Family
13-5x17-4
vaulted

Kitchen
15-5x14-9

MBr
13-8x17-5
coffered clg.

Dining
13-0x13-7
coffered clg

Br 2
12-0x13-7

Br 3
11-0x13-7

Living
13-5x13-8
coffered clg

Foyer

Br 4
13-9x11-6

Porch

Garage
23-5x25-8

72'-4"

79'-4"

**TO ORDER BLUEPRINTS USE THE FORM ON PAGE 15 OR CALL TOLL-FREE 1-877-671-6036**
View thousands more home plans online at www.familyhandyman.com/homeplans

247

**2,362 total square feet of living area**

## Front Porch Is An Inviting Entrance

### Special features

- A spacious kitchen with an oversized island, breakfast area and delightful screened porch combine for family enjoyment
- The second floor offers a computer area in addition to the two bedrooms
- Bonus room on the second floor has an additional 271 square feet of living area
- 3 bedrooms, 2 1/2 baths, 2-car side entry garage
- Basement foundation

### Price Code D

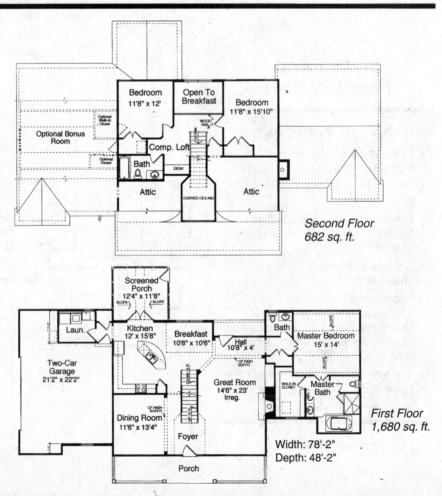

Second Floor
682 sq. ft.

First Floor
1,680 sq. ft.

Width: 78'-2"
Depth: 48'-2"

# Plan #717-056D-0005

© 2003, Garrell Associates, Inc.

## 2,111 total square feet of living area

---

## Open And Airy Grand Room

### Special features

- 9' ceilings throughout the first floor
- Formal dining room has columns separating it from other areas while allowing it to maintain an open feel
- Master bedroom has privacy from other bedrooms
- Bonus room on the second floor has an additional 345 square feet of living area
- 3 bedrooms, 2 baths, 2-car side entry garage
- Basement foundation

### *Price Code H*

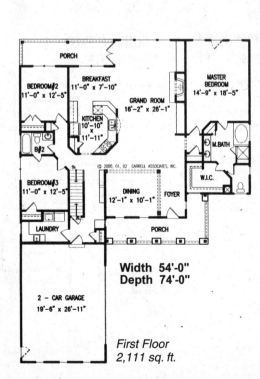

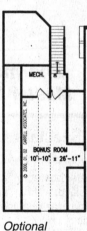

Width 54'-0"
Depth 74'-0"

*First Floor*
2,111 sq. ft.

*Optional Second Floor*

---

**TO ORDER BLUEPRINTS USE THE FORM ON PAGE 15 OR CALL TOLL-FREE 1-877-671-6036**
View thousands more home plans online at www.familyhandyman.com/homeplans

249

**3,556 total square feet of living area**

## Enormous Master Bath

### Special features

- Curved portico welcomes guests
- Master bedroom has a see-through fireplace, wet bar, private bath and sitting area opening to covered patio
- Cozy family room with fireplace has adjacent summer kitchen outdoors on patio
- 4 bedrooms, 3 1/2 baths, 3-car side entry garage
- Slab foundation

**Price Code F**

Width: 85'-0"
Depth: 85'-0"

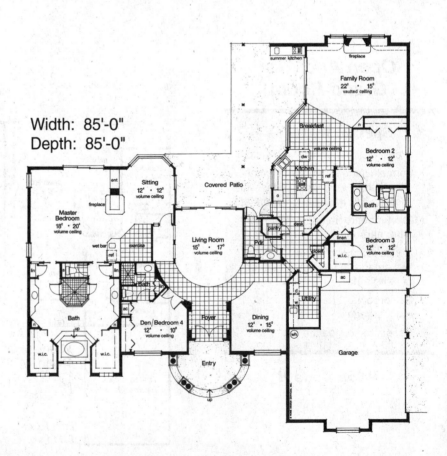

**2,073 total square feet of living area**

## Vaulted Ceilings Enhance This Spacious Home

### Special features

- Family room provides ideal gathering area with a fireplace, large windows and vaulted ceiling
- Private first floor master bedroom enjoys a vaulted ceiling and luxury bath
- Kitchen features an angled bar connecting the kitchen and breakfast area
- 4 bedrooms, 2 1/2 baths, 2-car side entry garage
- Basement foundation

*Price Code D*

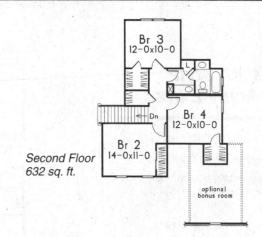

Br 3
12-0x10-0

Br 4
12-0x10-0

Br 2
14-0x11-0

*Second Floor
632 sq. ft.*

optional bonus room

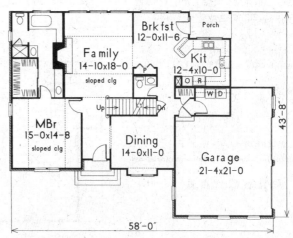

Brkfst
12-0x11-6

Porch

Family
14-10x18-0
sloped clg

Kit
12-4x10-0

MBr
15-0x14-8
sloped clg

Dining
14-0x11-0

Garage
21-4x21-0

43'-8"

58'-0"

*First Floor
1,441 sq. ft.*

**1,342 total square feet of living area**

## Ranch Style With Many Extras

### Special features

- 9' ceilings throughout the home
- Master suite has a tray ceiling and wall of windows that overlook the backyard
- Dining room includes a serving bar connecting it to the kitchen and sliding glass doors that lead outdoors
- Optional second floor has an additional 350 square feet of living area
- 3 bedrooms, 2 baths, 2-car garage
- Slab, walk-out basement or crawl space foundation, please specify when ordering

**Price Code A**

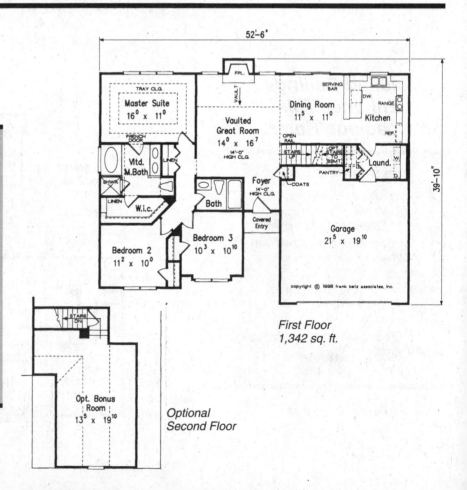

First Floor
1,342 sq. ft.

Optional
Second Floor

**2,307 total square feet of living area**

## Wonderful Open Great Room

### Special features

- The bayed breakfast area warms the home with natural light
- The spacious master bedroom boasts two walk-in closets, private bath and a bonus area ideal for an office or nursery
- The vaulted great room includes a grand fireplace, built-in shelves and a double-door entry onto the covered porch
- 3 bedrooms, 2 1/2 baths, 2-car side entry garage
- Basement, crawl space or slab foundation, please specify when ordering

**Price Code D**

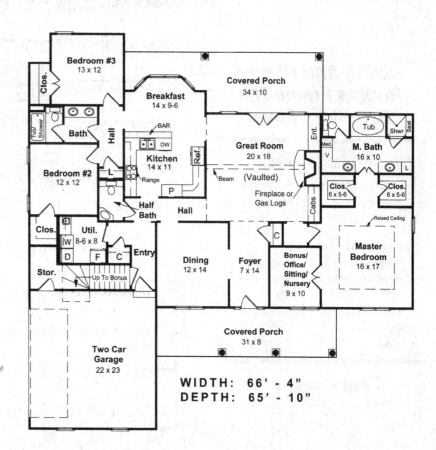

**WIDTH: 66' - 4"**
**DEPTH: 65' - 10"**

**TO ORDER BLUEPRINTS USE THE FORM ON PAGE 15 OR CALL TOLL-FREE 1-877-671-6036**
View thousands more home plans online at www.familyhandyman.com/homeplans

253

**2,733 total square feet of living area**

## Living And Dining Rooms Frame The Two-Story Foyer

### Special features

- 9' ceilings throughout the first floor
- Master bedroom features a double-door entry, large bay window and master bath with walk-in closet and separate tub and shower
- Efficiently designed kitchen adjoins an octagon-shaped breakfast nook, which opens to the outdoors
- 4 bedrooms, 2 1/2 baths, 2-car garage
- Basement foundation

**Price Code F**

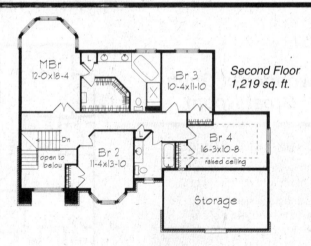

MBr
12-0x18-4

Br 3
10-4x11-10

*Second Floor*
*1,219 sq. ft.*

Dn
open to below

Br 2
11-4x13-10

Br 4
16-3x10-8
raised ceiling

Storage

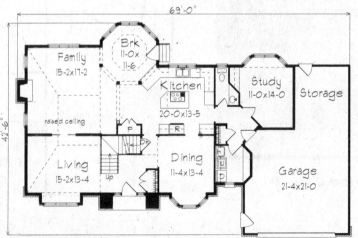

69'-0"

Family
15-2x17-2

Brk
11-0x
11-6

Kitchen
20-0x13-5

Study
11-0x14-0

Storage

42'-6"

raised ceiling

Living
15-2x13-4
up

Dining
11-4x13-4

Garage
21-4x21-0

*First Floor*
*1,514 sq. ft.*

**2,266 total square feet of living area**

## Wrap-Around Porch Creates A Comfortable Feel

### Special features

- Great room includes a fireplace flanked by built-in bookshelves and dining nook with bay window

- Unique media room includes a double-door entrance, walk-in closet and access to a full bath

- Master bedroom has a lovely sitting area and private bath with a walk-in closet, step-up tub and double vanity

- 3 bedrooms, 3 baths, 2-car side entry garage

- Basement foundation, drawings also include crawl space foundation

*Price Code D*

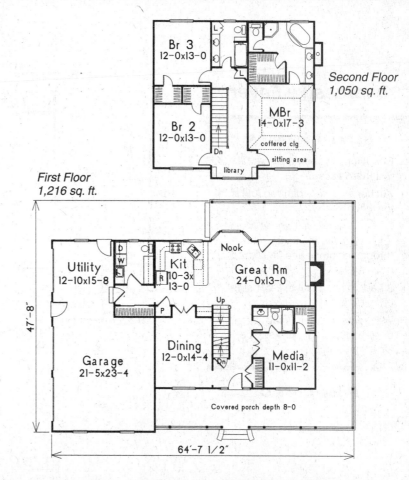

**1,856 total square feet of living area**

## Impressive Foyer

### Special features

- Beautiful covered porch creates a Southern accent
- Kitchen has an organized feel with lots of cabinetry
- Large foyer has a grand entrance and leads into the family room through columns and an arched opening
- 3 bedrooms, 2 baths, 2-car side entry garage
- Walk-out basement, crawl space or slab foundation, please specify when ordering

### Price Code C

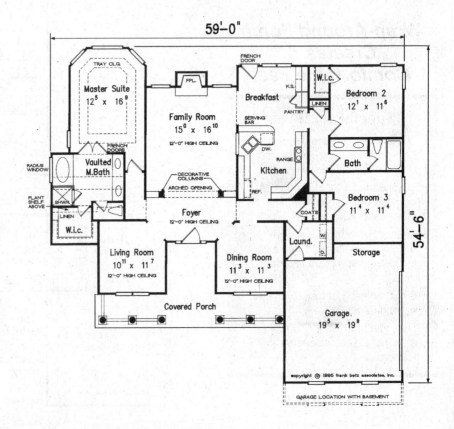

**1,883 total square feet of living area**

## Practical Layout

### Special features

- Large laundry room located off the garage has a coat closet and half bath
- Large family room with fireplace and access to the covered porch is a great central gathering room
- U-shaped kitchen has breakfast bar, large pantry and swing door to dining room for convenient serving
- 3 bedrooms, 2 1/2 baths, 2-car side entry garage
- Basement foundation

*Price Code C*

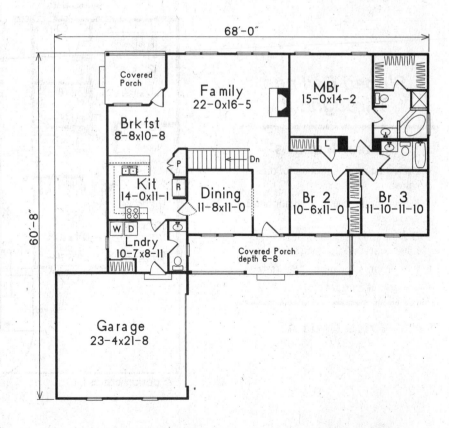

**TO ORDER BLUEPRINTS USE THE FORM ON PAGE 15 OR CALL TOLL-FREE 1-877-671-6036**
View thousands more home plans online at www.familyhandyman.com/homeplans

257

**1,341 total square feet of living area**

## Sloped Ceilings Throughout

### Special features

- Breakfast area is a cheerful dining retreat
- Master bath boasts a whirlpool tub and shower
- U-shaped kitchen is designed to have everything within reach
- 3 bedrooms, 2 baths, 2-car garage
- Basement foundation

### Price Code A

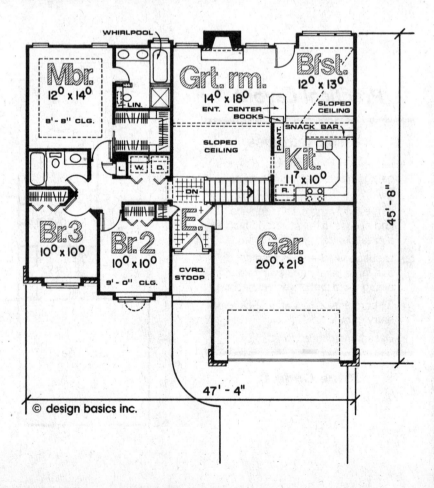

**2,975 total square feet of living area**

## Private Master Suite

### Special features

- Dining room has a 12' ceiling and butler's pantry nearby
- Second floor bedroom has access to a computer center making it an ideal space for a school-aged child or a home office area
- Bonus room has an additional 425 square feet of living area
- 5 bedrooms, 4 baths, 2-car side entry garage
- Crawl space or slab foundation, please specify when ordering

*Price Code E*

*Second Floor*
*445 sq. ft.*

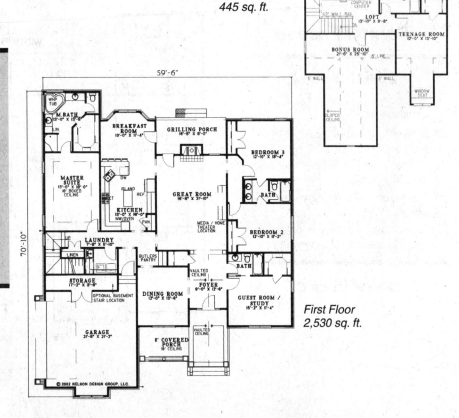

*First Floor*
*2,530 sq. ft.*

**TO ORDER BLUEPRINTS USE THE FORM ON PAGE 15 OR CALL TOLL-FREE 1-877-671-6036**
View thousands more home plans online at www.familyhandyman.com/homeplans

259

**1,890 total square feet of living area**

## Formal Facade

### Special features

- 10' ceilings give this home a spacious feel
- Efficient kitchen has a breakfast bar which overlooks the living room
- Master bedroom has a private bath with walk-in closet
- 3 bedrooms, 2 baths, 2-car side entry garage
- Crawl space foundation, drawings also include slab foundation

### Price Code C

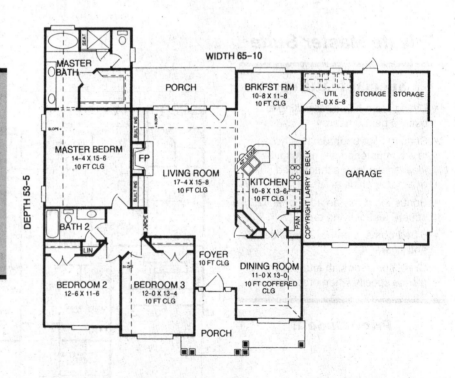

**1,818 total square feet of living area**

## Dormers Accent Country Home

### Special features

- Breakfast room is tucked behind the kitchen and has a laundry closet and deck access
- Living and dining areas share a vaulted ceiling and fireplace
- Master bedroom has two closets, a large double-bowl vanity and a separate tub and shower
- Large front porch wraps around the home
- 4 bedrooms, 2 1/2 baths, 2-car drive under garage
- Basement foundation

*Price Code C*

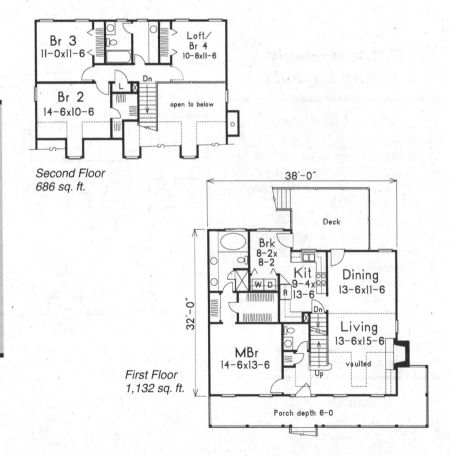

*Second Floor 686 sq. ft.*

*First Floor 1,132 sq. ft.*

**TO ORDER BLUEPRINTS USE THE FORM ON PAGE 15 OR CALL TOLL-FREE 1-877-671-6036**
View thousands more home plans online at www.familyhandyman.com/HOMEPLANS

261

**1,926 total square feet of living area**

## Optimal Family Living Layout

### Special features

- Large covered rear porch is spacious enough for entertaining
- L-shaped kitchen is compact yet efficient and includes a snack bar for extra dining space
- Oversized utility room has counterspace, extra shelves and space for a second refrigerator
- Secluded master suite has a private bath and a large walk-in closet
- 3 bedrooms, 2 baths, 2-car side entry garage
- Slab or crawl space foundation, please specify when ordering

**Price Code C**

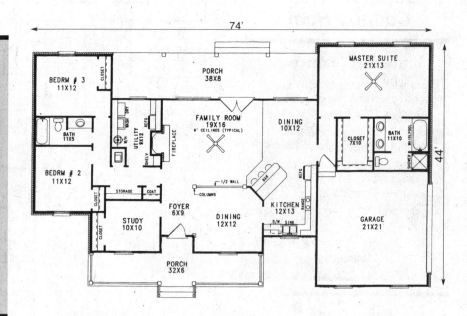

**TO ORDER BLUEPRINTS USE THE FORM ON PAGE 15 OR CALL TOLL-FREE 1-877-671-6036**
View thousands more home plans online at www.familyhandyman.com/homeplans

**2,477 total square feet of living area**

## Bayed Great Room

### Special features

- An arched soffit and decorative columns grace the entrance to the massive great room with fireplace
- The screened porch provides a relaxing atmosphere for outdoor entertaining
- The kitchen opens to the bayed nook and includes a large center island
- 4 bedrooms, 2 1/2 baths, 2-car garage
- Basement foundation

*Price Code E*

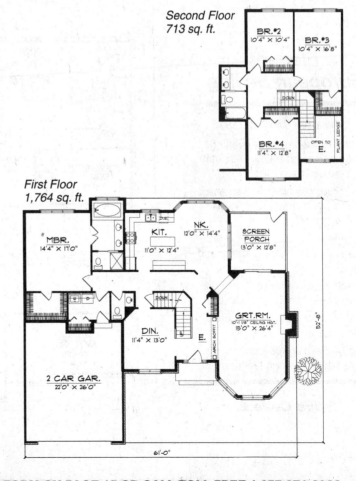

Second Floor
713 sq. ft.

BR. #2
10'4" × 10'4"

BR. #3
10'4" × 16'8"

BR. #4
11'4" × 12'8"

OPEN TO E.
PLANT LEDGE

First Floor
1,764 sq. ft.

MBR.
14'4" × 17'0"

KIT.
11'0" × 12'4"

NK.
12'0" × 14'4"

SCREEN PORCH
13'0" × 12'8"

DIN.
11'4" × 13'0"

GRT.RM.
10'1 1/8" CEILING HGT.
15'0" × 26'4"

2 CAR GAR.
22'0" × 26'0"

52'-8"

61'-0"

**2,600 total square feet of living area**

## Elegant European Styling

### Special features

- Formal entry has large openings to dining and great rooms both with coffered ceilings
- Great room has corner fireplace and atrium doors leading to rear covered porch
- Morning room with rear view and an angled eating bar is sunny and bright
- Exercise room could easily serve as an office or computer room
- 4 bedrooms, 2 1/2 baths, 3-car side entry garage
- Slab or crawl space foundation, please specify when ordering

**Price Code E**

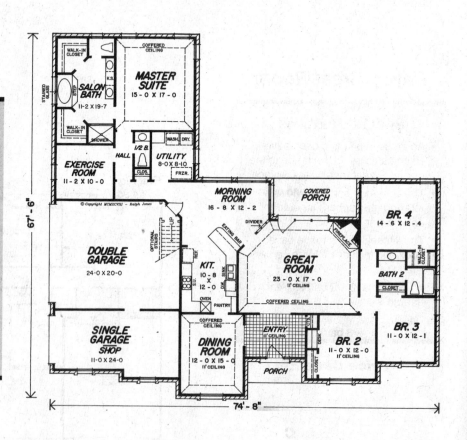

**1,929 total square feet of living area**

## The Plan That Has It All

### Special features

- A classic traditional exterior for timeless elegance
- More than a great room for this size home, the grand room features a vaulted ceiling, brick and wood mantle fireplace and double-doors to rear patio
- State-of-the-art U-shaped kitchen has a built-in pantry, computer desk, breakfast bar and breakfast room with bay window
- The master bedroom includes a vaulted ceiling, large walk-in closet, luxury bath and doors to rear patio
- 4 bedrooms, 3 baths, 3-car side entry garage
- Crawl space foundation, drawings also include slab and basement foundations

**Price Code C**

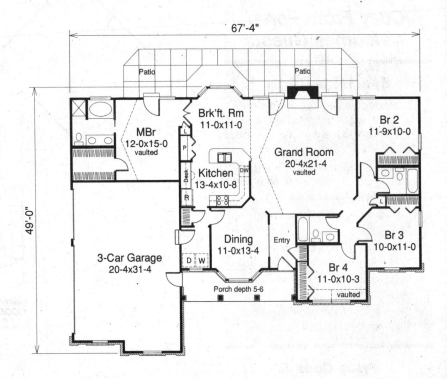

**1,393 total square feet of living area**

## Cozy Front Porch Welcomes Guests

### Special features

- L-shaped kitchen features a walk-in pantry, island cooktop and is convenient to the laundry room and dining area
- Master bedroom features a large walk-in closet and private bath with separate tub and shower
- Convenient storage/coat closet in hall
- View to the patio from the dining area
- 3 bedrooms, 2 baths, 2-car detached garage
- Crawl space foundation, drawings also include slab foundation

**Price Code B**

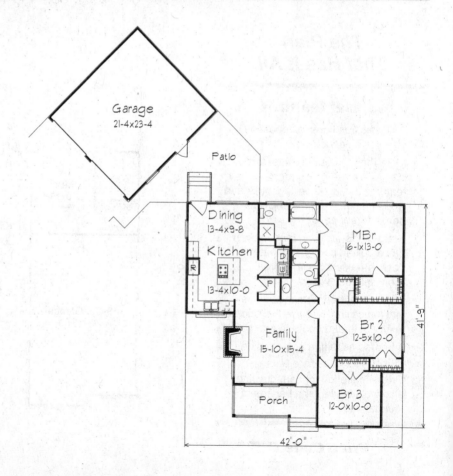

Garage
21-4x23-4

Patio

Dining
13-4x9-8

Kitchen
13-4x10-0

Family
15-10x15-4

Porch

MBr
16-1x13-0

Br 2
12-5x10-0

Br 3
12-0x10-0

41'-9"

42'-0"

**1,937 total square feet of living area**

*Rear View*

## Secluded Master Suite

### Special features

- Upscale great room offers a sloped ceiling, fireplace with extended hearth and built-in shelves for an entertainment center
- Gourmet kitchen includes a cooktop island counter and a quaint morning room
- Master suite features a sloped ceiling, cozy sitting room, walk-in closet and a private bath with whirlpool tub
- 3 bedrooms, 2 baths, 2-car side entry garage
- Crawl space foundation

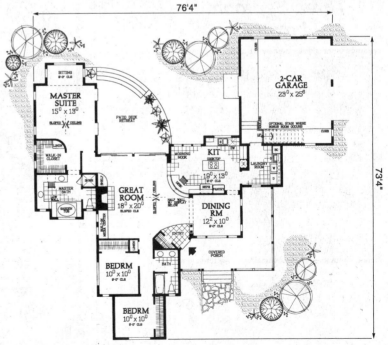

**Price Code C**

TO ORDER BLUEPRINTS USE THE FORM ON PAGE 15 OR CALL TOLL-FREE 1-877-671-6036
View thousands more home plans online at www.familyhandyman.com/homeplans

267

**1,161 total square feet of living area**

## Three Bedroom Luxury

### Special features

- Brickwork and feature window add elegance to home for a narrow lot
- Living room enjoys a vaulted ceiling, fireplace and opens to kitchen
- U-shaped kitchen offers a breakfast area with bay window, snack bar and built-in pantry
- 3 bedrooms, 2 baths
- Basement foundation

**Price Code AA**

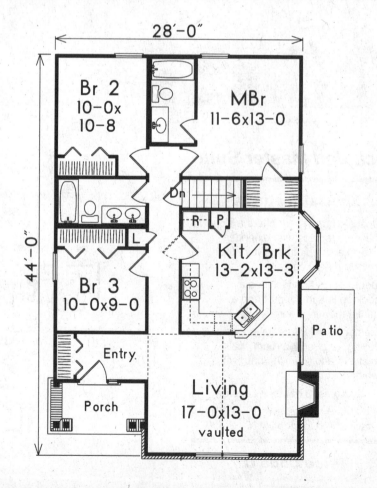

**1,865 total square feet of living area**

## Wonderful Great Room

### Special features

- The large foyer opens into an expansive dining area and great room
- Home features vaulted ceilings throughout
- Master bedroom features an angled entry, vaulted ceiling, plant shelf and bath with double vanity, tub and shower
- 4 bedrooms, 2 baths, 2-car garage
- Slab foundation, drawings also include crawl space foundation

*Price Code D*

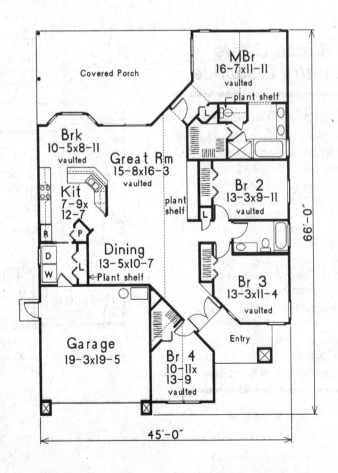

**TO ORDER BLUEPRINTS USE THE FORM ON PAGE 15 OR CALL TOLL-FREE 1-877-671-6036**
View thousands more home plans online at www.familyhandyman.com/homeplans

269

**1,787 total square feet of living area**

## Ranch Offers Country Elegance

### Special features

- Large great room with fireplace and vaulted ceiling features three large skylights and windows galore
- Cooking is sure to be a pleasure in this L-shaped well-appointed kitchen which includes a bayed breakfast area with access to the rear deck
- Every bedroom offers a spacious walk-in closet with a convenient laundry room just steps away
- 415 square feet of optional living area available on the lower level
- 3 bedrooms, 2 baths, 2-car drive under garage
- Walk-out basement foundation

*Price Code B*

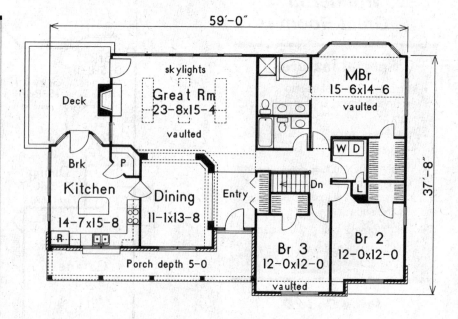

**2,076 total square feet of living area**

## Great Room Forms Core Of This Home

### Special features

- Vaulted great room has a fireplace flanked by windows and skylights that welcome the sun
- Kitchen leads to the vaulted breakfast room and rear deck
- Study located off the foyer provides a great location for a home office
- Large bay windows grace the master bedroom and bath
- 3 bedrooms, 2 baths, 2-car garage
- Basement foundation

*Price Code C*

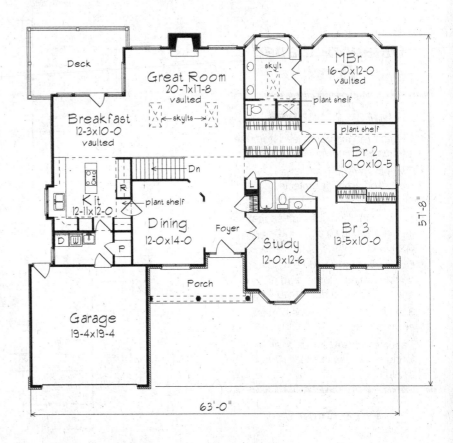

**TO ORDER BLUEPRINTS USE THE FORM ON PAGE 15 OR CALL TOLL-FREE 1-877-671-6036**
View thousands more home plans online at www.familyhandyman.com/homeplans

271

**2,044 total square feet of living area**

## Octagon-Shaped Porch

### Special features

- Elegant French doors lead from the kitchen to the formal dining room
- Two-car garage features a workshop area for projects or extra storage
- Second floor includes loft space ideal for an office area and a handy computer center
- Colossal master bedroom boasts double walk-in closets and a private bath with bay window seat
- 3 bedrooms, 2 1/2 baths, 2-car side entry garage
- Basement, crawl space or slab foundation, please specify when ordering

**Price Code C**

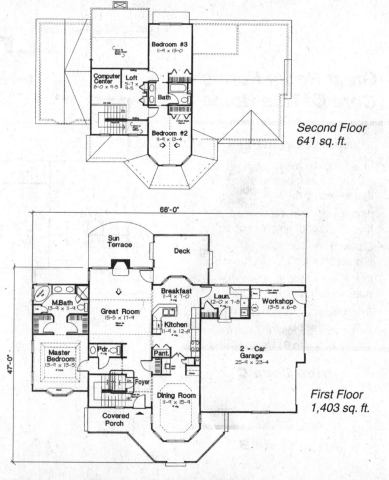

*Second Floor 641 sq. ft.*

*First Floor 1,403 sq. ft.*

**TO ORDER BLUEPRINTS USE THE FORM ON PAGE 15 OR CALL TOLL-FREE 1-877-671-6036**
View thousands more home plans online at www.familyhandyman.com/homeplans

**1,684 total square feet of living area**

*Rear View*

## A Special Home For Views

### Special features

- Delightful wrap-around porch is anchored by a full masonry fireplace
- The vaulted great room includes a large bay window, fireplace, dining balcony and atrium window wall
- Double walk-in closets, large luxury bath and sliding doors to exterior balcony are a few fantastic features of the master bedroom
- Atrium opens to 611 square feet of optional living area
- 3 bedrooms, 2 baths, 2-car drive under garage
- Walk-out basement foundation

***Price Code B***

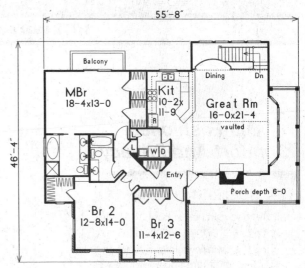

55'-8"

46'-4"

Balcony

MBr
18-4x13-0

Kit
10-2x
11-9

Dining    Dn

Great Rm
16-0x21-4
vaulted

Entry

Porch depth 6-0

Br 2
12-8x14-0

Br 3
11-4x12-6

*First Floor*
*1,684 sq. ft.*

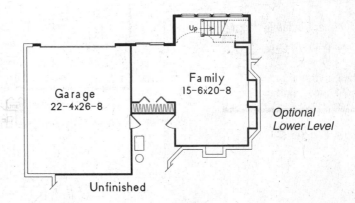

Up

Garage
22-4x26-8

Family
15-6x20-8

*Optional*
*Lower Level*

Unfinished

**1,772 total square feet of living area**

## Old-Fashioned Comfort And Privacy

### Special features

- Extended porches in front and rear provide a charming touch
- Large bay windows lend distinction to the dining room and bedroom #3
- Efficient U-shaped kitchen
- Master bedroom includes two walk-in closets
- Full corner fireplace in family room
- 3 bedrooms, 2 baths, 2-car detached garage
- Slab foundation, drawings also include crawl space foundation

*Price Code C*

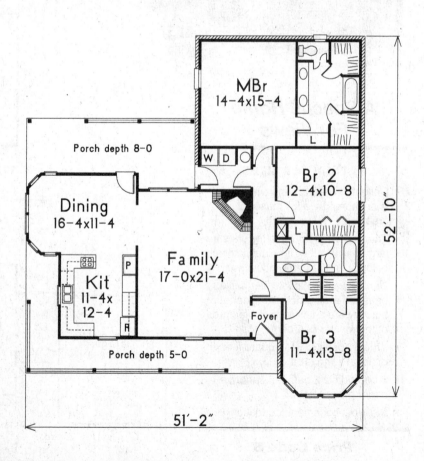

MBr 14-4x15-4
Porch depth 8-0
Dining 16-4x11-4
Br 2 12-4x10-8
Family 17-0x21-4
Kit 11-4x 12-4
P
R
Foyer
Br 3 11-4x13-8
Porch depth 5-0
52'-10"
51'-2"

**2,357 total square feet of living area**

## Attractive Entry Created By Full-Length Porch

### Special features

- 9' ceilings on the first floor
- Secluded master bedroom includes a private bath with double walk-in closets and vanity
- Balcony overlooks living room with large fireplace
- The future game room on the second floor has an additional 303 square feet of living area
- 4 bedrooms, 3 1/2 baths, 2-car side entry garage
- Slab foundation, drawings also include crawl space foundation

**Price Code D**

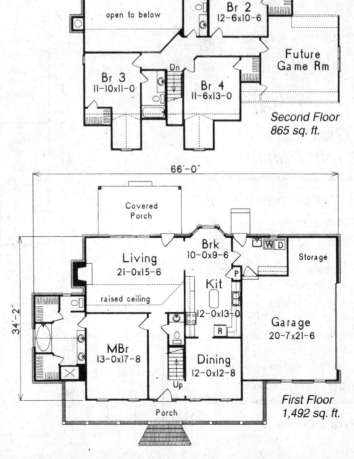

open to below

Br 2
12-6x10-6

Br 3
11-10x11-0

Dn

Br 4
11-6x13-0

Future Game Rm

*Second Floor*
*865 sq. ft.*

66'-0"

Covered Porch

34'-2"

Living
21-0x15-6

raised ceiling

Brk
10-0x9-6

W D

Storage

Kit
12-0x13-0

P

MBr
13-0x17-8

Dining
12-0x12-8

R

Garage
20-7x21-6

Up

Porch

*First Floor*
*1,492 sq. ft.*

**TO ORDER BLUEPRINTS USE THE FORM ON PAGE 15 OR CALL TOLL-FREE 1-877-671-6036**
View thousands more home plans online at www.familyhandyman.com/homeplans

275

**2,218 total square feet of living area**

**Rear View**

## Gracious Atrium Ranch

### Special features

- Great room has an arched colonnade entry and bay windowed atrium
- Kitchen has pass-through breakfast bar and walk-in pantry
- Breakfast room offers bay window and snack bar open to kitchen
- Atrium opens to 1,217 square feet of optional living area below
- 4 bedrooms, 2 baths, 2-car garage
- Walk-out basement foundation

### Price Code D

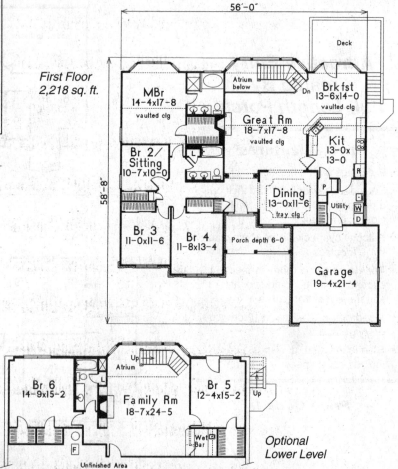

*First Floor*
*2,218 sq. ft.*

56'-0"

58'-8"

Deck

MBr
14-4x17-8
vaulted clg

Atrium
below

Dn

Brk fst
13-6x14-0
vaulted clg

Great Rm
18-7x17-8
vaulted clg

Kit
13-0x
13-0

Br 2/
Sitting
10-7x10-0

Dining
13-0x11-6
tray clg

Utility

Br 3
11-0x11-6

Br 4
11-8x13-4

Porch depth 6-0

Garage
19-4x21-4

Br 6
14-9x15-2

Up
Atrium

Family Rm
18-7x24-5

Br 5
12-4x15-2

Up

Wet Bar

Unfinished Area

*Optional Lower Level*

**276**

**TO ORDER BLUEPRINTS USE THE FORM ON PAGE 15 OR CALL TOLL-FREE 1-877-671-6036**
View thousands more home plans online at www.familyhandyman.com/homeplans

**2,605 total square feet of living area**

## Distinctive Two-Level Porch

### Special features

- Master bedroom boasts a vaulted ceiling and transom picture window which lights sitting area
- Country kitchen features appliances set in between brick dividers and a beamed ceiling
- Living room features built-in bookcases, fireplace and a raised tray ceiling
- 4 bedrooms, 2 1/2 baths, 2-car side entry garage
- Slab foundation, drawings also include crawl space and basement foundations

### *Price Code E*

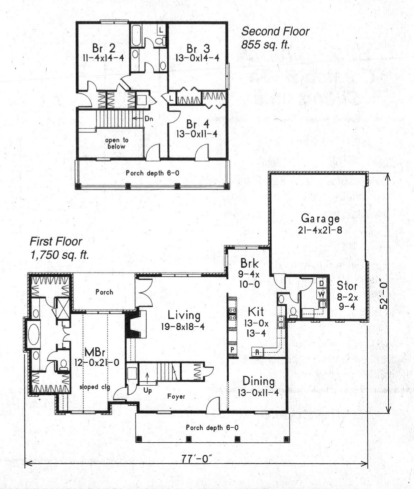

Second Floor
855 sq. ft.

Br 2
11-4x14-4

Br 3
13-0x14-4

Br 4
13-0x11-4

open to below

Dn

Porch depth 6-0

First Floor
1,750 sq. ft.

Garage
21-4x21-8

Brk
9-4x
10-0

Stor
8-2x
9-4

Porch

Living
19-8x18-4

Kit
13-0x
13-4

MBr
12-0x21-0

sloped clg

Up

Foyer

Dining
13-0x11-4

52'-0"

Porch depth 6-0

77'-0"

**TO ORDER BLUEPRINTS USE THE FORM ON PAGE 15 OR CALL TOLL-FREE 1-877-671-6036**
View thousands more home plans online at www.familyhandyman.com/homeplans

277

**2,246 total square feet of living area**

## Striking Turret Created By The Sitting Area

### Special features

- Two-story foyer is impressive
- Master suite has a sitting area with bay window
- Breakfast area is near the kitchen
- Bedroom #4 easily converts to an office
- Optional bonus room has an additional 269 square feet of living area
- 4 bedrooms, 3 baths, 2-car side entry garage
- Walk-out basement, slab or crawl space foundation, please specify when ordering

**Price Code D**

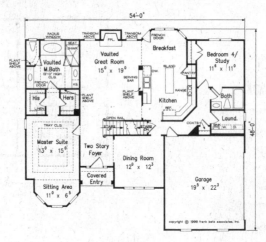

First Floor
1,688 sq. ft.

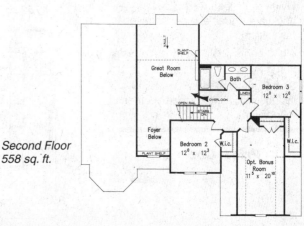

Second Floor
558 sq. ft.

278

**TO ORDER BLUEPRINTS USE THE FORM ON PAGE 15 OR CALL TOLL-FREE 1-877-671-6036**
View thousands more home plans online at www.familyhandyman.com/homeplans

**3,199 total square feet of living area**

*Rear View*

## Double Atrium Embraces The Sun

### Special features

- Kitchen features bay-shaped cabinetry built over an atrium overlooking two-story window wall
- A second atrium dominates the master bedroom that boasts a sitting area and a luxurious bath that has a whirlpool tub open to a garden and lower level study
- 3 bedrooms, 2 1/2 baths, 3-car side entry garage
- Walk-out basement foundation

*Price Code E*

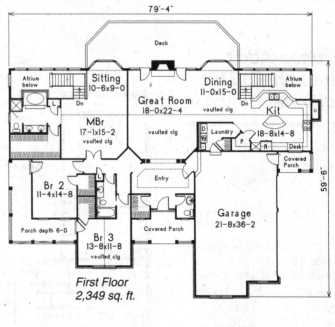

*First Floor*
*2,349 sq. ft.*

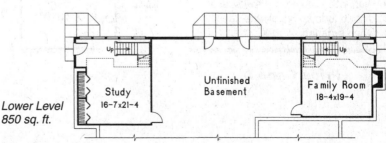

*Lower Level*
*850 sq. ft.*

**TO ORDER BLUEPRINTS USE THE FORM ON PAGE 15 OR CALL TOLL-FREE 1-877-671-6036**
View thousands more home plans online at www.familyhandyman.com/homeplans

279

2,350 total square feet of living area

## Stucco Adds Excitement To This Traditional Ranch

### Special features

- Luxurious master suite enjoys a large bath and an enormous walk-in closet
- Built-in hutch in breakfast room is eye-catching
- The terrific study is located in its own private hall and includes a half bath, two closets and a bookcase
- 3 bedrooms, 2 1/2 baths, 2-car side entry garage
- Walk-out basement, crawl space or slab foundation, please specify when ordering

**Price Code D**

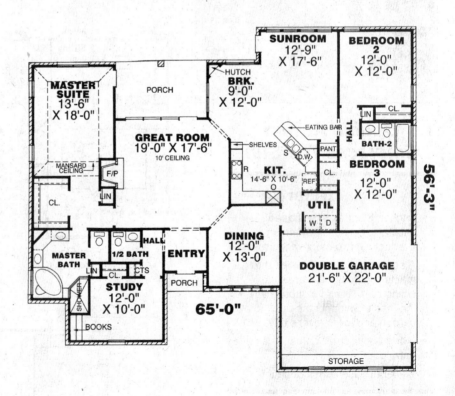

280

**TO ORDER BLUEPRINTS USE THE FORM ON PAGE 15 OR CALL TOLL-FREE 1-877-671-6036**
View thousands more home plans online at www.familyhandyman.com/homeplans

**1,791 total square feet of living area**

## Classic Exterior Employs Innovative Planning

### Special features

- Vaulted great room and octagon-shaped dining area enjoy the view of the covered patio
- Kitchen features a pass-through to dining area, center island, large walk-in pantry and breakfast room with large bay window
- Master bedroom is vaulted with sitting area
- 4 bedrooms, 2 baths, 2-car garage with storage
- Basement foundation, drawings also include crawl space and slab foundations

*Price Code C*

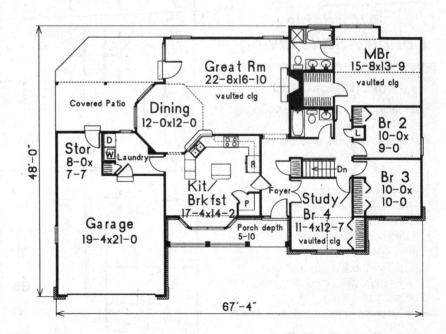

Covered Patio

Great Rm
22-8x16-10
vaulted clg

MBr
15-8x13-9
vaulted clg

Dining
12-0x12-0

Stor
8-0x
7-7

Laundry

D W

Kit/
Brk fst
17-4x14-2

Foyer

Br 2
10-0x
9-0

Dn

Br 3
10-0x
10-0

Garage
19-4x21-0

Porch depth
5-10

Study
Br 4
11-4x12-7
vaulted clg

48'-0"

67'-4"

**TO ORDER BLUEPRINTS USE THE FORM ON PAGE 15 OR CALL TOLL-FREE 1-877-671-6036**
View thousands more home plans online at www.familyhandyman.com/homeplans

281

**1,945 total square feet of living area**

## Affordable Country-Style Living

### Special features

- Great room has a stepped ceiling and a fireplace
- Bayed dining area enjoys a stepped ceiling and French door leading to a covered porch
- Master bedroom has a tray ceiling, bay window and large walk-in closet
- 3 bedrooms, 2 1/2 baths, 2-car side entry garage
- Basement, crawl space or slab foundation, please specify when ordering

### *Price Code D*

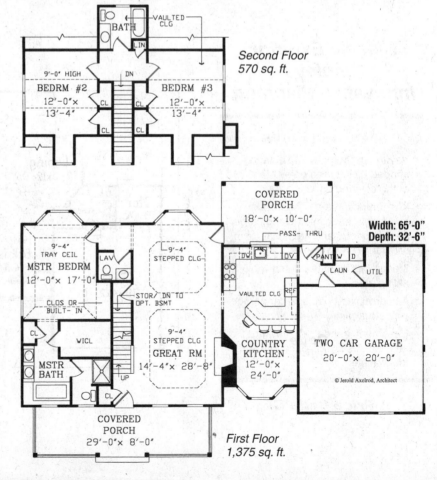

*Second Floor 570 sq. ft.*

BATH — VAULTED CLG
LIN
9'-0" HIGH  DN
BEDRM #2 12'-0" x 13'-4"  CL  CL  BEDRM #3 12'-0" x 13'-4"

Width: 65'-0"
Depth: 32'-6"

COVERED PORCH 18'-0" x 10'-0"
PASS-THRU

9'-4" TRAY CEIL
MSTR BEDRM 12'-0" x 17'-0"
LAV
9'-4" STEPPED CLG
DW
DV  PANT  W  D
LAUN  UTIL
VAULTED CLG  REF

CLOS OR BUILT-IN
STOR/ DN TO OPT. BSMT
9'-4" STEPPED CLG
GREAT RM 14'-4" x 28'-8"
COUNTRY KITCHEN 12'-0" x 24'-0"
TWO CAR GARAGE 20'-0" x 20'-0"
© Jerold Axelrod, Architect

CL  WICL
MSTR BATH
UP
CL

COVERED PORCH 29'-0" x 8'-0"

*First Floor 1,375 sq. ft.*

**2,586 total square feet of living area**

## Striking Great Room

### Special features

- Great room has an impressive tray ceiling and see-through fireplace into the bayed breakfast room
- Master bedroom has a walk-in closet and private bath
- 4 bedrooms, 3 baths, 2-car side entry garage
- Basement foundation, drawings also include crawl space and slab foundations

### Price Code D

WIDTH 64'-10"

DEPTH 61'-0"

*First Floor*
*2,028 sq. ft.*

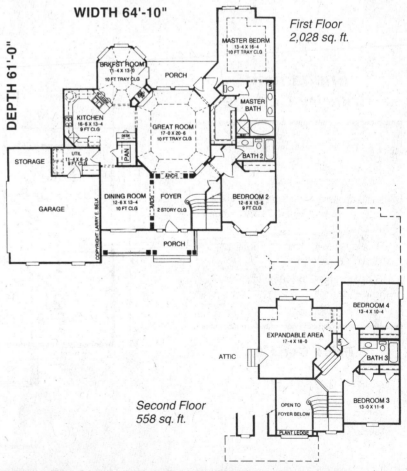

MASTER BEDRM
13-4 X 16-4
10 FT TRAY CLG

PORCH

BRKFST ROOM
11-4 X 13-0
10 FT TRAY CLG

MASTER BATH

KITCHEN
16-6 X 13-4
9 FT CLG

GREAT ROOM
17-0 X 20-6
10 FT TRAY CLG

BATH 2

STORAGE

UTIL
11-4 X 8-0
9 FT CLG

PAN

DESK

GARAGE

COPYRIGHT LARRY E. BELK

DINING ROOM
12-6 X 13-4
10 FT CLG

FOYER
2 STORY CLG

BEDROOM 2
12-6 X 13-6
9 FT CLG

ARCH

PORCH

BEDROOM 4
13-4 X 10-4

EXPANDABLE AREA
17-4 X 18-0

BATH 3

ATTIC

OPEN TO FOYER BELOW

BEDROOM 3
13-0 X 11-6

PLANT LEDGE

*Second Floor*
*558 sq. ft.*

**TO ORDER BLUEPRINTS USE THE FORM ON PAGE 15 OR CALL TOLL-FREE 1-877-671-6036**
View thousands more home plans online at www.familyhandyman.com/homeplans

283

# Plan #717-007D-0030

**1,140 total square feet of living area**

## Enchanting Country Cottage

### Special features

- Open and spacious living and dining areas for family gatherings
- Well-organized kitchen with an abundance of cabinetry and a built-in pantry
- Roomy master bath features a double-bowl vanity
- 3 bedrooms, 2 baths, 2-car drive under garage
- Basement foundation

### *Price Code AA*

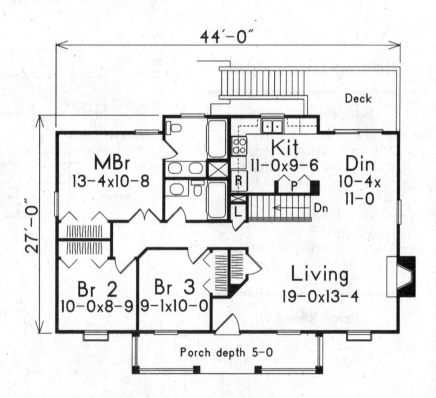

**1,992 total square feet of living area**

## Triple Dormers Create Terrific Curb Appeal

### Special features

- Interesting angled walls add drama to many of the living areas including the family room, master bedroom and breakfast area

- Covered porch includes a spa and the outdoor kitchen with sink, refrigerator and cooktop

- Enter the majestic master bath to find a dramatic corner oversized tub

- 4 bedrooms, 3 baths, 2-car side entry garage

- Basement, crawl space or slab foundation, please specify when ordering

**Price Code C**

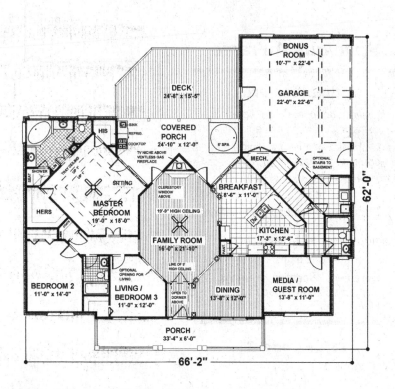

**TO ORDER BLUEPRINTS USE THE FORM ON PAGE 15 OR CALL TOLL-FREE 1-877-671-6036**
View thousands more home plans online at www.familyhandyman.com/homeplans

285

**1,769 total square feet of living area**

## Spacious A-Frame

### Special features

- Living room boasts an elegant cathedral ceiling and fireplace
- U-shaped kitchen and dining area combine for easy living
- Secondary bedrooms include double closets
- Secluded master bedroom features a sloped ceiling, large walk-in closet and private bath
- 3 bedrooms, 2 baths
- Basement foundation, drawings also include crawl space and slab foundations

### Price Code B

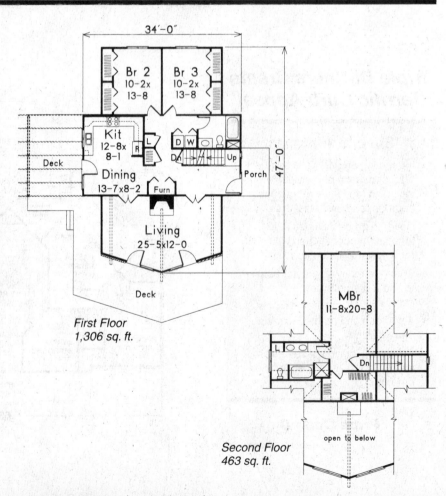

**First Floor**
**1,306 sq. ft.**

**Second Floor**
**463 sq. ft.**

**2,531 total square feet of living area**

*Rear View*

## Traditional Exterior Boasts Exciting Interior

### Special features

- Porch with dormers leads into vaulted atrium great room
- Well-designed kitchen and breakfast bar adjoin an extra-large laundry/mud room
- Double sinks, tub with window and plant shelf complete master bath
- 4 bedrooms, 2 1/2 baths, 2-car side entry garage
- Walk-out basement foundation

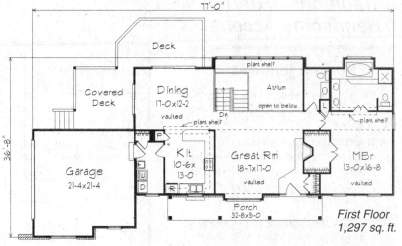

First Floor 1,297 sq. ft.

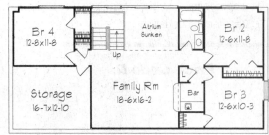

Lower Level 1,234 sq. ft.

*Price Code D*

# Plan #717-001D-0013

**1,882 total square feet of living area**

## Traditional Exterior, Handsome Accents

### Special features

- Wide, handsome entrance opens to the vaulted great room with fireplace
- Living and dining areas are conveniently joined but still allow privacy
- Private covered porch extends breakfast area
- Practical passageway runs through the laundry room from the garage to the kitchen
- Vaulted ceiling in master bedroom
- 3 bedrooms, 2 baths, 2-car garage
- Basement foundation

**Price Code D**

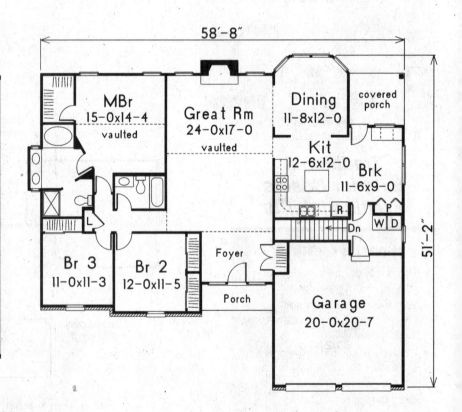

**2,665 total square feet of living area**

## Distinctive Facade

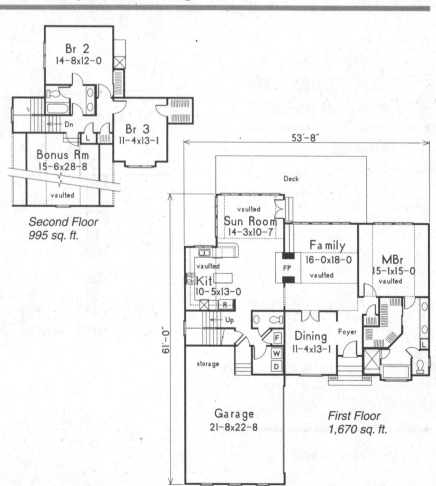

Br 2
14-8x12-0

Br 3
11-4x13-1

Bonus Rm
15-6x28-8
vaulted

*Second Floor*
*995 sq. ft.*

53'-8"

Deck

vaulted
Sun Room
14-3x10-7

Family
16-0x18-0
vaulted

MBr
15-1x15-0
vaulted

FP

vaulted
Kit
10-5x13-0

61'-0"

Up

Dining
11-4x13-1

Foyer

storage

F
W D

Garage
21-8x22-8

*First Floor*
*1,670 sq. ft.*

**TO ORDER BLUEPRINTS USE THE FORM ON PAGE 15 OR CALL TOLL-FREE 1-877-671-6036**
View thousands more home plans online at www.familyhandyman.com/homeplans

289

1,400 total square feet of living area

## Classic Ranch Has Grand Appeal With Expansive Porch

### Special features

- Master bedroom is secluded for privacy
- Large utility room has additional cabinet space
- Covered porch provides an outdoor seating area
- Roof dormers add great curb appeal
- Living room and master bedroom feature vaulted ceilings
- Oversized two-car garage has storage space
- 3 bedrooms, 2 baths, 2-car garage
- Basement foundation, drawings also include crawl space foundation

*Price Code B*

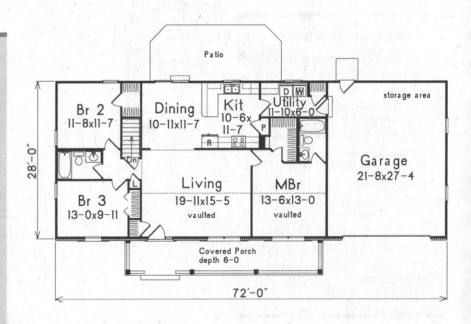

**1,170 total square feet of living area**

## Brick And Siding Enhance This Traditional Home

### Special features

- Master bedroom enjoys privacy at the rear of this home
- Kitchen has an angled bar that overlooks the great room and breakfast area
- Living areas combine to create a greater sense of spaciousness
- Great room has a cozy fireplace
- 3 bedrooms, 2 baths, 2-car garage
- Slab foundation

*Price Code AA*

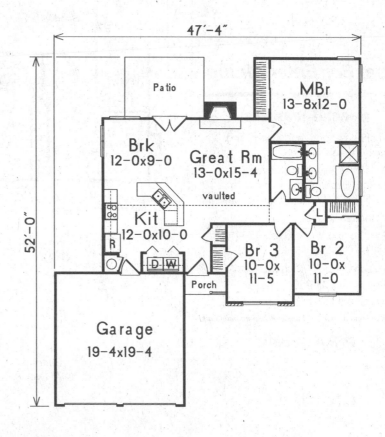

**1,870 total square feet of living area**

## Ideal For Entertaining

### Special features

- Kitchen is open to the living and dining areas
- Breakfast area has cathedral ceiling creating a sunroom effect
- Master bedroom is spacious with all the amenities
- Second floor bedrooms share hall bath
- 3 bedrooms, 2 1/2 baths, 2-car drive under garage
- Basement foundation

### Price Code C

First Floor
1,159 sq. ft.

Sundeck
16-0 x 12-0

Brkfst.
10-6 x 7-6

Kit.
10-6 x 10-0

Dining
10-10 x 8-10

Lav.

M.Bath

Living Area
20-6 x 13-6

Master Bedroom
17-6 x 14-6

Entry

44-4

38-0

6-0

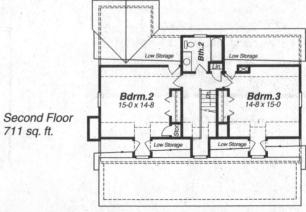

Bth.2

Low Storage    Low Storage

Bdrm.2
15-0 x 14-8

Bdrm.3
14-8 x 15-0

Low Storage    Low Storage

Second Floor
711 sq. ft.

**3,169 total square feet of living area**

## Grand-Scale Elegance

### Special features

- Formal areas include an enormous entry with handcrafted stairway and powder room, French doors to living room and open dining area with tray ceiling
- Informal areas consist of a large family room with bay window, fireplace, walk-in wet bar and kitchen open to breakfast room
- Stylish master bedroom is located on the second floor for privacy
- Front secondary bedroom includes a private study
- 4 bedrooms, 2 1/2 baths, 3-car side entry garage
- Basement foundation

**Price Code F**

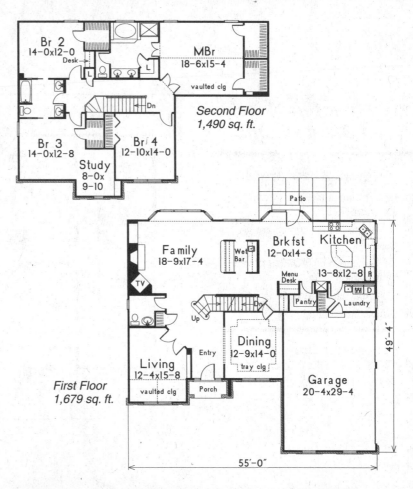

Second Floor
1,490 sq. ft.

First Floor
1,679 sq. ft.

**TO ORDER BLUEPRINTS USE THE FORM ON PAGE 15 OR CALL TOLL-FREE 1-877-671-6036**
View thousands more home plans online at www.familyhandyman.com/homeplans

293

**1,642 total square feet of living area**

## Corner Fireplace In Great Room

### Special features

- Built-in cabinet in dining room adds a custom feel
- Secondary bedrooms share an oversized bath
- Master bedroom includes private bath with dressing table
- 3 bedrooms, 2 baths, 2-car garage
- Crawl space foundation

**Price Code B**

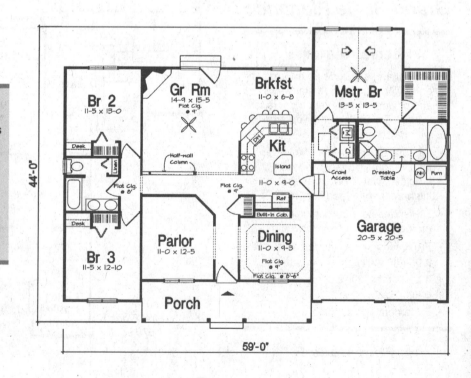

**2,416 total square feet of living area**

## Lots Of Charm Inside And Out

### Special features

- Octagon-shaped formal dining room makes an impact on the exterior of this home
- Angled walls add interest to the floor plan throughout this home
- Future playroom on the second floor has an additional 207 square feet of living area
- 4 bedrooms, 2 1/2 baths, 2-car side entry garage
- Slab foundation

*Price Code D*

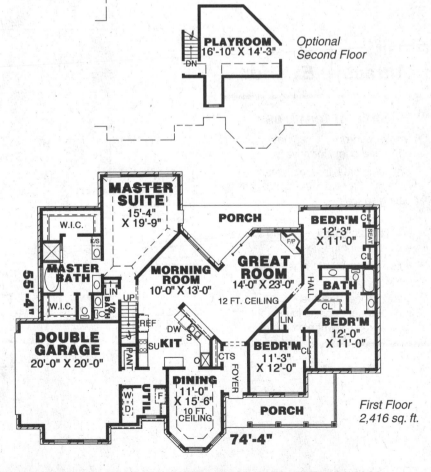

PLAYROOM
16'-10" X 14'-3"

*Optional Second Floor*

MASTER SUITE
15'-4" X 19'-9"

PORCH

BEDR'M
12'-3" X 11'-0"

W.I.C.

MASTER BATH

W.I.C.

MORNING ROOM
10'-0" X 13'-0"

GREAT ROOM
14'-0" X 23'-0"

12 FT. CEILING

BATH

BEDR'M
12'-0" X 11'-0"

55'-4"

DOUBLE GARAGE
20'-0" X 20'-0"

REF

KIT

BEDR'M
11'-3" X 12'-0"

FOYER

DINING
11'-0" X 15'-6"
10 FT. CEILING

PORCH

74'-4"

*First Floor 2,416 sq. ft.*

**TO ORDER BLUEPRINTS USE THE FORM ON PAGE 15 OR CALL TOLL-FREE 1-877-671-6036**
View thousands more home plans online at www.familyhandyman.com/homeplans

295

**2,107 total square feet of living area**

## Attractive Exterior

### Special features

- Master bedroom is separate from other bedrooms for privacy
- Spacious breakfast room and kitchen include center island with eating space
- Centralized great room has fireplace and easy access to any area in the home
- 4 bedrooms, 2 1/2 baths, 2-car garage
- Crawl space, basement, walk-out basement or slab foundation, please specify when ordering

**Price Code C**

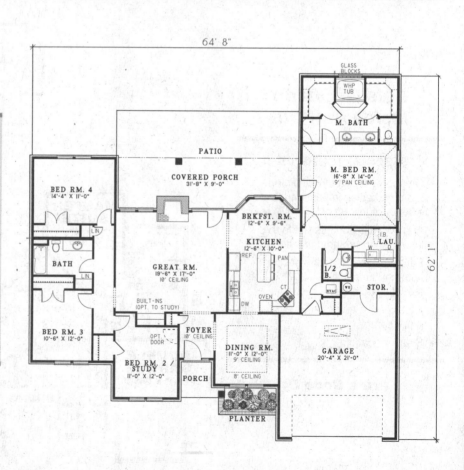

**296**

**TO ORDER BLUEPRINTS USE THE FORM ON PAGE 15 OR CALL TOLL-FREE 1-877-671-6036**
View thousands more home plans online at www.familyhandyman.com/homeplans

**3,171 total square feet of living area**

## Outdoor Covered Deck Warmed By Fireplace

### Special features

- An enormous walk-in closet is located in the master bath and dressing area

- The great room, breakfast area and kitchen combine with 12' ceilings to create an open feel

- The optional lower level has an additional 1,897 square feet of living area and is designed for entertaining featuring a wet bar with seating, a billiards room, large media room, two bedrooms and a full bath

- 3 bedrooms, 2 1/2 baths, 3-car side entry garage

- Walk-out basement foundation

### *Price Code E*

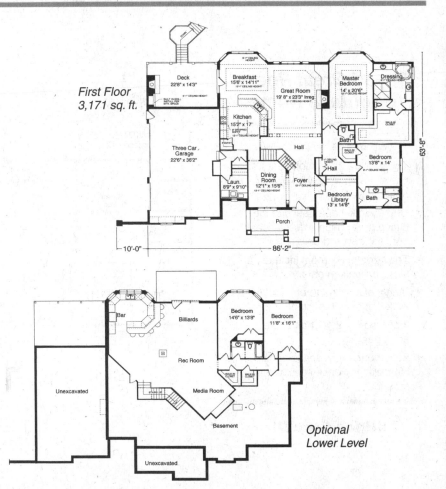

First Floor
3,171 sq. ft.

Optional
Lower Level

**TO ORDER BLUEPRINTS USE THE FORM ON PAGE 15 OR CALL TOLL-FREE 1-877-671-6036**
View thousands more home plans online at www.familyhandyman.com/homeplans

297

**1,896 total square feet of living area**

## Bayed Great Room Brightens Home

### Special features

- The vaulted great room features a grand fireplace flanked by built-in bookshelves

- U-shaped kitchen opens to the dining area which enjoys access onto the covered porch

- The large utility room includes a sink and walk-in pantry

- Plenty of storage throughout with a walk-in closet in each bedroom

- 3 bedrooms, 2 1/2 baths, 2-car side entry garage

- Basement, crawl space or slab foundation, please specify when ordering

*Price Code D*

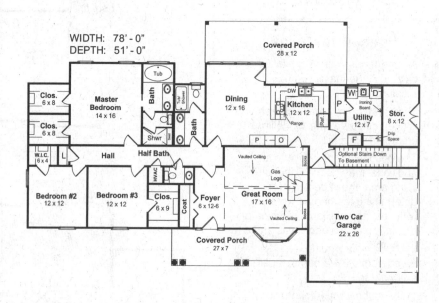

WIDTH: 78' - 0"
DEPTH: 51' - 0"

Covered Porch 28 x 12

Clos. 6 x 8
Clos. 6 x 8

Master Bedroom 14 x 16

Tub
Bath

Dining 12 x 16

DW
Kitchen 12 x 12
Range
Ref.

W D
Ironing Board
P
Utility 12 x 7
Stor. 8 x 12
Drip Space

W.I.C. 6 x 4
Hall
Half Bath
Bath
Tub/Shower
Seat
Shwr

P O
Vaulted Ceiling
Books
F

Optional Stairs Down To Basement

Bedroom #2 12 x 12
Bedroom #3 12 x 12
HVAC
Clos. 6 x 9
Coat
Foyer 6 x 12-6

Gas Logs
Great Room 17 x 16
Books

Two Car Garage 22 x 26

Vaulted Ceiling

Covered Porch 27 x 7

**2,716 total square feet of living area**

## Amenity-Full Master Bath

### Special features

- Master suite has lots of privacy from other bedrooms
- 10' ceiling in the formal dining room makes an impression
- Bonus room on the second floor has an additional 438 square feet of living area
- 4 bedrooms, 4 baths, 2-car side entry garage
- Crawl space or slab foundation, please specify when ordering

### Price Code E

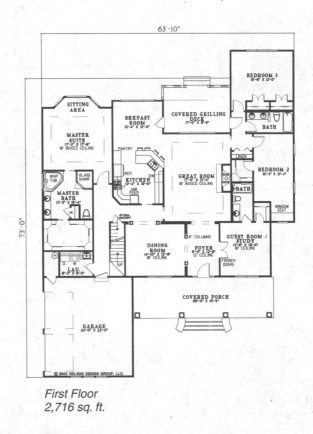

*First Floor*
*2,716 sq. ft.*

*Optional Second Floor*

**TO ORDER BLUEPRINTS USE THE FORM ON PAGE 15 OR CALL TOLL-FREE 1-877-671-6036**
View thousands more home plans online at www.familyhandyman.com/homeplans

299

**3,814 total square feet of living area**

Rear View

## Ultimate Atrium For A Sloping Lot

### Special features

- Great room with vaulted ceiling includes exciting balcony overlook of towering atrium window wall

- Breakfast bar adjoins open "California" kitchen

- Seven vaulted rooms for drama and four fireplaces for warmth

- Master bath is complemented by colonnade and fireplace

- 3 bedrooms, 2 1/2 baths, 3-car side entry garage

- Walk-out basement foundation

- 3,566 square feet on the first floor and 248 square feet on the lower level atrium

**Price Code G**

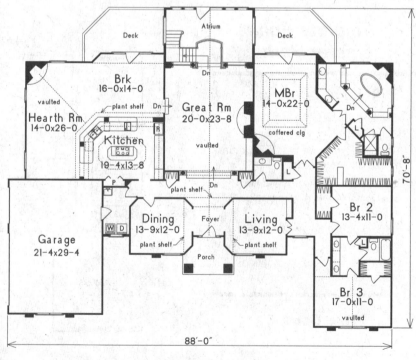

300

**TO ORDER BLUEPRINTS USE THE FORM ON PAGE 15 OR CALL TOLL-FREE 1-877-671-6036**
View thousands more home plans online at www.familyhandyman.com/homeplans

300

**4,380 total square feet of living area**

## Lower Level Designed Perfectly For An In-Law Suite

### Special features

- 11' ceilings on the first floor and 9' ceilings on the second floor
- Intricate porch details display one-of-a-kind craftsmanship
- Impressive foyer has a curved staircase creating a grand entry
- Second floor bedroom accesses private balcony for easy outdoor relaxation
- Optional lower level has an additional 1,275 square feet of living area
- 4 bedrooms, 3 1/2 baths, 3-car drive under garage
- Walk-out basement foundation

**Price Code H**

First Floor
2,974 sq. ft.

Width: 57'-0"
Depth: 72'-0"

Second Floor
1,406 sq. ft.

Optional Lower Level

**TO ORDER BLUEPRINTS USE THE FORM ON PAGE 15 OR CALL TOLL-FREE 1-877-671-6036**
View thousands more home plans online at www.familyhandyman.com/homeplans

301

**1,785 total square feet of living area**

## Traditional Southern-Style Home

### Special features

- 9' ceilings throughout home
- Luxurious master bath includes a whirlpool tub and separate shower
- Cozy breakfast area is convenient to the kitchen
- 3 bedrooms, 3 baths, 2-car detached garage
- Basement, crawl space or slab foundation, please specify when ordering

*Price Code B*

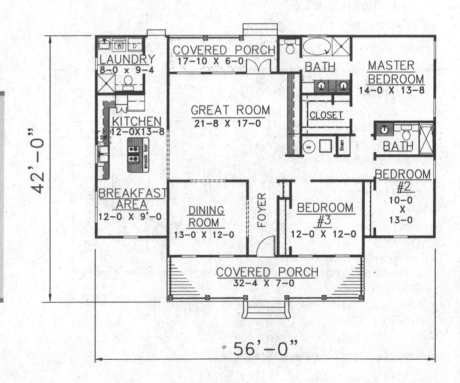

**2,890 total square feet of living area**

## Lots Of Bay Windows Fill Home With Sunlight

### Special features

- Formal dining and living rooms in the front of the home create a private place for entertaining
- Kitchen is designed for efficiency including a large island with cooktop and extra counterspace in route to the dining room
- A stunning oversized whirlpool tub is showcased in the private master bath
- Bonus room on the second floor has an additional 240 square feet of living area
- 3 bedrooms, 2 1/2 baths, 3-car side entry garage
- Crawl space foundation

**Price Code E**

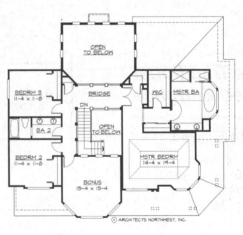

*Second Floor 1,260 sq. ft.*

*First Floor 1,630 sq. ft.*

**TO ORDER BLUEPRINTS USE THE FORM ON PAGE 15 OR CALL TOLL-FREE 1-877-671-6036**
View thousands more home plans online at www.familyhandyman.com/homeplans

303

# Plan #717-053D-0017

**2,529 total square feet of living area**

## Handsome Traditional With Gabled Entrance

### Special features

- Distinguished appearance enhances this home's classic interior arrangement
- Bonus room over the garage, which is included in the square footage, has direct access from the attic and the second floor hall
- Garden tub, walk-in closet and coffered ceiling enhance the master bedroom suite
- 4 bedrooms, 2 1/2 baths, 2-car garage
- Basement foundation

**Price Code E**

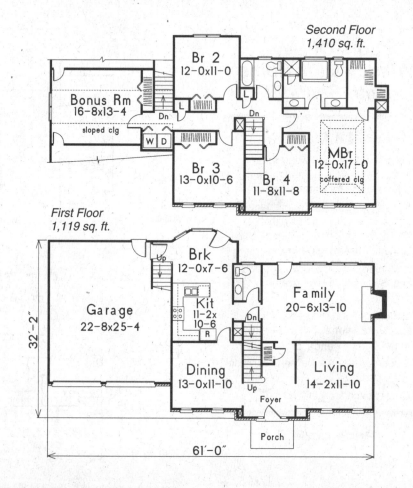

Second Floor
1,410 sq. ft.

Bonus Rm
16-8x13-4
sloped clg

Br 2
12-0x11-0

Br 3
13-0x10-6

Br 4
11-8x11-8

MBr
12-0x17-0
coffered clg

First Floor
1,119 sq. ft.

Garage
22-8x25-4

Brk
12-0x7-6

Kit
11-2x
10-6

Family
20-6x13-10

Dining
13-0x11-10

Living
14-2x11-10

Foyer

Porch

32'-2"

61'-0"

**TO ORDER BLUEPRINTS USE THE FORM ON PAGE 15 OR CALL TOLL-FREE 1-877-671-6036**
View thousands more home plans online at www.familyhandyman.com/homeplans

# Family Handyman

**1,285 total square feet of living area**

## Layout Creates Large Open Living Area

### Special features

- Accommodating home with ranch-style porch
- Large storage area on back of home
- Master bedroom includes dressing area, private bath and built-in bookcase
- Kitchen features pantry, breakfast bar and complete view to the dining room
- 3 bedrooms, 2 baths
- Crawl space foundation, drawings also include basement and slab foundations

**Price Code B**

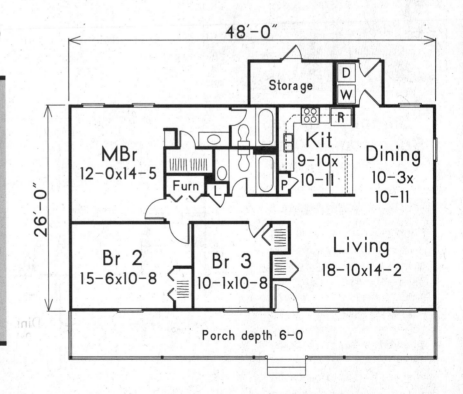

48'-0"

26'-0"

Storage

D
W

MBr
12-0x14-5

Furn

Kit
9-10x
10-11

R

P

Dining
10-3x
10-11

L

Br 2
15-6x10-8

Br 3
10-1x10-8

Living
18-10x14-2

Porch depth 6-0

**2,806 total square feet of living area**

Rear View

## Balcony Enjoys Spectacular Views In Atrium Home

### Special features

- Harmonious charm throughout
- Sweeping balcony and vaulted ceiling soar above spacious great room and walk-in bar
- Atrium with lower level family room is a unique touch, creating an open and airy feeling
- 4 bedrooms, 2 1/2 baths, 2-car garage
- Walk-out basement foundation

**Price Code E**

*First Floor*
*1,473 sq. ft.*

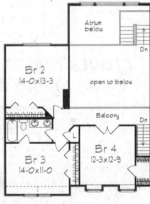

*Second Floor*
*785 sq. ft.*

*Lower Level*
*548 sq. ft.*

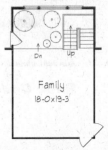

**TO ORDER BLUEPRINTS USE THE FORM ON PAGE 15 OR CALL TOLL-FREE 1-877-671-6036**
View thousands more home plans online at www.familyhandyman.com/homeplans

**3,321 total square feet of living area**

## Victorian Exterior With Custom-Feel Interior

### Special features

- Cozy den has two walls of bookshelves making it a quiet retreat
- A useful screen porch is located off dining room for dining and entertaining outdoors
- Varied ceiling heights throughout bedrooms on second floor add interest
- 4 bedrooms, 2 1/2 baths, 2-car side entry garage
- Basement foundation

*Price Code F*

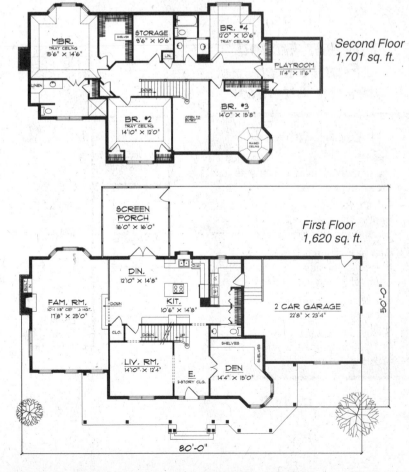

*Second Floor 1,701 sq. ft.*

*First Floor 1,620 sq. ft.*

**TO ORDER BLUEPRINTS USE THE FORM ON PAGE 15 OR CALL TOLL-FREE 1-877-671-6036**
View thousands more home plans online at www.familyhandyman.com/homeplans

307

**1,992 total square feet of living area**

## Elegant Arched Front Porch Attracts Attention

### Special features

- Bayed breakfast room overlooks the outdoor deck and connects to the screened porch
- Private formal living room in the front of the home could easily be converted to a home office or study
- Compact, yet efficient kitchen is conveniently situated between the breakfast and dining rooms
- 3 bedrooms, 2 1/2 baths, 3-car side entry garage
- Basement, crawl space or slab foundation, please specify when ordering

*Price Code C*

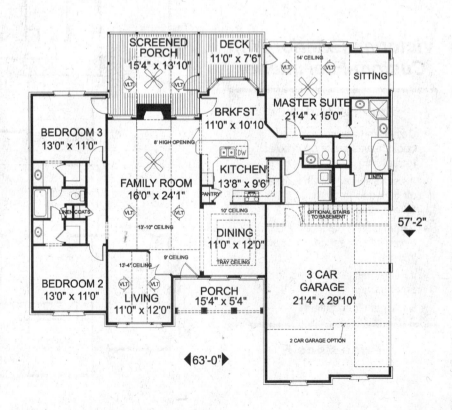

SCREENED PORCH 15'4" x 13'10"

DECK 11'0" x 7'6"

14' CEILING

SITTING

MASTER SUITE 21'4" x 15'0"

BEDROOM 3 13'0" x 11'0"

BRKFST 11'0" x 10'10"

8' HIGH OPENING

LINEN

KITCHEN 13'8" x 9'6"

DW

FAMILY ROOM 16'0" x 24'1"

PANTRY

13'-10" CEILING

LINEN COATS

10' CEILING

OPTIONAL STAIRS TO BASEMENT

57'-2"

DINING 11'0" x 12'0"

TRAY CEILING

9' CEILING

13'-4" CEILING

BEDROOM 2 13'0" x 11'0"

LIVING 11'0" x 12'0"

PORCH 15'4" x 5'4"

3 CAR GARAGE 21'4" x 29'10"

2 CAR GARAGE OPTION

◄ 63'-0" ►

**TO ORDER BLUEPRINTS USE THE FORM ON PAGE 15 OR CALL TOLL-FREE 1-877-671-6036**
View thousands more home plans online at www.familyhandyman.com/homeplans

**2,967 total square feet of living area**

## Picture Perfect For A Country Setting

### Special features

- An exterior with charm graced with country porch and multiple arched projected box windows
- Dining area is oversized and adjoins a fully equipped kitchen with walk-in pantry
- Two bay windows light up the enormous informal living area to the rear
- 4 bedrooms, 3 1/2 baths, 3-car side entry garage
- Basement foundation

*Price Code E*

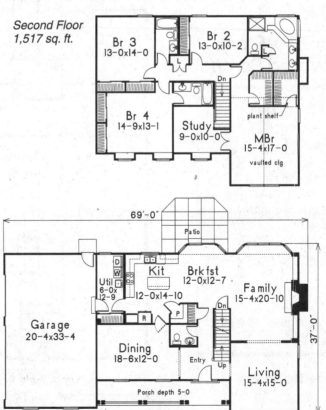

*Second Floor 1,517 sq. ft.*

Br 3 13-0x14-0
Br 2 13-0x10-2
Br 4 14-9x13-1
Study 9-0x10-0
plant shelf
MBr 15-4x17-0
vaulted clg
Dn

*First Floor 1,450 sq. ft.*

69'-0"
Patio
Util 6-0x12-9
Kit 12-0x14-10
Brk fst 12-0x12-7
Family 15-4x20-10
D W
R
P
Dn
Garage 20-4x33-4
Dining 18-6x12-0
Entry
Up
Living 15-4x15-0
Porch depth 5-0
37'-0"

**TO ORDER BLUEPRINTS USE THE FORM ON PAGE 15 OR CALL TOLL-FREE 1-877-671-6036**
View thousands more home plans online at www.familyhandyman.com/homeplans

309

**1,600 total square feet of living area**

## Roomy Two-Story Has Covered Porch

### Special features

- Energy efficient home with 2" x 6" exterior walls
- First floor master bedroom is accessible from two points of entry
- Master bath dressing area includes separate vanities and a mirrored makeup counter
- Second floor bedrooms have generous storage space and share a full bath
- 3 bedrooms, 2 baths, 2-car side entry garage
- Crawl space foundation, drawings also include slab foundation

*Price Code B*

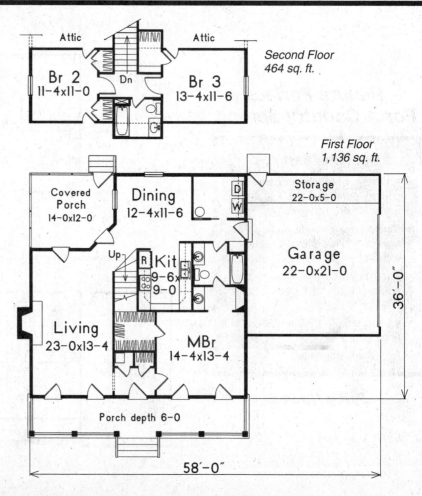

Attic

Br 2
11-4x11-0

Dn

Br 3
13-4x11-6

Attic

*Second Floor*
*464 sq. ft.*

*First Floor*
*1,136 sq. ft.*

Covered Porch
14-0x12-0

Dining
12-4x11-6

D W

Storage
22-0x5-0

Up

R Kit
9-6x
9-0

Garage
22-0x21-0

Living
23-0x13-4

MBr
14-4x13-4

36'-0"

Porch depth 6-0

58'-0"

**2,269 total square feet of living area**

## Delightful One-Level Home

### Special features

- An open atmosphere encourages an easy flow of activities
- Grand windows and a covered porch offer a cozy atmosphere
- The master bedroom boasts a double vanity, whirlpool tub and spacious walk-in closet
- 3 bedrooms, 2 baths, 2-car garage
- Basement foundation

*Price Code D*

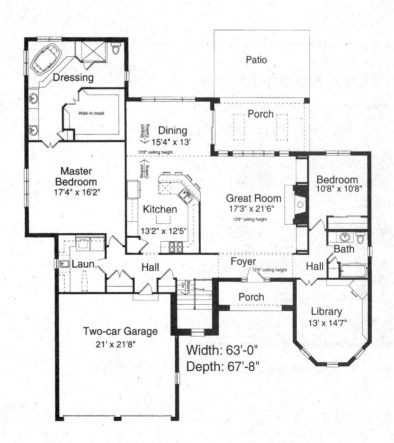

Dressing

Walk-in closet

Patio

Porch

Dining
15'4" x 13'

Sloped Ceiling

12'8" ceiling height

Master Bedroom
17'4" x 16'2"

Sloped Ceiling

Kitchen
13'2" x 12'5"

Great Room
17'3" x 21'6"
12'8" ceiling height

Bedroom
10'8" x 10'8"

Bath

Laun.

Hall

Foyer
12'8" ceiling height

Hall

Porch

Two-car Garage
21' x 21'8"

Library
13' x 14'7"

Width: 63'-0"
Depth: 67'-8"

**TO ORDER BLUEPRINTS USE THE FORM ON PAGE 15 OR CALL TOLL-FREE 1-877-671-6036**
View thousands more home plans online at www.familyhandyman.com/homeplans

311

**1,818 total square feet of living area**

## Open Family Living

### Special features

- Spacious breakfast area extends into the family room and kitchen
- Master suite has a tray ceiling and vaulted bath with walk-in closet
- Optional bonus room above the garage has an additional 298 square feet of living area
- 3 bedrooms, 2 1/2 baths, 2-car garage
- Walk-out basement, slab or crawl space foundation, please specify when ordering

**Price Code C**

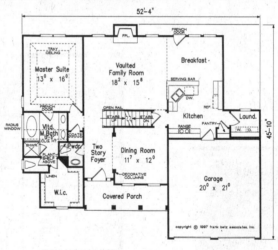

*First Floor*
*1,382 sq. ft.*

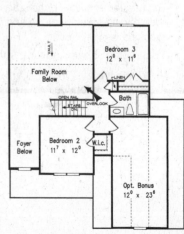

*Second Floor*
*436 sq. ft.*

**3,006 total square feet of living area**

## Third Floor All-Purpose Room

### Special features

- Energy efficient home with 2" x 6" exterior walls
- Large all-purpose room and bath on third floor
- Efficient U-shaped kitchen includes a pantry and adjacent planning desk
- 4 bedrooms, 3 1/2 baths, 2-car side entry garage
- Basement foundation, drawings also include slab foundation

### Price Code E

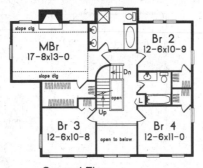

MBr 17-8x13-0
Br 2 12-6x10-9
Br 3 12-6x10-8
Br 4 12-6x11-0
open to below
slope clg
open
Dn
Up

*Second Floor 1,138 sq. ft.*

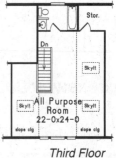

Stor.
Dn
Skylt
Skylt
Skylt
All Purpose Room 22-0x24-0
slope clg
slope clg

*Third Floor 575 sq. ft.*

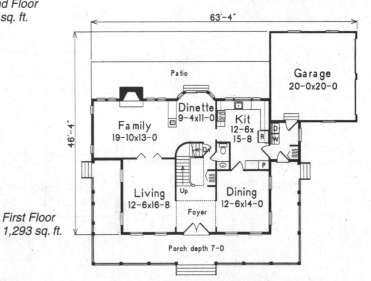

63'-4"
46'-4"
Patio
Garage 20-0x20-0
Family 19-10x13-0
Dinette 9-4x11-0
Kit 12-6x15-8
Living 12-6x16-8
Dining 12-6x14-0
Foyer
Up
D
W
R
P

*First Floor 1,293 sq. ft.*

Porch depth 7-0

**TO ORDER BLUEPRINTS USE THE FORM ON PAGE 15 OR CALL TOLL-FREE 1-877-671-6036**
View thousands more home plans online at www.familyhandyman.com/homeplans

313

**1,874 total square feet of living area**

## Breezeway Joins Living Space With Garage

### Special features

- 9' ceilings throughout the first floor
- Two-story foyer opens into the large family room with fireplace
- First floor master bedroom includes a private bath with tub and shower
- 4 bedrooms, 2 1/2 baths, 2-car garage
- Basement foundation, drawings also include slab foundation

### Price Code C

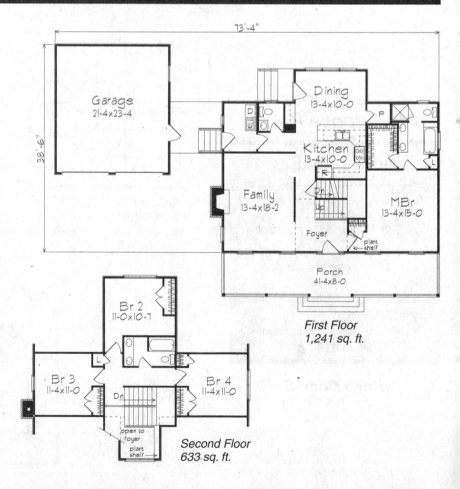

73'-4"

38'-6"

Garage
21-4x23-4

Dining
13-4x10-0

Kitchen
13-4x10-0

Family
13-4x18-2

MBr
13-4x15-0

Foyer

plant shelf

Porch
41-4x8-0

*First Floor*
*1,241 sq. ft.*

Br 2
11-0x10-7

Br 3
11-4x11-0

Br 4
11-4x11-0

Dn

open to foyer
plant shelf

*Second Floor*
*633 sq. ft.*

**TO ORDER BLUEPRINTS USE THE FORM ON PAGE 15 OR CALL TOLL-FREE 1-877-671-6036**
View thousands more home plans online at www.familyhandyman.com/homeplans

**1,630 total square feet of living area**

## Open Ranch Design
## Gives Expansive Look

### Special features

- Crisp facade and full windows front and back offer open viewing
- Wrap-around rear deck is accessible from breakfast room, dining room and master bedroom
- Vaulted ceilings in living room and master bedroom
- Sitting area and large walk-in closet complement master bedroom
- 3 bedrooms, 2 baths, 2-car garage
- Basement foundation

*Price Code B*

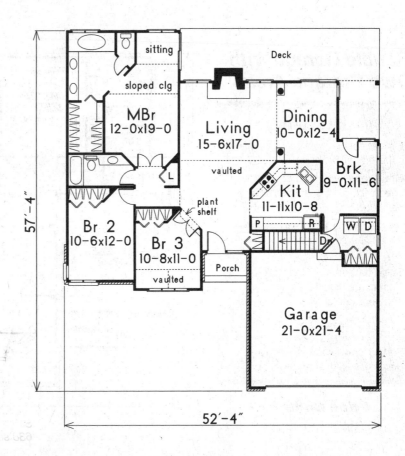

**TO ORDER BLUEPRINTS USE THE FORM ON PAGE 15 OR CALL TOLL-FREE 1-877-671-6036**
View thousands more home plans online at www.familyhandyman.com/homeplans

**315**

**2,281 total square feet of living area**

## Double Garage With Two Storage Areas

### Special features

- Formal dining room features a coffered ceiling
- Great room with fireplace and coffered ceiling overlooks covered back porch
- Kitchen with angled eating bar adjoins angled morning room with bay window
- Salon bath has double walk-in closets and vanities, step-up tub and separate shower
- 3 bedrooms, 2 baths, 2-car side entry garage
- Slab or crawl space foundation, please specify when ordering

*Price Code D*

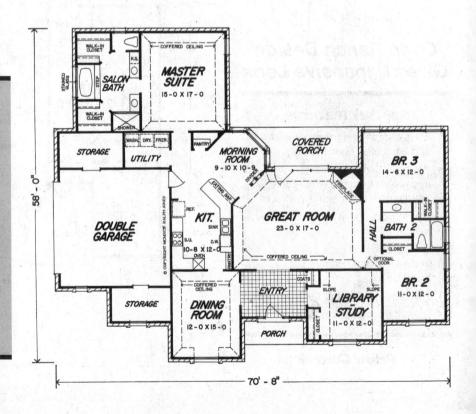

**1,791 total square feet of living area**

## Attractive Styling

### Special features

- Dining area has a 10' high sloped ceiling
- Kitchen opens to the large living room with fireplace and has access to a covered porch
- Master suite features a private bath, double walk-in closets and whirlpool tub
- 3 bedrooms, 2 baths, 2-car garage
- Slab or crawl space foundation, please specify when ordering

### Price Code B

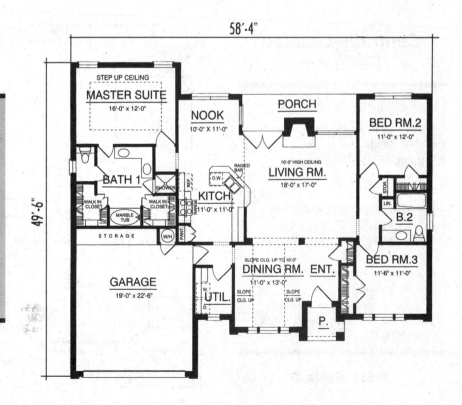

**2,024 total square feet of living area**

## Centrally Located Bedroom

### Special features

- Covered porches offer a relaxing atmosphere
- Bedrooms are separated for privacy
- The formal dining room provides an elegant space for entertaining
- The second floor living area and optional bath are ideal for a guest suite
- 3 bedrooms, 2 baths, 2-car side entry garage
- Basement, crawl space or slab foundation, please specify when ordering

*Price Code D*

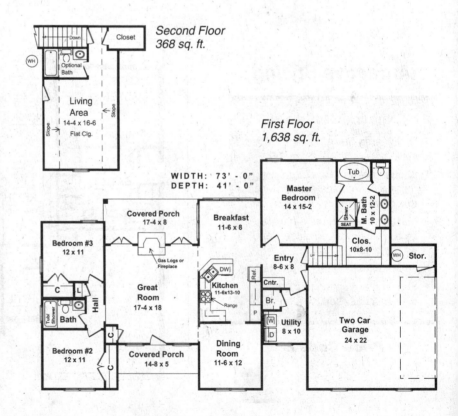

Second Floor
368 sq. ft.

WH

Optional Bath

Down

Closet

Living Area
14-4 x 16-6
Flat Clg.

Slope

First Floor
1,638 sq. ft.

WIDTH: 73' - 0"
DEPTH: 41' - 0"

Master Bedroom
14 x 15-2

Tub

M. Bath
10 x 12-2

Shwr.

SEAT

Clos.
10x8-10

WH

Stor.

Covered Porch
17-4 x 8

Breakfast
11-6 x 8

Entry
8-6 x 8

Up

Bedroom #3
12 x 11

Gas Logs or Fireplace

Kitchen
11-6x13-10

DW

Ref.

Cntr.

C

L

Great Room
17-4 x 18

Range

Br.

P

Two Car Garage
24 x 22

Hall

Tub/Shower

Bath

C

W

D

Utility
8 x 10

Bedroom #2
12 x 11

C

Covered Porch
14-8 x 5

Dining Room
11-6 x 12

**1,711 total square feet of living area**

*Rear View*

## Ideal Home For Lake, Mountain Or Seaside

### Special features

- Great room has exposed beams, two-story window wall, fireplace, wet bar and balcony
- Breakfast room shares the fireplace with the kitchen
- Vaulted master bedroom has two closets and bookshelves
- Spiral stairs and balcony dramatize the loft
- 2 bedrooms, 2 1/2 baths
- Basement foundation

### *Price Code B*

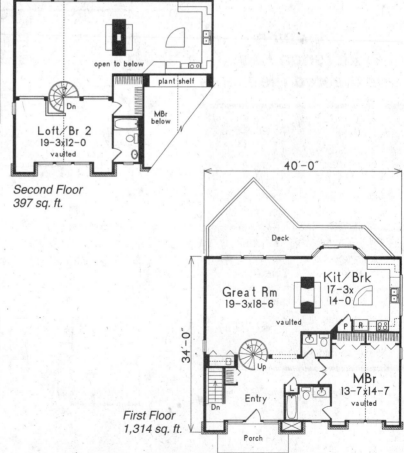

*Second Floor*
*397 sq. ft.*

Loft/Br 2
19-3x12-0
vaulted

open to below

plant shelf

MBr
below

Dn

40'-0"

Deck

Great Rm
19-3x18-6
vaulted

Kit/Brk
17-3x
14-0
vaulted

34'-0"

Up

MBr
13-7x14-7
vaulted

Entry

Dn

Porch

*First Floor*
*1,314 sq. ft.*

**TO ORDER BLUEPRINTS USE THE FORM ON PAGE 15 OR CALL TOLL-FREE 1-877-671-6036**
View thousands more home plans online at www.familyhandyman.com/homeplans

**319**

**2,935 total square feet of living area**

## Charming Victorian Has Unexpected Pleasures

### Special features

- Gracious entry foyer with handsome stairway opens to separate living and dining rooms
- Kitchen has vaulted ceiling and skylight, island worktop, breakfast area with bay window and two separate pantries
- Large second floor master bedroom features a fireplace, raised tub, dressing area with vaulted ceiling and skylight
- 4 bedrooms, 2 1/2 baths, 2-car side entry garage
- Basement foundation

*Price Code E*

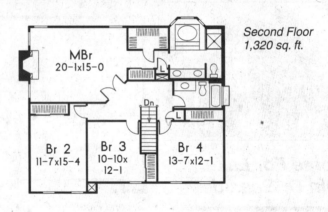

Second Floor 1,320 sq. ft.

MBr 20-1x15-0

Br 2 11-7x15-4

Br 3 10-10x 12-1

Br 4 13-7x12-1

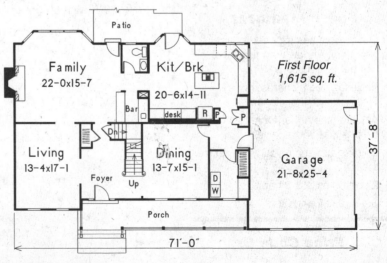

First Floor 1,615 sq. ft.

Patio

Family 22-0x15-7

Kit/Brk 20-6x14-11

Bar

Living 13-4x17-1

Dining 13-7x15-1

Foyer

Garage 21-8x25-4

Porch

71'-0"

37'-8"

320

**TO ORDER BLUEPRINTS USE THE FORM ON PAGE 15 OR CALL TOLL-FREE 1-877-671-6036**
View thousands more home plans online at www.familyhandyman.com/homeplans

# 5-minute
### Guaranteed
# Bugle
## Course

Price
# 25¢

Martino Publishing
Mansfield Centre, CT
2010

*Martino Publishing*
*P.O. Box 373,*
*Mansfield Centre, CT 06250 USA*

www.martinopublishing.com

ISBN 1-57898-966-3

© *2010 Martino Publishing*

Cover design by T. Matarazzo

*Printed in the United States of America On 100% Acid-Free Paper*

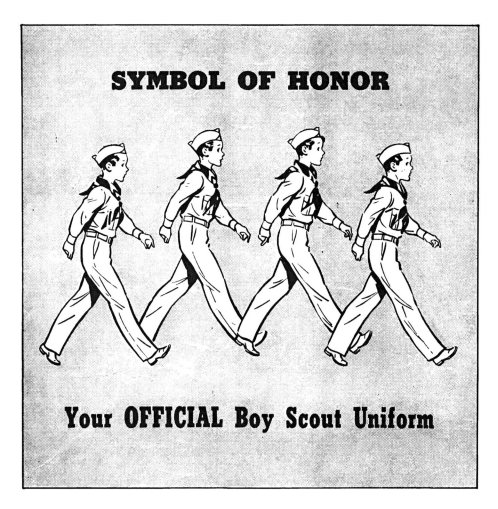

**SYMBOL OF HONOR**

**Your OFFICIAL Boy Scout Uniform**

Respected by a nation, honored by all, your official Boy Scout Uniform symbolizes the flower of American youth.

Wear it proudly . . . wear it correctly. You and your Uniform are a part of traditional America. In you are summed up the men and ideals which pioneered this country . . . from Daniel Boone to Daniel Carter Beard . . . a rich heritage which is yours to carry on.

In all the land only the official Boy Scout Uniform has earned this respected position because the Boy Scouts have been ever true to their trust. Since you are privileged to wear the *official* Boy Scout Uniform it is up to you to wear it correctly . . . wear it proudly. It is a symbol of honor.

# National Supply Service · Boy Scouts of America

2 Park Avenue, New York 16, N. Y. · 231 South Greene Street, Chicago 7, Ill. · 755 Market Street, San Francisco 3, Calif.

# FIRST READ THIS

The Bugle has played a prominent part in all the great wars of history. Its martial notes have been heard in battle, and in the thick of the fray the Buglers have stood ready to sound the "Charge" or "Recall."

In Revolutionary times the Bugles sounded the "Spirit of '76" and many a drummer boy and Bugler marched with Washington's "Minute Men."

The Civil war saw Buglers wearing both the Blue and the Gray, and a visit to any large museum will show us the bugles they used. Not so very different in appearance from the ones used today, but not by any means as easy to blow as our modern ones.

Colonel Roosevelt's "Rough Riders" had Buglers attached to them, and a Bugle sounded the "Charge" at San Juan Hill.

In the recent Great War, and along the Mexican border today, the Bugle plays its part. Ready at the command to blow "Boots and Saddles" and at the close of the day, to sound "Taps."

"Young America" today is rapidly taking the Bugle for its own, and this movement is not by any means confined to the Boy Scouts. Boys of all ages, from 6 to 60 are interested in learning the Bugle, and are finding in its simplicity an easy step to the Cornet, Trombone and other brass instruments.

By carefully reading this book, and applying its principles, you can readily understand how to play the Bugle in "5 Minutes."

# THE BUGLE

As the illustrations show, there are two types of Bugles in common use. Both are played exactly the same; the only practical difference is the appearance and in the key in which they are tuned when made. Your choice of an instrument depends entirely upon personal preference; it does not really matter which one you possess. If you acquire mastery of one you will be able to play the other, as they are both played exactly the same.

An understanding of your Bugle, its parts and their purpose, will enable you to take better care of the instrument, and will also help in the ease with which it may be played.

The Cavalry model Bugle in G, has a slide at the back, just under the mouthpiece, by which the entire notes of this type of Bugle may be changed or lowered to the Key of F, one whole tone lower than its normal range with the slide in. This enables you to play the instrument in two different keys, G, in which it is built, and by pulling out the slide, in F. It is a change sometimes to play in a lower key and is also used in Bugle Bands when playing two part selections.

The Army type Bugle is fixed in pitch and can only be played in the key in which it is made. It is shorter and more compact than the Cavalry model and is the regulation type used by the U. S. and British Infantry and Marine forces.

# CARE OF THE BUGLE

If you desire your Bugle to look its best at all times, keep it polished with a good metal or brass cleaner.

Use the best or you will find scratches marring the bright new finish of your instrument.

When through playing wipe off carefully with a chamois or soft cloth and put your Bugle away in a flannel bag. This can be obtained from any music store, or you can have one made at home quite easily. Covering the instrument and putting it away helps to keep it clean and protects it from dents which will spoil the tone.

For good tone and ease of playing, your Bugle should also be cleaned inside occasionally. This is done by first removing the mouthpiece, then **pouring cold** water in the bell and allowing it to drain through the coils and out at the mouthpiece shank. If desired, the bell and mouthpiece shank may be plugged with a large and small cork respectively; **then with the cold** water inside, shake as though cleaning a bottle. The **cold water washes out the** saliva and dust, that if allowed to accumulate, would cause corrosion.

In the Cavalry Bugle the slide should be lubricated occasionally with vaseline, which will keep it in proper working condition. If the slide fits snugly and does not easily pull out, loop a handkerchief through it and pull gently but firmly, straight out, away from the mouthpiece. Do not attempt to wiggle it out, or you may b e n d the tubing.

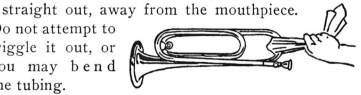

# MAKING TONES

Tones are produced on a Bugle by the vibration of the lips on the mouthpiece. The brass tubing and bell merely amplify these vibrations or tones, and bring them out in greater volume. You can, if you so desire, carry the mouthpiece about with you and practice at odd times. This will prove very helpful in training the lip, and for practice purposes is just as effective as performing on the complete instrument.

**To make a tone,** stand or sit in an upright position, tighten the lips by stretching over the teeth as shown. Place the mouthpiece against the lips—not too hard. Open the teeth slightly, with the tongue forward and just back of the lips.

Take a moderately deep breath, and with the mouthpiece in position on the lips, pronounce the word "tu." Use a fair amount of air and prolong the tone as long as possible. This method of attack is very similar to ejecting a small hair from the mouth.

The five notes on a Bugle are obtained by tightening or loosening the lips, according to the tone desired. On lower notes the lips are relaxed a trifle, and on high tones they are tightened.

It is not necessary to use a lot of air and get red in the face in order to play a Bugle; tone is made **only** by the vibration of the lips against the mouthpiece, plus a little air.

All the blowing in the world will not make a musical sound unless your lips are vibrating properly. Do not puff out the cheeks and attempt to force the tone; much better results will be obtained by using a steady flow of air and a light pressure on the mouthpiece.

If your lips get tired, give them a rest. Remember, you are using muscles that have probably never been called upon to work before.

Consistent practice will develop them and enable you to produce any tone on the Bugle at will.

SHOWING MOUTHPIECE IN POSITION

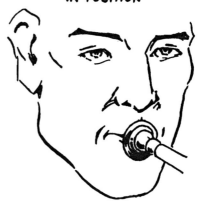

SHOWING POSITION OF LIPS

**DON'T DO THIS**

# Only Five Notes to Learn

C     G     C     E     G

The lowest note C is used very seldom in Bugle calls and for the first tone, we will sound  G,  the next highest, and also the easiest tone to play on the instrument.

Have someone sound G on the piano or some other instrument, and adjust your lips on the mouthpiece as you blow, until your Bugle is sounding the same tone.

Practice playing this note, and then by tightening the lips a trifle more,  attempt  the  next higher one C

Try to prolong the length of the tone on both of these, keeping the lips steady  while  you count 1-2-3-4-5-6 etc.

Go from one to the other of these notes until you can play either one at will.

Start on G again and take the note below, which is C then practice C  with the other two already learned, making a three note combination.  Practice these until a reasonable dexterity is obtained.

Using the three learned so far,   attempt E then the last and  highest note G

On the last two notes mentioned E and G, remember to tighten the lips and if necessary, apply a slight presure on the mouthpiece.

# Training Your Lip

Practise is necessary in training your lip, so that you may be able at will, to play any one of the five notes on the Bugle.

When playing the following exercises, attack each note firmly and always try to get a full, round, clear tone.

Play each exercise at least 20 times before attempting the next.

**Adding the C to the G, making a two note exercise.**

Count 1-2-3-4, 1-2-3-4, 1-2-3-4, etc.

Count 1-2-3-4, 1-2-3-4, etc.

**A 3 note combination for practice, adding the E.**

Count    1-2    1-2    1-2    1-2    1-2    1-2    1-2 etc.

**Play this one 20 times, paying special attention to the high G.**

Count    1-2    1-2    1-2 etc.

**The following exercises use the complete range of the Bugle, from C to G.    Watch the count.**

Count    1    2    3    4    1    2    3    4    1    2    3    4 etc.

# Learning Time

Time is to music, what grammar and punctuation are to literature. A story or poem without these two essentials would not make sense. The same thing applies to music, if some tones did not sound for a longer or shorter period than others, they would not make a melody.

Therefore time is a very necessary part of music, and fortunately also, it is easy to learn.

The first note, (see bottom of page) in square No.1 is called a whole note and for it count four times, as: 1·2·3·4. Whether you count the 4 beats fast or slow depends on the character of the music, that is if it is a fast or slow tune. The oblong character in the same square, is called a whole rest, and gets the same count as the whole note. A rest is used in music when no note is being played, more or less on the idea of "marking time."

The next note in square No. 2 is a half note, as is the rest in the same measure, and these both get 2 counts each.

The note and rest in the 3rd measure are called quarter($\frac{1}{4}$)notes and rests and are given 1 count.

No.4 is an eighth ($\frac{1}{8}$) note and rest, and these get half a count each.

No.5 is a sixteenth ($\frac{1}{16}$) note and rest, and these get only a quarter of a count apiece.

The small flags or tails on the sixteenth and eighth notes are sometimes joined together as:

A dot behind any note makes it half as long again, or increases its time value by half what it would get without the dot.

For example the note illustrated in No.6., is a half note and gets 2 counts. The dot behind it adds one more count making three altogether.

Measure No. 7 illustrates a triplet, which is 3 notes played all in one count. An example of this is in Irving Berlin's "The song is ended, but the mel-o-dy lingers on." The triplet occurs on the word, "melody."

| Square No.1. | Square No.2. | Square No.3. | Square No.4. | Square No.5. | Square No.6. | Square No.7. |
|---|---|---|---|---|---|---|

# Play These

This Bugle call is in Common or $\frac{4}{4}$ time.   $\frac{4}{4}$ means four quarter notes, or beats to the measure.

Count slowly 1    2    3-4    1    2    3-4    1    2    3    4    1    2    3-4

This one is in $\frac{3}{4}$ or Waltz time. Let's say it another way, count 3 beats to the measure.

Count slowly 1    2    3    1    2    3    1    2    3    1-2-3    1    2    3    1-2    3    1-2   3

This is in $\frac{2}{4}$ time, count 2 beats to every measure.

Count     1    2    1    2    1    2    1    2    1    2    1    2    1   &   2    1-2

The next one is in $\frac{6}{8}$ time. Count 6 to the measure, and play as though Waltz time, very fast, as 1·2·3 ____ 4·5·6

Count     1    2    3    4    5    6    1    2    3    4    5    6    1-2-3    4-5   6

# Easy Bugle Calls

The following calls are used in lieu of spoken commands.

This sign ⌢ indicates a pause, or hold as long as desired.

Practice these easy ones

Practice the triplets in the following. Triplets are played with a 1-2-3 count similar to pronouncing the words "mel-o-dy" or "ripp-l-ing."

Boy Scouts use regular Bugle calls in manoeuvers,  and if  in  camp with soldiers,the following calls should precede the regular one,identifying it for the Scouts only.

## THE SCOUTS CALL

Count    1-2-3 - 4-5-6   1-2 - 3 - 4-5 - 6    1-2-3 - 4-5 - 6   1-2-3-4-5-6

In the following call "Overcoats," the first beat of the measure is divided between two  8th notes.  Count 1 & 2 and play as if pronouncing the word itself, holding the last syllable  "coats" for the longest count.

## OVERCOATS

Count    1    &    2    1    &    2    1    &    2

Before playing the next call, notice the triplet in the first measure. Count this as explained on the previous page,and go over both measures. You will find this very helpful before playing.

## WATER

Count    1    -    &  -  2  -  &  -  3  -  &  -  4    1-2 - 3-4

The following one is in Waltz or $\frac{3}{4}$ time. Count  1-2-3.

## CHEERS

Count    3    1-2 - 3  .  1-2 - 3    1 - 2 - 3

# Triple Tongueing

Triple Tongueing is used very largely in calls that have fast triplets or sixteenth notes in quick tempo.

Pronounce the words "tu, tu, ku" with the tongue when playing, giving it a fast 1-2-3 count.

Practice the tongueing slowly and repeat previous exercises. After your tongue has acquired the right motion, and you can "tongue" with ease, the speed can be gradually increased.

# The Slur

The Slur is easily made. It consists of running one note into another, as follows.

# Bugle Calls

## RETREAT

## RECALL

## SWIMMING CALL

# 200 Ukulele Song Book

The Standard Endorsed Ukulele book is being used in thousands of schools as a text-book on the Ukulele.

The book contains 200 songs in the Key of C. Only 3 chords necessary to learn in order to play any of the songs.

This is the greatest little book ever published for the Ukulele player and the beginner.

# 200 Harmonica Songs

## With New System

This book is the greatest ever published for the harmonica.

Contains a new system adapted for teaching with 200 songs.

Endorsed by the M. Hohner Co. and used by thousands of public schools.

# STAMP OF APPROVAL

## ... THE OFFICIAL SEAL

## *Look for it on all Boy Scout equipment!*

This seal is your guarantee that your Uniform and other Scout equipment has been tested and approved. It is your protection because this seal is stamped only on authorized Uniforms and equipment.

Look for it before you buy. Only in this way can you be sure that you are getting *Official* equipment . . . authorized and approved by the Boy Scouts of America and your local Scout Dealer.

As a Scout or Scouter you are privileged to wear the finest. Buy *Official* . . . with the stamp of approval . . . and you get the finest.

## National Supply Service · Boy Scouts of America

2 Park Avenue, New York 16, N. Y. · 231 South Greene Street, Chicago 7, Ill. · 755 Market Street, San Francisco 3, Calif.

CPSIA information can be obtained at www.ICGtesting.com
Printed in the USA
BVOW08s0352161213

339064BV00003B/123/P

# An account of remarkable cures, performed by the use of Maredant's antiscorbutic drops, prepared by John Norton, Surgeon, in Golden-Square, London.

John Norton

PRINT EDITIONS

Eighteenth Century
Collections Online
Print Editions

**Gale ECCO Print Editions**

Relive history with *Eighteenth Century Collections Online*, now available in print for the independent historian and collector. This series includes the most significant English-language and foreign-language works printed in Great Britain during the eighteenth century, and is organized in seven different subject areas including literature and language; medicine, science, and technology; and religion and philosophy. The collection also includes thousands of important works from the Americas.

The eighteenth century has been called "The Age of Enlightenment." It was a period of rapid advance in print culture and publishing, in world exploration, and in the rapid growth of science and technology – all of which had a profound impact on the political and cultural landscape. At the end of the century the American Revolution, French Revolution and Industrial Revolution, perhaps three of the most significant events in modern history, set in motion developments that eventually dominated world political, economic, and social life.

In a groundbreaking effort, Gale initiated a revolution of its own: digitization of epic proportions to preserve these invaluable works in the largest online archive of its kind. Contributions from major world libraries constitute over 175,000 original printed works. Scanned images of the actual pages, rather than transcriptions, recreate the works *as they first appeared.*

Now for the first time, these high-quality digital scans of original works are available via print-on-demand, making them readily accessible to libraries, students, independent scholars, and readers of all ages.

For our initial release we have created seven robust collections to form one the world's most comprehensive catalogs of 18th century works.

*Initial Gale ECCO Print Editions collections include:*

### History and Geography
Rich in titles on English life and social history, this collection spans the world as it was known to eighteenth-century historians and explorers. Titles include a wealth of travel accounts and diaries, histories of nations from throughout the world, and maps and charts of a world that was still being discovered. Students of the War of American Independence will find fascinating accounts from the British side of conflict.

## Social Science

Delve into what it was like to live during the eighteenth century by reading the first-hand accounts of everyday people, including city dwellers and farmers, businessmen and bankers, artisans and merchants, artists and their patrons, politicians and their constituents. Original texts make the American, French, and Industrial revolutions vividly contemporary.

## Medicine, Science and Technology

Medical theory and practice of the 1700s developed rapidly, as is evidenced by the extensive collection, which includes descriptions of diseases, their conditions, and treatments. Books on science and technology, agriculture, military technology, natural philosophy, even cookbooks, are all contained here.

## Literature and Language

Western literary study flows out of eighteenth-century works by Alexander Pope, Daniel Defoe, Henry Fielding, Frances Burney, Denis Diderot, Johann Gottfried Herder, Johann Wolfgang von Goethe, and others. Experience the birth of the modern novel, or compare the development of language using dictionaries and grammar discourses.

## Religion and Philosophy

The Age of Enlightenment profoundly enriched religious and philosophical understanding and continues to influence present-day thinking. Works collected here include masterpieces by David Hume, Immanuel Kant, and Jean-Jacques Rousseau, as well as religious sermons and moral debates on the issues of the day, such as the slave trade. The Age of Reason saw conflict between Protestantism and Catholicism transformed into one between faith and logic -- a debate that continues in the twenty-first century.

## Law and Reference

This collection reveals the history of English common law and Empire law in a vastly changing world of British expansion. Dominating the legal field is the *Commentaries of the Law of England* by Sir William Blackstone, which first appeared in 1765. Reference works such as almanacs and catalogues continue to educate us by revealing the day-to-day workings of society.

## Fine Arts

The eighteenth-century fascination with Greek and Roman antiquity followed the systematic excavation of the ruins at Pompeii and Herculaneum in southern Italy; and after 1750 a neoclassical style dominated all artistic fields. The titles here trace developments in mostly English-language works on painting, sculpture, architecture, music, theater, and other disciplines. Instructional works on musical instruments, catalogs of art objects, comic operas, and more are also included.

**The BiblioLife Network**

This project was made possible in part by the BiblioLife Network (BLN), a project aimed at addressing some of the huge challenges facing book preservationists around the world. The BLN includes libraries, library networks, archives, subject matter experts, online communities and library service providers. We believe every book ever published should be available as a high-quality print reproduction; printed on-demand anywhere in the world. This insures the ongoing accessibility of the content and helps generate sustainable revenue for the libraries and organizations that work to preserve these important materials.

The following book is in the "public domain" and represents an authentic reproduction of the text as printed by the original publisher. While we have attempted to accurately maintain the integrity of the original work, there are sometimes problems with the original work or the micro-film from which the books were digitized. This can result in minor errors in reproduction. Possible imperfections include missing and blurred pages, poor pictures, markings and other reproduction issues beyond our control. Because this work is culturally important, we have made it available as part of our commitment to protecting, preserving, and promoting the world's literature.

**GUIDE TO FOLD-OUTS MAPS and OVERSIZED IMAGES**

The book you are reading was digitized from microfilm captured over the past thirty to forty years. Years after the creation of the original microfilm, the book was converted to digital files and made available in an online database.

In an online database, page images do not need to conform to the size restrictions found in a printed book. When converting these images back into a printed bound book, the page sizes are standardized in ways that maintain the detail of the original. For large images, such as fold-out maps, the original page image is split into two or more pages

Guidelines used to determine how to split the page image follows:

• Some images are split vertically; large images require vertical and horizontal splits.
• For horizontal splits, the content is split left to right.
• For vertical splits, the content is split from top to bottom.
• For both vertical and horizontal splits, the image is processed from top left to bottom right.

# AN
# ACCOUNT
### OF

## Remarkable Cures,

Performed by the Use of

# MAREDANT'S
## Antiscorbutic Drops,

### PREPARED BY
## *JOHN NORTON,*
## SURGEON, in GOLDEN-SQUARE,
## LONDON.

### PRINTED IN THE YEAR
#### MDCCLXXIV.

As a Proof of the superior Efficacy of MAREDANT's DROPS, (prepared by Mr. *Norton*, Surgeon, of *Golden-Square, London*) to any Medicine, hitherto known, for the Cure of the *Scurvy, Leprosy, Ulcers, the Evil, Fistula, Piles,* long-continued *Inflammations of the Eyes,* and every other Disorder arising from a Foulness in the Blood, the following extraordinary *Cures* are referred to.

N. B. Be pleased to read this Pamphlet with Attention, and take Care of it.

---

To Mr. NORTON, *Surgeon,* in *Golden-Square.*

SIR, *Middleton, Warwickshire, Dec.* 1, 1773.

I Have the unspeakable pleasure to acquaint you that I have received a most extraordinary Cure from the taking of a few Bottles of your valuable *Maredant's Drops.* I was, for several Years, violently afflicted with a scorbutic Humour, which broke out in Blotches all over me, and caused so violent an Itching and Smarting, that I could hardly rest either Night or Day. The Humour increased to that Degree, that my Arms and Legs became like the Bark of a Tree, and greatly swelled; but, thank God, I am now perfectly recovered, and desire you will publish this extraordinary Cure, in justice to the Medicine and for the Benefit of those afflicted as I was.

*I am, Sir, your humble Servant,*

ALICE ROGERS.

P. S. It is above a Year since I left off the Drops, so that I have not the least Apprehension of the Disorder's returning.

B

*To*

To Mr. NORTON, *Surgeon*, in *Golden-Square, London.*

SIR,

THE Cure I have obtained, by the Use of your *Maredant's Drops,* (after having been afflicted, for many Years, with a most inveterate Scurvy, which appeared in large Blotches and other Eruptions in most Parts of my Body, and after having been in an Hospital for three Months, and discharged from thence as incurable) merits my most sincere Acknowledgements. I beg you will publish this extraordinary Cure; it may be the Means of relieving others afflicted in the like Manner.

*I am, with great Respect, Sir,*
*Your very humble Servant,*
AMELIA PRIOR.

*Hay-street Hill, Cold-bath-fields, Nov.* 30, 1773.

Witnesses to the above Cure.

*Geo. Underwood,* Bath-street, Cold-bath-fields.
*John Fowler,* Warner-street, Cold-bath-fields.
*Robert Dowley,* Coin-factor, Dorrington-street, Cold-bath-fields.

To Mr. NORTON, *Surgeon*, in *Golden-Square, London.*

SIR,                                     *Nov.* 8, 1773.

I Have happily experienced the Efficacy of your *Maredant's Drops,* by the most extraordinary Cure obtained by their Use. My Case was as follows: I was taken ill with the Scurvy, which appeared in great Blotches and other Eruptions all over my Body, attended with so violent an Itching, that it almost deprived me of Sleep at Nights, and made me continually uneasy in the Daytime. The Drops created me an Appetite, which I much wanted. I am, at this Time, perfectly recovered, and enjoy my rest as usual, and am willing to satisfy any Person, of the Truth of this, by calling at my House.

*I am, Sir, your most humble Servant,*
WILLIAM POTIER,

*Wine Merchant, in Grafton-street, near*
*Litchfield-street, St. Ann's, Soho.*

*To*

*To* Mr. NORTON, *Surgeon*, in *Golden-Square.*

SIR,            *Glasgow, Nov.* 8, 1773.

I Should think it an Act of the greatest Ingratitude if I did not acquaint you of the Cure I have received from the Use of your *Maredant's Drops.* My Case was as follows : I was seized with a violent scorbutic Disorder in my Legs, which rendered them useless to me, having tried many Things to no Purpose ; I was at last advised to take your Drops by a Friend who had obtained a perfect Cure by them. I am now in perfect Health, and have the Use of my Limbs as well as ever, the Disorder being entirely eradicated. You have my Leave to publish this extraordinary Cure.

*I am your very humble Servant,*
JAMES TULLOCH.

*To* Mr. NORTON, *Surgeon*, in *Golden Square.*

SIR,            *Cambridge, August* 6, 1773.

IN Justice to your Medicine, and for the Good of Mankind, I am induced to make public a Cure which your *Maredant's Drops* effected on me.

Know, then, Sir, I had for many Years been more or less tormented with a scorbutic Disorder, attended with frequent Eruptions, variously intersperfed, till at length my whole frame was attacked.

I was covered with Blotches and an universal Scurf, attended with a perpetual scalding Humour, which discharged itself from my Head. An Aching in all my Bones, a general Laxity of Constitution, Lowness of Spirits, and various other Symptoms, that occasioned nothing less than the Expectation of a speedy Dissolution ; but, being fortunately recommended to try your Drops, I began them ; and by persevering some Time, my Complaints were removed, so that I now enjoy a perfect State of Health.

*I am your obedient humble Servant,*
JOHN BRAMPTON.

*To* Mr. **NORTON**, *Surgeon,* in *Golden-Square.*

SIR,

ABOUT fix Years ago I got a Surfeit by bathing when I was extremely hot, which threw me into a Fever, attended with a fevere racking Pain in my Bowels, that made me weary of Life, having tried the moſt eminent of the Faculty to no Purpoſe. In reading the News-papers one Day, I happened to fee a moſt extraordinary Cure performed by your *Maredant's Drops,* which induced me to try them ; and, after taking a few Bottles, I am, thank God, perfectly reſtored to my former Health.

*Mile-end,*      *From your humble Servant,*
*July* 29, 1773.      RICHARD TOOVEY.

P. S. I defire you will publiſh this extraordinary Cure for the Benefit of others.

*To* Mr. **NORTON**, *Surgeon,* in *Golden-Square.*

SIR,

I Have, for above fix Years, laboured under a moſt dreadful Pain in my Stomach, a Lowneſs of Spirits, and the Scurvy, attended with a moſt fevere Pain in my Head, which made me weary of Life, having tried many of the Faculty to no Purpoſe. Hearing of the many extraordinary Cures by your *Maredant's Drops,* it induced me to try them ; after taking them fome Time, I am, thank God, reſtored to my perfect Health. I defire you will publiſh this moſt extraordinary Cure for the Benefit of Mankind.

*Long-lane, Southwark,*    I am, Sir,
*May* 21, 1773.      *Your moſt humble Servant,*
         EDWARD MARQURE.

*To* Mr. **NORTON**, *Surgeon,* in *Golden-Square.*

SIR,             *May* 14, 1773.

I Am cured, by the Uſe of your *Maredant's Drops,* of a moſt afflicting Diſorder, of the fcorbutic Kind, after trying every Medicine that could be thought of for my Relief in vain ; my Cafe was as follows · I firſt had ſmall Pimples come out on my Head, Face, Hands, and
Legs ;

Legs; in a little Time after, my Face and Body were covered with large Blotches, which difcharged a Kind of watery Humour, attended with exceffive Itching: I was in this Situation till about January, 1766, when I was recommended by a Gentleman, who was cured by the Ufe of your Drops, of an inveterate dry Scurvy all over his Body. I am now in perfect Health, and am continually praying for the Welfare of the Author of fo valuable a Medicine. In Juftice to you, and for the Good of Mankind, I give you Leave to make what Ufe you pleafe of this.

*I am, with great Efteem, Sir,*

*Cork-ftreet,*    *Your obedient humble Servant,*

*Liverpool.*    CHARLES COOK.

*To* Mr. NORTON, *Surgeon,* in *Golden-Square.*

S I R,       *March* 14, 1773.

HAVING been afflicted with a violent Scurvy, for the Space of 17 Years, and having tried many Medicines, and the Surgeons in an Hofpital, without Effect, I was, at the laft, (by a Book, containing an Account of the many excellent Cures performed by your *Maredant's Drops,* being left at the Houfe where I lived, and recommended by a Friend who knew their Efficacy) prevailed on to Experience the fame; and, after taking a few Bottles thereof, am, through the Bleffing of God, perfectly reftored to my former Health. In Gratitude to you, and for the Benefit of Mankind, I defire you will publifh this Cure.

*I am, Sir, your much obliged and*

No. 6, St. *Andrew's-hill,*    *Moft humble Servant,*

 *Black-Friars.*    THOMAS CHOWNING.

*Witneffes*—W. Bull.——William Roberts, St. Andrew's-hill.——John Dobfon, at the three Caftles, St. Andrew's-hill, Black-Friars.

*To* Mr. NORTON, *Surgeon, in Golden-Square, London.*

S I R,

IT is almoft three Years fince I was cured, by the Ufe of your Drops, of a moft inveterate Scurvy; which fhewed itfelf in Blotches and Ulcers all over my

Body. It affected me to that Degree, so as to deprive me of the Use of my Limbs : Besides which, I was severely afflicted with the Piles, a bilious Cholic and Indigestion. Any Person may be convinced of the Truth of this, by enquiring at Mr. Gibson's, No. 7, and at Mr. Broome's, in Charles-street, Hatton-street, Holborn ; at Mr. Taberrer's, Grocer, in Hatton-street ; and at Mrs. Bird's, Clarges-street, Piccadilly ; or (if desirous of seeing me) at Mrs. Norman's, in Clarges-street.

January 12, *I am, Sir, your obedient humble Servant,*

1773.                     ELIZ. STRINGER.

To Mr. NORTON, *Surgeon, in Golden-Square.*

SIR,

THE great Cure I have received by taking your *Maredant's Drops,* merits my public Thanks ; being perfectly restored to Health, after an Illness of eight Years. At first I was taken with a violent nervous Fever, which rendered me unable to get my Bread ; after having taken many Medicines without Effect for a long Time, I was advised by the Physicians, to try whether my native Air would be of Service ; I tried, but found none. Soon after a Swelling appeared in my right Knee : being then at Shrewsbury, I was persuaded to take the Advice of the Infirmary ; where my Knee was cured ; but I had the Misfortune to get a violent Cold, by a Window's being left open when I was in a Sweat : I was then seized with a Soreness in my Head, Collar-bone, and one of my Arms, which was immediately succeeded by a most acute Pain in those Parts. In this situation I returned to London, and took every Medicine the Physicians or my Friends advised, for the Rheumatism, as the Faculty then pronounced that to be my Case ; but without finding the least Benefit. I then was ordered to go to Margate ; where I drank the Waters, and bathed in the Sea for some Time, but found no Relief. I returned to London much worse than I left it, and continued very ill for some Time, and then my Disorder took another Turn ; for there appeared several Lumps on my Head, Face, Neck, and Arms ; two of them

them on my Head broke, and lay open two Years. In this deplorable State (a Burthen to myself, and a real Grief to my Friends) was I, when an Acquaintance, who had received a Cure in her Leg, by the Use of *Maredant's Drops*, advised me to take them : In the Course of my taking them, two large Pieces of Bone worked out of the Wound. It is a Year and three Quarters since I discontinued the Medicine, and still remain in perfect Health.

*I am your obedient humble Servant,*

December 17, 1772.  MARY LUTE,

*At Mr. Field's, in Castle-street, near Leicester-fields.*

*Witnesses*—Thomas Field, Castle-street.—— Henry Hide, Butcher, St. James's Market.

To Mr. NORTON, *Surgeon,* in *Golden-Square.*

SIR,  *November 28, 1772.*

I Return you my most sincere Thanks for the Cure I have obtained, by the Use of your most excellent Drops, of an inveterate scorbutic Humour in my Face. Its Virulency so affected my Eyes, as to render me almost incapable of seeing for above twelve Months. I also was severely afflicted with the Piles, which I have entirely got rid of by the same Means. Any doubtful Person may be convinced of this, by applying at the Music Shop, No. 78, Snow-hill, near West Smithfield.

*I am, Sir, your very humble Servant,*

MARY BRIDE.

To Mr. NORTON, *Surgeon,* in *Golden-Square.*

SIR,  *November 19, 1772.*

I Return you my most sincere Thanks for the Cure I have obtained by the Use of your *Maredant's Drops;* which, in Justice to you, and for the Benefit of others afflicted in like Manner, I desire may be made public. My Case was as follows : About thirty Years ago, a violent scorbutic Complaint broke out in one of my Legs, which soon after spread over most Part of my Body, and caused such an Itching, that I seldom could

B 4  get

get any Reft at Night; when one Leg feemed near well the Humour would break out in rh     . _ have had the Advice of the moft er.        i the Faculty, without Effect : After which, I was adviied to two Hofpitals, where I continued for near two Years ; from both which I was difcharged as incurable.  I co t nued in this miferable Condition till about two Years and a Half ago, when I began to take your Drops ; by which I have obtained a perfect Cure, as I have been en-tirely free from any fcorbutic Complaint above two Years.  Any Perfon defirous of knowing the Truth of this, may be convinced, by applying at Mr. Kennei-ley's, Warwick-ftreet, Golden-fquare.

*Leicefter-ftreet, Swallow-*     I am, Sir,
    *ftreet, Golden-fquare.*      *Your very humble Servant,*

GRACE BRITTAIN,

*Witneffes* to the above Cure — Thomas Kenneiley. James Wingfield, Hatter, in Brewer-ftreet.——Richard Andrews, Grocer and Oilman, Swallow-ftreet.——Henry Savory, Coal-merchant, Leicefter-ftreet.——Jofeph Thompfon, Grocer, in Warwick-ftreet.

*To* Mr. NORTON, *Surgeon,* in *Golden-Square.*

SIR,                          *November* 3, 1772.

I Should think myfelf wanting in Gratitude to you, and Humanity to my Fellow Creatures, if I any longer omitted acquainting the Public of the Cure I have ob-tained by taking your *Maredant's Drops.* It is nine Years fince the Scurvy firft appeared in my Hands, in the Manner following : There appeared fome fmall Pimples in the Palms of my Hands, which ran one into another, and fo became one large Sore, which took away the Ufe of one Finger and both my Thumbs. I remained in this Condition five Years, during which Time I tried many Things without Effect.

*I am, Sir, your moft obedient*

No. 18, *Magpye-Ally,*          *Humble Servant,*
    *Fetter-lane.*            WILLIAM JONES.

*To*

*To* Mr. NORTON, *Surgeon*, in *Golden-Square, London.*

SIR, *Brompton, October* 30, 1772.

ABOUT two Years and a Half ago, I was seized with a violent Hoarseness and Shortness of Breath. I sent for a Physician, who ordered me to be bled: I also took a great many Medicines, but grew worse instead of better. My Head ached so violently, that it prevented my getting any Rest; my Face and Head broke out in large Blotches, which spread so much that I was in daily Fear of losing my Eye-sight. The Humour which discharged from my Face was so very offensive, that I could hardly bear it myself; but, by the Use of your *Maredant's Drops*, am effectually cured. Any Person, doubting of this, may be convinced of the Truth, by calling on Mrs. Copson, at Brompton; or by enquiring of Mr. Orton, Coal Merchant, in Whitcomb-street, near Leicester Fields.

> *I am, with great Respect,*
> *Sir, your most humble Servant,*
> MARY COPSON.

*To* Mr NORTON, *Surgeon*, in *Golden-Square, London.*

SIR, *Mitcham in Surry, Sept.* 28, 1772.

I Should think myself wanting in Gratitude to you, and Humanity to my Fellow Creatures, if I longer omitted acquainting the Public of a most remarkable Cure I have obtained by the Use of your *Maredant's Drops*. About seven Years ago, I got a Surfeit by riding in wet Weather: Soon after which I was taken very ill, and there appeared great Blotches and other Eruptions all over my Hands, Legs, and Body. I have had the Advice of the most eminent Physicians in London, and have taken various Medicines, Diet Drinks, &c. in vain. I hope the Publication of this extraordinary Cure may be the Means of relieving others afflicted as I was.

> *I am, Sir, your very humble Servant,*
> A. RAYMOND.

*Witness*—Jerom Guiliard, at the Hercules Pillars, in Greek-street, St. Ann's, Soho.

*To*

To Mr. NORTON, *Surgeon*, in *Golden-Square*.

SIR, September 19, 1772.

I Am now cured of a moſt inveterate ſcorbutic Humour, which broke out in large Ulcers in my Legs, attended with a Loſs of Appetite, &c. by taking your *Maredant's Drops.* I have recommended them to ſeveral of my Friends, who have alſo received great Benefit by them. You have my Leave to publiſh this Cure, as it may be the Means of relieving others afflicted in the like Manner. *I am, Sir,*

*Dolphin Inn,*   *Your moſt humble Servant,*
*Kingſton upon Thames.*   JOHN CREW, Inn Keeper.


To Mr. NORTON, *Surgeon*, in *Golden-Square*.

SIR, Auguſt 15, 1772.

I Should think myſelf wanting in Gratitude to you, and Humanity to my Fellow Creatures, if I longer omitted acquainting the Public of a moſt remarkable Cure I have obtained by the Uſe of your *Maredant's Drops.* About forty Years ago I got a Surfeit, by drinking a Quantity of Small Beer when I was exceſſive hot; ſoon after which I was taken very ill, and there appeared great Blotches, and other Eruptions, all over my Head, my Hands, and my Body, much like the Bark of a Tree. I have had the Advice of the moſt eminent Phyſicians in London, and have taken various Medicines, Diet Drinks, &c. without Relief, till I took your Drops by which, thank God, I am now perfectly cured. As my Diſorder appears to be of longer Standing than any mentioned in your Paper, you have my Leave to publiſh it. *I am, Sir,*

*Your very humble Servant,*
*Berwick-Street, Soho.*   JOHN HAINES.


To Mr. NORTON, *Surgeon*, in *Golden-Square*.

SIR, July 9, 1772.

IT is above two Years ſince my Son was cured of an inveterate Scurvy by the Uſe of your Drops. He was one entire Scab, from the Crown of his Head to the

Soles

Soles of his Feet; befides which, he had feveral Holes in one of his Legs and Arms. I employed feveral Surgeons, and fent him by their Direction, to bathe and drink the Sea Water, without Effect. As I think this is a moft extraordinary Cure, I defire you will publifh it for the Good of others.

*I am, Sir, your obedient humble Servant,*

## NATHANIEL LANE.

*Woolen Draper, Great Ruffell-Court, Covent-Garden.*

MAREDANT's Antifcorbutic Drops.

To Mr. JAMES WILLIAMS, *Bookfeller,* in *Skinner Row, Dublin,* Mr. NORTON's *Agent* in *Ireland.*

S I R,

ABOUT eight Months ago, I was afflicted with a dreadful Scurvy which broke out in large Blotches all over my Body, my Legs in particular were fo much fwelled, that the fmall Part of them were as Thick as the Calf, and feveral Holes in them, which caufed an Inflammation fo great that I was unable to walk for near three Months, I took many Medicines, and had the Advice of feveral eminent Phyficians, but in vain; at laft I was advifed to take *Maredant's Drops,* prepared by Mr. Norton, Surgeon, in London, which you fell, and have the Satisfaction to inform you, that by taking feven Bottles of thefe valuable Drops, I find myfelf perfectly cured. I fhould think myfelf deficient in Gratitude to the Author of thefe valuable Drops, did I not make my Cafe public, that others of my Fellow Creatures, labouring under fuch a dreadful Diforder, may know where to get immediate Relief.

*Crampton Court,*      *I am, your humble Servant,*

*May 1, 1773.*      STEPHEN ARMITAGE.

*To* Mr. NORTON, *Surgeon, in* Golden-Square, London.

SIR, *Pill, near Briftol, March* 18, 1772.

I Think I fhould be undeferving the Benefit I have received, and greatly deficient in Point of Gratitude to
you, did I not lay before the Public my late deplorable
Situation, and the Benefit I have received by your
*Maredani's Drops.* My Cafe was this: About a Year
and a Half fince, I got a Cold, (by riding to Bath in a
rainy Day) fucceeded by a malignant Fever, which,
with difficulty I furvived: Some Months after this, I
perceived an Eruption on my Arms and Legs, and afterwards on my Face, to fuch a violent Degree, that it
was one entire Scab, and fmelt intolerably; my Eyes,
Nofe, and Mouth, were almoft clofed up, which obliged me for fome Time to live on Spoon Meat only: I
had alfo three inveterate Ulcers on my left Leg, and
was reduced to a mere Skeleton. I had the Advice of
the moft eminent of the Faculty at Briftol, to no Purpofe. In this deplorable Situation was I, when I heard
of the almoft incredible Cures performed by your Drops:
By taking them, the Ulcers in my Leg are healed, the
Eruption has difappeared, and I enjoy a better State of
Health than I have for thefe feveral Years paft. I defire you will make this public, for the Benefit of my
Fellow Sufferers. *I am, with Gratitude,*
*Your much obliged humble Servant,*

ROBERT SHIELDS,

*Witneffes—*Thomas Rawlins.——William Hodds.


*To* Mr. NORTON, *Surgeon,* in Golden-Square.

*Pound-Lane, Clapton, St. John's, Hackney,*

SIR, *February* 24, 1772.

I Return you my moft fincere Thanks for the Cure I
have obtained (by the Ufe of your moft excellent
Drops) of an inveterate Scurvy, which afflicted me almoft twenty Years: My left Leg was fo violently inflamed all over, that it appeared like the St. Anthony's
Fire; attended with large Blotches and the moft extreme
Pain; the Veins were alfo greatly enlarged and knotted.

In

In this melancholy Condition, I applied to several eminent Physicians, and to two of the principal Hospitals
without Relief: Relating my unhappy Case to a Gentleman, he advised me to take your Drops; he said a
Friend of his had been cured by them, after every other
Means had failed; on which I immediately began to
take them, and by continuing for some Time, am restored to perfect Health, my Disorder having entirely
left me.

*I am, your obedient and very humble Servant,*

ANN JOYCE.

Witnesses to the Cure. } Claude Croquée, Esq. John Webb, Corn-Factor. } Hackney.

*To* Mr. NORTON, *Surgeon, in* Golden-Square, *London.*

SIR, *Guernsey, February* 4, 1772.

I Was afflicted with a violent scorbutic Humour, upwards of twenty Years, which affected me as follows:
My Legs, that were greatly swelled, were covered with
Scabs and Ulcers, which caused such a Heat I was unable to keep them in Bed; neither could I walk without
a Stick; and notwithstanding I used every Means that
could be thought of, such as Purges, bathing in the
Sea, &c. I still grew worse; insomuch that I thought I
should have lost the Use of them; but seeing one of
your Bills, and knowing Mr. Stoddard, of Ash, in
Kent, who was cured of the Scurvy by the Use of your
Drops, induced me to apply to them, by which I have
obtained a perfect Cure. You have my Leave to publish this, in Justice to you, and for the Benefit of others.

*I am, Sir, your very humble Servant,*

JOHN WILLIAMS, Cabinet Maker.

*To* Mr. JAMES WILLIAMS, *Bookseller,* Skinner-
row, *Dublin,* (Mr. NORTON's *Agent in* Ireland).

SIR, *Castletown, in the* Queen's *County.*

THE taking of *Maredant's Drops* (after trying
many other Medicines to no Purpose) has effectually cured me of a most inveterate Scurvy and Rheumatism,

tifm, with which I was affected near fix Years; my
Reft, Spirits, and Appetite were entirely gone; but
now, by God's Affiftance, and the Application of this
very efficacious Medicine, I am perfectly well; I did
not chufe to inform you of this, until I had paffed laft
Autumn and Spring, for Fear of a Return of the Diforder at thofe trying Seafons of the Year, but I have
not had the leaft.—You may make what Ufe of this
you pleafe for the Benefit of the Public, as I fhall always be ready and willing to atteft the Truth.

*I am, Sir, your very humble Servant,*
    A. SEYMOUR.


## To the PUBLIC.

HENRY PHILIPS, of the Parifh of Lanftinan, in
the County of Pembroke, is perfectly cured of an
inveterate Scurvy, (by the ufe of *Maredant's Drops*,
prepaied by Mr. Norton, Surgeon,) which appeared in
Pimples all over his Body, Arms, and Legs. He had
bathed and drank the Sea-Water, without Effect.


## A MOST EXTRAORDINARY CURE BY THE USE OF MAREDANT's DROPS.

*To* Mr. NORTON, *Surgeon, in Golden-Square, London.*

SIR,         *September* 26, 1771.

I Take this Method of returning you my moft fincere
Thanks for the Cure of my Son, which was effected
by your moft excellent Drops. Two Years and a Half
ago, he had the Small-Pox; immediately after that, a
moft violent Humour fettled in both his Hands, which
were fo bad that he entirely loft the Ufe of them; the
Bones were fo much affected that two Pieces feparated
and came away. The Humour in his Hands was attended with almoft as violent a one in his Face, which for-
med an entire Scab over the whole, and fmelt intolerably: In fhort, he was in fo much Mifery, and without
Hopes of Recovery, (as I had had the Opinion of the
             moft

moſt Eminent withcut Effeɛt, who called it the King's Evil, that I deſpaired of his Life. In Gratitude for ſo extraordinary a Cure, I have defii ed this to be made public. Any Perſon, by calling at my Houſe, the Talbot-Inn, in the Strand, may be infoi med of every Paiticular, and ſee the Child.

CHARLES ASHLEY.

*To* Mr. NORTON, *Surgeoa,* in *Golden-Square, London.*

  S I R,

IN Gratitude to you, and for the good of others, I ſend you the following Caſe to publiſh.—I was af-fliɛted for above ſix Years with a moſt violent Inflam-mation in my Face and Aims, attended with white Bliſters and extreme Pain, which cauſed them to ſwell to an immoderate Size; this Diſorder brought me ſo low, that I was believed to be in a Conſumption. I ap-plied to many without Succeſs, till Providence direɛted me to take your Drops; by which Means I am ieſtored to perfeɛt Health, the above-mentioned Complaints having long ſince left me.—Any Peiſon, by applying to Mr. Le Febvre's, in Cogdell-Couit, Silvei-ſtreet, Gulden-Squaie, may be convinced of the Truth of this.

*I am your humble Servant,*

*Auguſt* 5, 1771.           ANN BOWIE.

## A MOST EXTRAORDINARY CURE BY THE USE OF MAREDANT's DROPS.

*To* Mr. NORTON, *Surgeon,* in *Golden-Square, London.*

  S I R,             *Oxford, December* 16, 1771.

IN Giatitude to you, and for the Good of the Public, I beg Leave to ſend you the following miraculous Account of a Cuie which does Honour to yourſelf and you invaluable Medicine, and which I defiie you will publiſh for the Good of Mankind in general.

My youngeſt Son, about twelve Years of Age, had been affliɛted, for above two Years, with a violent ſcoibutic Humoui in the Teeth and Gums; by which

the

the falival Glands were fo fwelled and inflamed that it
was with Difficulty he could open his Mouth to receive
the fmalleft Nourifhment, which could only be convey-
ed by a fmall Spoon. I had the timely Advice of more
than one able Phyfician and Surgeon; but the Methods
they ufed were fo inefficacious, and the Diforder gained
fo much Ground, notwithftanding all their Prefcriptions,
that I had refolved to take him to London, where, if
poffible, I might meet with better Advice and Succefs.
I fhould have put this Defign into Execution, had not a
Gentleman of Oxford informed me of the great Benefit
he had received from the Ufe of your Drops, which I
immediately refolved to make Trial of; and had the
Satisfaction of feeing my Son gradually mend, and, in
lefs than a Month, perfectly cured : He is now in Oxford, where many People of Credit are ready to teftify
the Truth of this Cure.

*I am, Sir, your ever moft obliged,*

*And grateful humble Servant,*

THOMAS WILKINS.

To Mr. N O R T O N, *Surgeon,* in *Golden-Square.*

S I R,

I Have happily experienced the Efficacy of your
*(Maredant's) Drops,* in a very painful Humour and
Diforder, which I laboured under near twenty Years,
in both my Legs, accompanied with a violent Inflammation, and profufe Difcharge, the fharpnefs of which
fleaed off the Skin, and prevented my getting (but at
very fhort Intervals) either Sleep or Reft.—After trying Stoops of Herbs, Diet Drinks, and innumerable
Medicines, in vain, almoft wearied out with Pain and
Grief, I was recommended to make Trial of your Drops;
which I took, and have the Pleafure to inform you,
that they have effectually removed the Complaint, fo as
to leave no Appearance of the Diforder.—Pleafe to accept my Thanks for the fame, and my fincere Wifhes
that this Teftimony of the Efficacy of your invaluable
Drops may be fo publicly known as that others, labouring

bouring under the like affliction, may find the same Relief.

*I am, with great Respect,*
*Your most humble Servant,*

*March* 14, 1771.     ESTHER WRIGHT.

*At Mr. Cox's, Shoe-Lane, Fleet-Street.*

*To* Mr. NORTON, *Surgeon, in Golden-Square.*

SIR,        *Prescot-street, August* 24, 1770.

I Should think myself wanting in Gratitude to you, and Humanity to my Fellow-Creatures, if I longer omitted acquainting the Public of the most extraordinary Cure I have obtained by the Use of your *(Maredant's) Drops.* It is twenty-two Years since I was first taken ill with the Scurvy, which appeared in great Blotches, and other Eruptions, all over my Body: I have had the Advice of many Physicians of Eminence, from some of whom I received temporary Relief, which (and bathing in the Sea) only enabled me to support a most miserable Life. I was in the most afflicting Situation, without Hopes of Recovery, when, luckily, reading the News-Papers, I saw the Cure of Mr. Hall, Attorney, in Johnson's-court, Fleet-street, whom I had known for many Years; that induced me to begin your Drops; in taking a few Bottles I found great Benefit, particularly in my Constitution and Appetite; and by continuing them, am effectually cured; which I have no Reason to doubt, as it is above two Years since I took any, and remain in perfect Health, though I can justly and truly say, I was in as deplorable a Condition as ever Man was.

*I am, with great Esteem,*
*Your most obedient humble Servant,*

HENRY TRENCHARD GOODENOUGH.

Steward to the Magdalen-Hospital.

P. S. When I took the Drops I was a Clerk in the Prerogative Office, Doctors-Commons.

*To* Mr. JAMES WILLIAMS, *Bookseller, in Skinner-Row, Dublin,* (Mr. NORTON's *Agent in Ireland.*)

SIR, *Kilkenny, June 25, 1771.*

IF Mankind in general were ready to communicate to the Public the Benefit they receive from Remedies by which they have got Relief, many Persons, labouring under dreadful Complaints, might be relieved at a small Expence.

My Wishes for the general Good of Mankind, as well as my Gratitude for the Benefits I have received, have induced me to send you my Case, which you would do well to make public.

About twenty-five Years ago, I was afflicted with a most violent Scurvy in my Arms, which afterwards broke out in my Face, in large Ulcers and Blotches, spreading so fast as to affect even my Eyes, accompanied with a lost Appetite, and Pains in my Back and Breast; during the said Term of twenty-five Years, I applied to several eminent Physicians, and tried various Medicines prescribed by them, to little or no Effect, which is well known to most of the Inhabitants of the City of Kilkenny, where I have resided for upwards of thirty Years past. At length, on seeing *Maredant's Drops* advertized by you Correspondent, Edmund Finn, Printer, in Kilkenny, as being a powerful Medicine for such Disorders as mine, I was advised to try them, and accordingly bought four Bottles, which I have taken, and have now the Pleasure to acquaint you that my Appetite is quite restored, the Scurf and Pimples have gradually left my Face, and all Parts of my Body; and I now, thank God, find myself perfectly cured, and my Skin as clear as ever it was. THOMAS HEWITT.

We certify the above ⎤ ANTHONY BLUNT, Mayor.
Case to be Fact, ⎦ LUKE MEAGHER.

*To* Mr. NORTON, *Surgeon, in Golden-Square, London.*

SIR,

HAVING some Time since been greatly afflicted, with the Scurvy, which appeared in great Blotches and other Eruptions, all over my Body, and having had

the

the Advice of several eminent Physicians without Relief, I was at last advised by a Friend to try your *(Maredant's) Drops*, which I accordingly did, and am now perfectly restored to my former Health by no other Means. If you think proper to publish this, I have no Objection.

*I am,*

Chancery-lane,      *Your very humble Servant,*

December 5, 1770.    THOMAS WILLIAM PINCK.


*To* Mr. NORTON, *Surgeon, in* Golden-Square, *London.*

SIR,          *Pontefract, October* 1, 1769.

HAVING been afflicted with a violent scorbutic Disorder ever since I was eleven Years old, occasioned by a severe Surfeit I then got, every Spring and Fall since that Time, I have either had ulcerous sore Legs, or a violent Fever, till I took your Drops, which have entirely cured me. It is a Twelvemonth since I left off taking them, and have had no Return of my Disorder; on the contrary, I now enjoy a better State of Health than ever. You have my Leave to publish this, in Justice to your Medicine, and for the good of Mankind.     *I am your humble Servant,*

THOMAS SMITH.

Besides the above, there is a Number of People in the Town and Neighbourhood of Pontefract, who, to my Knowledge, are cured by Mr. Norton's Drops; and who, though they will not allow their Cures to be published, may be referred to by applying to me.

JOHN LINDLEY.

Bookseller, at Pontefract, Yorkshire.


*To* Mr. NORTON, *Surgeon,* in *Golden-Square.*

SIR,          *London, February* 17, 1769.

I Have the Pleasure to acquaint you that I have taken of your valuable Drops, which have entirely cured me of a dangerous and obstinate Fistula, I have been

         afflicted

affliſted with ſince September, 1767. I have not the leaſt Objeſtion to your making this public, as it may be the Means of doing Service to the Community in general.  *I am, Sir,*
*Your humble Servant,*
J O H N  G O O D.
Late Surgeon to his Majeſty's Sloop Ferrit.

*To* Mr. NORTON, *Surgeon, in* Golden-Square, London.

S I R,                                          *September* 23, 1768.

HAVING received ſo much Benefit from your Drops as to convince me I am indebted to them for the Recovery of my Health, I give you the Liberty I promiſed in my laſt Letter, and have great Pleaſure in declaring to the World how truly valuable your Medicine is. When I firſt took the Drops I was reduced to the loweſt State of Illneſs by a violent Pain in my Side, and almoſt a continual Fever, both of which attended me for four or five Years, but at that Time was very bad, ſo that I had no Spirits, very little Strength, and no Appetite; the latter I recovered by taking two Bottles of Drops, and by the frequent Uſe of them, I gained Eaſe and Strength daily; as mine is different from every Caſe I have ſeen publiſhed, I conſider it as a Duty incumbent on me to publiſh it; happy, could I be the Means, through this Declaration, of aſſiſting one human Being in the State which I have ſuffered.

*From, Sir,*
Shepton-Montagu,        *Your humble Servant,*
Somerſetſhire,                M A R Y  K I N G S T O N.

*The* CASE *of a* Clergyman's Daughter, *cured by* MAREDANT's DROPS.

*To* Mr. NORTON, *Surgeon, in* Golden-Square, London.

S I R,

I Return you my moſt ſincere Thanks for the extraordinary Cure my Daughter has received by your *Maredant's Drops.* She was afflicted with a moſt inveterate Leproſy, which rendered her a moſt ſhocking Spectacle

to

to all who beheld her. The Winter before it broke out, she was troubled with a Sickness and a violent Spitting; in the Beginning of March the Disorder appeared in Blotches and Scurf about her Neck, attended with excessive itching; her Body was also swelled all over; the loose dry Scurf continued to spread all over her Body, followed by a violent sharp Humour, which took away the Skin from every Part. The inflammation was so great as to be sensibly felt by the Hand some Distance from her, which remained twenty-four hours; then the Humour dried up, and was followed with great loose Scales, which fell off by Handfuls in a most surprising Manner, for the Space of a Week, which at last increased till they became as hard as the Bark of a Tree; all this was followed with such a Smell, that few could bear the Room where she was: In short the Fever and loss of Appetite brought her so low, that no one expected her Life. In taking your Medicine the Humour gradually ceased, after that the Scales became thinner and thinner, till the natural Skin appeared, and now she has not the least Blemish on any Part of her Body. —You have my Leave to publish this most extraordinary Cure for the Benefit of Mankind.

*I am, your humble Servant,*

CORIOLANUS COPPLESTONE,

*At Cobham in Surry.*

*Witnesses to this Cure*—John Hone,——Dinah Wheatly.

P. S. The Girl is nine Years old.

To Mr. NORTON, *Surgeon*, in *Golden-Square.*

SIR,

I Have the Pleasure to acquaint you that my Wife has received a perfect Cure of a most inveterate scorbutic Disorder, by taking your *Maredant's Drops,* which I should think an Omission of Justice to your Medicine and self to conceal from the Public, as it is a Disorder so incident to the human Frame. I here enclose you the Case: About the Year 1758, she was violently afflicted

with

with a Kind of an Inflammation in her Face and Arms, which appeared like what is called St. Anthony's Fire, attended with large red Blotches and extreme Pain. She applied to several of the Faculty, but without Success, except one, who was a Foreigner; he administered a Kind of a Diet-Drink, prepared from Herbs, which gave her some small Relief for about two Years. The next Turn the Disorder took, it appeared in her Stomach, attended with a most dreadful bilious Cholic, which she was afflicted with every six Weeks or two Months; the Pain of which was so violent in her Stomach and Back, that it generally used to last her eight or ten Hours, that to all Appearance she was like a Person under the greatest Torture, and when that Pain ceased, it was succeeded by violent Reachings, which continued five or six Days; after this, her Complexion used to be as yellow as a Person in the Jaundice, which seldom disappeared in less than a Fortnight or three Weeks. She still continued with a bad Digestion, her Stomach swelling, with violent hysterical Complaints, &c. We then again consulted several of the Faculty, but without Relief. About three Years ago it pleased God her Disorder appeared again in her Face and Arms, but in a more corrosive Manner, and much more swelled, her Face being covered all over with Blotches, as bad as a Person in the Small-Pox, and her Eyes very much affected with the Inflammation; her Hands and Arms, from her Fingers to her Elbows, were swelled to an immoderate Size, and covered with Blisters, the extreme Pain of which obliged her to apply a Poultice to each Arm, which discharged full three Pints of the most corrosive Matter in a few Hours; this she repeated several Times, without the least Appearance of abating the Disorder, then went under a Course of Physic and Diet for near four Months, and every internal and external Application we cou'd think of, with little or no Success, till she found her Constitution was decaying, and her Disorder not much abated. At that Time I was so happy as to read your Advertisement, I then persuaded her to take your Drops; she did so, and soon found Relief from every Complaint in her Stomach; this induced her to keep wholly to your Medicine and Advice,

until

until her Cure was completed, which is now near twelve Months ago.—I fhould far exceed the Limits of a Letter, if I offered any Thanks for your genteel and kind Behaviour in your Advice, her Diforder ever taking the Turn you told her. My wife prefents her Compliments, and chearfully throws in the Mite of her Wifhes for the Succefs of your Medicine. And you have my Leave to make what Ufe you pleafe of this, for the Satisfaction of thofe afflicted with the like Diforder.

*And am, Sir,*
>*Your much obliged humble Servant,*
>### THOMAS FORREST.

*Great Kirby-ftreet, Hatton-Garden,*
>*March* 19, 1767.

*A moft amazing Cure, by the Ufe of Maredant's Antifcorbutic Drops, prepared by* Mr. NORTON, *Surgeon, in Golden-Square.*

## To the PUBLIC.

ABOUT twenty Years fince, I got a violent Surfeit, by leaping into the Water when hot; after trying many Things to no Purpofe, was advifed to drink Salt-Water, and go into the Sea, which I complied with fome Years, when my Diforder ftruck in: I afcribed it to my going into the Water in the Month of February, it being then at a long Diftance from the Shore; from which Time I date the lofs of Health. I then had an Iffue cut, which I thought did me Service. In a Morning I was greatly afflicted with violent Reachings, which greatly weakened my Spirits, and kept increafing till February, 1765. My Head was fo greatly affected, that I pitched out of a Chair, as if in a Fit of Apoplexy; I was now perfuaded to have two more Iffues cut betwixt my Shoulders. About June, 1765, I had the Advice of an eminent Phyfician, whofe Directions were followed, but no Benefit received; I grew

worfe,

worfe, had fuch a prodigious Uneafinefs in my Stomach, that I was almoft diftracted; a Blifter was applied to my Head; I don't think I had 6 Hours Sleep in 6 Months; Laudanum was now given to compofe me: Another famous Phyfician ordered bathing in the Sea, to omit one Drop of Laudanum daily, and take certain Things; it did me this Service, that, after fix Weeks bathing, &c. I got fairly rid of the Laudanum; I have been ever fince perhaps in the moft miferable Manner ever known, hardly ever any Sleep till the late hard Froft ended. I was perfuaded, by a Friend, to try *Maredant's Drops*, he made me this (I think) juft Remark, that it was almoft impoffible for me to be worfe, and that there was a Poffibility of their doing me good. The Night the Thaw came on, I had fuch Sleep, that I had not met with before for three Year. The time I was fo extreme bad, generally what I difcharged upwards, in the Nature of Spittle, fo congealed, that it would not diffolve for fome Days, it now came from me by Stool, which gave me great Eafe; I continued fleeping, from the firft Night's Reft, till the 28th of February, much the fame; my Belly, hard like a Drum's Head, was now very pliant, and furprizingly eafed; Water now iffued from my Groins, that were fo fore, it was a trouble to fit, ftand, or lie; in four Days afterwards this abated, and the Humour came out on my Thighs and Legs, which was thought, by the Phyficians, to be impoffible. Thank God, I am fo unexpectedly relieved, that I have been to fee feveral Friends, and begin, after three Years Mifery and Confinement, to fee after my Affairs. If it was in the Power of any Perfon to give me the whole national Debt of England, to remain in the State I was in before I took thefe Drops, I would not accept of it. I don't publifh this with any View of ferving Mr. Norton, nor did he ever requeft it of me, but entirely for the Benefit of the Public.

D. STODDARD,

*March* 30, 1768.

Late Brewer at Afh, Sandwich, Kent.

*To*

## TO THE PUBLIC.

MY Daughter is effectually cured by the Ufe of *Maredant*'s *Drops*, (prepared by Mr. Norton, Surgeon, of Golden-Square) of an inveterate Humour, occafioned by the Relics of the Small-Pox, which cauf-ed feveral Ulcers in her Knees, Legs, &c. With one Knee fhe was fo violently bad, that the Lotion, which was injected to cleanfe the Wound, on one Side, came out at the other. In the Courfe of five Yeais, I employed feveral of the moft eminent Surgeons in London, without the Child's receiving the leaft Benefit from any of them; one of whom (who is of the greateft Repute among the Faculty) declared, that, if ever the Virulence of the Humour could be corrected, the Patient would have a ftiff Knee for Life That Knee is now quite flexible, and the Child, in all other Refpects, happily cured to the Aftonifhment of the many Surgeons that attended her, and every Body elfe that knew her in her deplorable Situation. All which I impute to the powerful Influence of Maiedant's Drops, which Mr. Norton is at Liberty to make public, in Order to promote the Sale of his Medicine, as well as for the Afflicted to know where to find a Remedy under the like unhappy Circumftances.

*Ijlington-Road, Oct.* 1767.          D. D A V I S.

## To Mr. NORTON, *Surgeon*, in *Golden-Square*.

S I R,

HAVING been for feveral Years paft much af-flicted with a fcoibutic Diforder, which fhewed it-felf externally on my Shoulders, Neck, and Ears, in-fomuch that my Ears have been often ulcerated, and my Neck overfpread with Scales, like the Scales of a Fifh: I had almoft a continued Pain and Diforder, with a Pain at my Stomach; I loft my Appetite, my Complection changed to a yellow Hue, and, in fhort, I was in a very bad State of Health, but am now, by the Ufe of your *Maredant's Drops*, perfectly recovered. You may fhew

this

this Letter to any of your Patients, or make what other
Ufe of it you pleafe, as I think in Gratitude I ought to
acknowledge to you, and to the World, how much I
owe to your Medicine the Recovery of my Health from
that of a very bad Conftitution.

*I am, with great Efteem, Sir,*

*Your obedient and very humble Servant,*

*July* 3, 1766.                             J O H N  H A L L.

*Attorney,* in *Johnfon's-Court, Fleet-Street.*


*The Cafe of* J O S E P H  F E Y R A C, *Efq; late
Lieutenant-Colonel to his Majefty's* 18th *or Royal Re-
giment of Foot, in Ireland, cured by the Ufe of*
M A R E D A N T's D R O P S.


*To* Mr. N O R T O N, *Surgeon,* in *Golden Square.*

S I R.                              *London, Sept.* 20, 1765.

I Have at laft the very great Pleafure of acquainting
you, that I am perfectly recovered from my late Ill-
nefs by taking your Drops, and perfifting in them fince
the firft of February laft; as this Remedy muft be of
great Benefit to the Public, in Juftice to them and to
you, I here fend you the Particulars of my Diftemper,
for the Perufal of all fuch as chufe to be informed of
the Certainty of their Effects.—In the Years 1751 and
1759, I was attacked by a violent Scurvy, having no
Part free from Pimples, Scurf, and Ulcers, but the Palms
of my Hands, my Face, and Breaft; attended by a total
Want of Appetite, Sleep, and Spirits; to fuch a Degree
was I afflicted, that I wifhed myfelf dead, having followed many different Prefcriptions to no Manner of Purpofe. From this Situation I was relieved by an old Wo-
man, who undertook to cure me; and accordingly all
this was carried off by the Juice of Herbs, preceded by
violent Bleedings, followed by Diet Drinks and outward
Applications, when I was to all outward Appearance,
well for about a Year, but ever fince I have been ailing,
without any vifible Signs, being greatly diftreffed by

Want

Want of Sleep, great lowneſs of Spirits, and Loſs of Appetite; when, about ſixteen Months ſince, I was ſuddenly taken ill with the moſt ſharp and acute Pains in my Back and Side; this was followed by violent Inflammations in my Eyes, ſwelling of Limbs, &c. I kept my Room three Months before I could ſtir; was ſent to Bath, found a bad Effect from the Waters; a Humour, after my ſickneſs fell into my Heel, I was ordered to pump, but all to no Purpoſe; at laſt I could neither walk nor ride, when I was adviſed to bliſter it, and half a Pint of the moſt corroſive matter came out, but was thirty Days a healing, on account of a violent ſcorbutic Habit the Surgeon then ſaw I was in. As ſoon as healed, I went out, and returned Home with my Leg greatly inflamed, not being able to ſtand upon it or kneel; I was then kept in Poultices for a Month, from my Knee to my Heel, before I could walk; I then to all Appearance, was outwardly well, but ſtill violently low in Spirits, want of Appetite, Sleep, &c. It happened, I read your Advertiſement in the Bath Papers, and making the ſtricteſt Enquiry on the Spot, of Mr. Attwood's Cure, I found it atteſted by every one there. I came to London the latter End of January laſt, have taken your Drops ever ſince the Firſt of February; a Week after I began, it drove out the Humour in the ſmall of my Leg, and in different Parts, from my Heel to ſomewhat beneath the Calf, and upon the Back of both my Hands; the Matter that came out of my Leg was ſo corroſive, that the Cloth that was on, when waſhed, became full of Holes, the Matter or Spots could not be waſhed out, but burnt the Piece out. This Humour has gradually come out, cruſted, and then peeled off, and has ſlowly decreaſed in Violence, until it came to mere Water, and is now perfectly healed: My Hands were ſhocking to the Sight, but dried by Degrees, then peeled off; more came out, and went off in like Manner ſucceſſively, but have been well long ſince, and I am now well recovered, my Strength is returned, my Spirits good, my Stomach the ſame, and Sleep well; in ſhort I thought myſelf ſo bad as obliged me to leave the Service, deſpairing entirely of a perfect Recovery.

I have

I have nothing farther to add, than that I am moſt ſincerely obliged to you, not only for the Recovery of my Health, for your very genteel and diſintereſted Behaviour, but alſo for your plain Dealing and Truth ; my Diſtemper having taken the Courſe you have, from Time to Time, told me it would ; and if it is in my Power ever to be of any Service to you, I ſhall be happy in an Opportunity of convincing you how much

I am, Sir,

*You very obliged humble Servant,*

JOSEPH FEYRAC.

*In good Health, Auguſt* 14, 1768

## To *the* P U B L I C.

JAMES SELF, Bricklayer, in Great St. Ann's-Lane, oppoſite the White Hart, Weſtminſter, has obtained a moſt extraordinary Cure, by the Uſe of *Maredant's Drops,* prepared by Mr. Norton, Surgeon, in Golden-Square. His Caſe was as follows· He had fourteen Holes in one of his Legs attended with rheumatic Pains He had been under the Care of ſeveral eminent Surgeons, and had alſo been an out-patient in an Hoſpital ſix Months, without receiving the leaſt Benefit. He was adviſed to have his Leg cut off.

## To *thoſe afflicted with the Scurvy.*

MRS. DARE, at Mrs. Proudman's, No. 25, in Walbrook, London, is perfectly cured by the Uſe of *Maredant's Drops,* (prepared by John Norton, Surgeon) of an inveterate ſcorbutic Humour in her Face, Arms, and Legs. Her Arms, from her Fingers to her Elbows, were one continued Scab ; and one of her Legs had many Holes in it ; ſhe had alſo a very bad State of Health, occaſioned by the Violence of the Humour, and the ineffectual Medicines ſhe had made Uſe of before ſhe took the Drops.

To

*To* Mr. N O R T O N, *Surgeon,* in *Golden–Square.*

S I R,      *Marlborough, Wilts, Feb.* 14, 1765

I Have a Girl, five Years old, that is effectually cured
by the Use of your *Maredant's Drops,* of a moſt inveterate Scurvy. It firſt broke out in little Pimples all
over the Body, the Palms of her Hands and Soles of
her Feet, not excepted; her Head was one entire Scab,
and ſmelt intolerably: The Pimples ſoon grew to large
Blotches, or Scabs, as big as a Silver Three-pence, and
ſome bigger. When ſhe was almoſt well, the Scabs
grew dry and came off like the Scales of a Fiſh, and
left red Places behind, which ſoon diſappeared, and now
her Skin is as clear as ever. If this will be of any Service to you or the Public, I beg you will advertiſe it:
This is a Truth, and well known to the whole Neighbourhood.      I am, Sir,
*With a Heart full of Gratitude,*
*Your Well-wiſher,*
J O H N  S A L W A Y.

I am Witneſs to the above Truth,
     William Crouch.

*To* Mr. N O R T O N, *Surgeon,* in *Golden–Square.*

   S I R,

T H E following is a Deſcription of the Diſorder I
was afflicted with before I took *Maredant's Drops,*
by which Medicine I am perfectly cured, viz. My
Thighs and Legs were an entire Scab, ſo that walking
became intolerable; my Hands, Head, and Face, broke
out in Sores, to the Amazement of every Body. My
Head was ſo light and giddy, that I was not able to look
up long together. I daily grew worſe, the Humour
ſcalded me intolerably, and when in Bed I had ſuch a
Heat in my Legs and Feet, that oftentimes I was obliged
to get up and walk about the Chamber to cool them: My
Diſorder was attended with ſo diſagreeable a Smell, that
I became in a Manner hateful to myſelf. In the End,
I was reduced to ſo very low an Ebb, that I could walk
but a very little Way without ſitting or lying down to
Reſt, attended with violent rheumatic Pains in my Legs.
By

By the Ufe of the above-mentioned Drops, I have now gained my Strength; I can walk, eat, drink, and fleep, as well as ever I could in my Life, after being under the Care of many eminent Hofpital-Practitioners, as well as others in vain.

WILLIAM PRIOR,
*Farmer, at Eynsford, in Kent.*

I Was afflicted with a moft fhocking Leprofy, attended with violent rheumatic Pains, fo that my Life was quite miferable: I tried every Thing that could be thought of for my Relief in vain. I am now perfectly cured by the Ufe of *Maredant's Drops*, as my Neighbours can teftify, who knew the fhocking Condition I was in.

JOHN FORSTER,
*At the Rofe, at Welling, in Kent.*

*To* Mr. NORTON, *Surgeon,* in *Golden-Square.*
SIR,

I Am cured by the Ufe of *Maredant's Drops*, of a moft afflicting Diforder of the fcorbutic Kind, after trying every Medicine that could be thought of for my Relief, in vain. My Cafe was as follows: I firft had fmall Pimples came out on my Head and Face; in a little Time after, my Face was covered with Blotches, and on the Side of my Nofe, fpungy Flefh grew as big as a fmall Nut; the fame round my Eyes and Mouth, tho' not fo large, with Blotches on my Body, Arms, and in the Palms of my Hands, attended with fo violent a Pain in my Head, that I had almoft loft the Sight of my left Eye, the Pain being moftly on that Side. I was in this Situation till January laft, when, by Providence, I met a Gentleman, who was then at Bath, but is fince gone to the Weft Indies; he recommended Mr. Norton's Drops to me, by which Medicine he had been cured of moft fhocking ulcerated Legs. I am now in perfect Health, and am continually praying for the Welfare of the Author of fo valuable a Medicine.

JOHN ATTWOOD,
*Tiy-maker, Market-place, Bath.*

✢ As

CPSIA information can be obtained at www.ICGtesting.com
Printed in the USA
BVOW08s0352161213

339064BV00003B/124/P